John Marshall

The House that John Marshall Built:
The United States Supreme Court. (LIBRARY OF CONGRESS)

John Marshall

THE CHIEF JUSTICE WHO SAVED THE NATION

HARLOW GILES UNGER

DA CAPO PRESS
A Member of the Perseus Books Group

Designed by Trish Wilkinson
Set in 11.5 point Adobe Garamond Pro by The Perseus Books Group

Library of Congress Cataloging-in-Publication Data

Unger, Harlow G., 1931–   author.
    John Marshall : the chief justice who saved the nation / Harlow Giles Unger.
        pages   cm
    Includes bibliographical references and index.
    ISBN 978-0-306-82220-9 (hardback) — ISBN 978-0-306-82221-6 (e-book)
1. Marshall, John, 1755–1835. 2. Judges—United States—Biography. 3. United States. Supreme Court—Biography. I. Title.
KF8745.M3U54 2014
347.73'2634—dc23
[B]   2014008405

First Da Capo Press edition 2014

Published by Da Capo Press
A Member of the Perseus Books Group
www.dacapopress.com

Da Capo Press books are available at special discounts for bulk purchases in the U.S. by corporations, institutions, and other organizations. For more information, please contact the Special Markets Department at the Perseus Books Group, 2300 Chestnut Street, Suite 200, Philadelphia, PA 19103, or call (800) 810-4145, ext. 5000, or e-mail special.markets@perseusbooks.com.

10 9 8 7 6 5 4 3 2 1

Contents

List of Illustrations

Acknowledgments

My deepest thanks to former deputy US Attorney General Edward C. Schmults and to New York attorney Andrew Bab for reviewing the manuscript of this book before its publication. Both were most gracious and generous in sharing their knowledge of history and their understanding of the Constitution. Attorney A. Reading Van Doren Jr., was also kind enough to review the manuscript. I am grateful as well to the staffs at the Supreme Court Historical Society, the John Marshall House, the Massachusetts Historical Society, and the Library of Congress Prints and Photographs Division for their help. And although their names do not appear on the cover, the members of the great publishing and editorial team at Da Capo Press of the Perseus Books group are as responsible as I am for this book. I am truly grateful for and honored by their help and support—especially, John Radziewicz, Publisher; Robert Pigeon, Executive Editor; Lissa Warren, Vice President, Director of Publicity; Kevin Hanover, Vice President, Director of Marketing; Sean Maher, Marketing Manager; Fred Francis, Managing Editor; Cisca Schreefel, Manager, Editorial Production; Justin Lovell, Editorial Assistant; Trish Wilkinson, Designer; and Josephine Mariea, Copy Editor; Robert Swanson, Indexer. My warmest thanks to you all and to the wonderful sales team of the Perseus Books Group.

Introduction

CLOUDS OF DOOM SHROUDED THE NATION IN 1800.

George Washington was dead.

For the first time in their twenty-five-year struggle to govern themselves, Americans faced a future without the father of their country to lead them.

And they lost their way.

Absent their commander-in-chief, the men who had helped him lead the nation to independence went mad. Chaos engulfed the land as surviving Founding Fathers—Adams, Burr, Hamilton, Jefferson, Monroe, and others—turned on each other as they clawed at Washington's fallen mantle.

In a drama not unlike a classical Greek or Shakespearean tragedy, arrogance and lust for power gripped the souls of national heroes, perverting their patriotism, spurring them to spring on each other, fangs bared, spitting venom. Defying the Declaration of Independence and Constitution they had written and sworn to uphold, they ignored the commandments their religions demanded they obey. Madness swept them into its arms, with congressmen wrestling each other to the floor of the House, pummeling each other. Former battlefield comrades and close friends challenged each other to deadly duels, and high government officials plotted to disgrace, imprison, or murder those they perceived as political foes.

1

Presidents were not immune from the madness. John Adams and Thomas Jefferson, both signers of the Declaration of Independence, blatantly violated their oaths of office, stripping the Bill of Rights from the Constitution and, in Jefferson's case, urging states to consider secession. The madness affected heroes as well. Virginia Senator James Monroe, a hero at the Battle of Trenton, plotted to disgrace Treasury Secretary Alexander Hamilton, who had helped save Monroe's life at Trenton. Hamilton, in turn, plotted to disgrace Aaron Burr Jr., who had also fought at Trenton and rode with both Monroe and Hamilton at Monmouth Courthouse. In the postwar struggle for power, Hamilton's scheming unseated President Adams in the 1800 presidential election and provoked the most dangerous constitutional conflict in early American history. Later, Hamilton's insane feuding with Burr—by then vice president of the United States—ended in a disastrous duel that sent him to his grave and Burr to exile in Europe.

As scandal and ignominy tarred his former wartime comrades, one man stood apart from the chaos engulfing the government—as heroic in peace as he had been in war. Like Burr, Hamilton, and Monroe, John Marshall had charged into enemy lines in New York, Trenton, and Monmouth and shared their suffering through the bitter winter at Valley Forge. Content to practice law at home in Richmond, Virginia, after the war he won national acclaim as a delegate to Virginia's ratification convention. In one of the most dramatic debates in American history, Marshall challenged America's legendary patriot Patrick Henry and championed ratification of the Constitution—a document designed to quell America's political chaos with a new and powerful central government. Virginia sided with Marshall and, rejecting Henry's objections, ratified the Constitution and sent Marshall's star soaring in the political firmament as a fearless attorney, state legislator, and congressman.

In 1793, however, the French Revolution sparked another outbreak of political madness in the United States. After France declared war on Britain, fighting between the two nations spilled into the Atlantic Ocean, with French and British warships attacking American vessels to prevent them from carrying cargoes to enemy ports. Together the French and English seized hundreds of millions of dollars' worth of ships and cargoes and impressed or imprisoned thousands of innocent American crewmen and helpless passengers.

President Washington and his successor, John Adams, tried steering the United States into neutral waters, but the French and British ship seizures further enraged and divided Americans. Alexander Hamilton demanded that Adams declare war on France to protect America's vital trade with England, while Hamilton's bitter foe Thomas Jefferson called for war against Britain on the side of America's Revolutionary War ally, France.

As street rioting convulsed the nation, President Adams chose a middle course, urging Congress to strengthen American defenses while he sent a commission that included John Marshall to France to talk peace. Hamilton then turned on Adams, calling him a coward "unfit to govern" and presenting an alternative candidate in the presidential elections of 1800. To crush growing dissent, the President fired cabinet members who sided with Hamilton and rammed the infamous Alien and Sedition Acts through Congress, effectively suspending the Bill of Rights and criminalizing oral and printed criticism of the President and his government.

Burning with ambition to replace Adams as President, Vice President Jefferson urged state legislatures in Kentucky and Virginia to undermine congressional powers by nullifying the new federal laws—in effect, calling for secession.

As a Hamilton puppet candidate siphoned votes from President Adams in the presidential election of 1800, Jefferson and Aaron Burr Jr. garnered the most votes, and Jeffersonians—now calling themselves "Republicans"*—gained control of both houses of Congress.

Left with only a few weeks in office and Jefferson pledging to dismantle much of the federal structure, President Adams reinforced as much of the national government as he could, "packing" the federal judiciary with

---

*Jeffersonian "Republicans" had nothing to do with the founding of the modern Republican party.

"federalist" judges pledged to preserving the powers of the central government. He then stunned the nation by appointing a champion of federalism, Secretary of State John Marshall, Chief Justice of the Supreme Court.

In the more than three decades that would follow his appointment, Marshall's pronouncements would ensure the integrity and eminence of the Constitution and the federal government and catapult him into the pantheon of American Founding Fathers as father of the American federal justice system. He would become the longest serving Chief Justice in US history, signing 1,180 decisions and writing 549 of them, or nearly one-half, himself.

"He hit the Constitution much as the Lord hit the chaos, at a time when everything needed creating," constitutional scholar John Paul Frank attested. "Only a first-class creative genius could have risen so magnificently to the opportunity of the hour."[1]

The British authority Lord Bryce insisted that Marshall's "legal judgments . . . have never been surpassed and rarely equaled by the most famous jurists of modern Europe or ancient Rome."[2]

In the course of his Supreme Court leadership Marshall stood at the center of the most riveting—and most important—courtroom dramas in the nation's formative years. Case by case he defined, asserted, and, when necessary, invented the authority he and the Court needed to render justice, stabilize the federal government, and preserve the Union and its Constitution.

Marshall and his fellow Supreme Court justices established the Constitution—and the Supreme Court's interpretations of the Constitution—as "the supreme law of the land" and a bulwark against tyranny from within by ambitious American officials.

Some Marshall decisions provoked presidential anger, others infuriated Congress, and still others outraged governors and state governments, with some states threatening secession. In effect Marshall's court—its members unelected and unaccountable to "We the People"—rewrote both the Constitution and the laws written by the nation's elected representatives in Congress.

During Marshall's tenure his decisions provoked many citizen protests—even rioting—and twenty-five years after his death those decisions plunged the nation into civil war. But the judicial edifice he built—and the Constitution he defended—survived. The US Supreme Court—Marshall's "Marble Palace"*—stands today as the third separate and equal branch of government alongside the executive and legislative branches. Together with the US Code of Laws and the Constitution, the Marshall Court's decisions form the foundation of the American legal system, ensuring "justice . . . and the blessings of liberty to ourselves and our posterity."[3]

Off the bench Marshall was a warm, loyal friend—beloved by every Founding Father except his cousin Thomas Jefferson, who became a bitter lifelong enemy. Marshall was a devoted father of six, and his forty-eight-year marriage to the lady he called "My dearest Polly" is one of the memorable love stories in early American history.

As John Adams looked back on his own life of public service, he called his appointment of John Marshall as Chief Justice his greatest gift to the nation and "the pride of my life."[4]

Marble Palace is the title of the legal scholar John Paul Frank's work on the Supreme Court, *Marble Palace: The Supreme Court in American Life* (New York: Alfred A. Knopf, 1958).

CHAPTER 1

Chaos!

"As this government stands," Patrick Henry thundered, "I despise and abhor it. . . . It will oppress and ruin the people. . . . The rights of conscience, trial by jury, liberty of the press, all your immunities and franchises, all pretensions to human rights and privileges are rendered insecure."[1]

Not since his plea for liberty or death in the spring of 1775 had the legendary Virginia patriot roused such passions among his countrymen. Eight states had held special conventions and ratified a new constitution to try to unite the confederation of thirteen sovereign states under a strong new central government. As Henry spoke, approval by only one more state—the ninth—would produce the two-thirds majority needed to create a new American government and, indeed, a new nation.

Henry knew, however, that even if twelve other states approved, the new nation would be impotent without Virginia. Virginia was the nation's largest, richest, and most heavily populated state, with one-fifth of America's population, one-third of its commerce, and a land mass that stretched from the Atlantic Ocean to the Mississippi River. Elected Virginia's first governor after it declared independence from Britain in 1775, Henry opposed ceding his state's sovereignty to a new Congress in Philadelphia as much he had opposed ceding it to London's Parliament.

"We are come hither to preserve the poor Commonwealth of Virginia," he cried out to Virginia's ratification convention. "The confederation carried us through a long and dangerous war. It rendered us victorious in that bloody conflict with a powerful nation. . . . Shall a government which has been this strong and vigorous be . . . abandoned for want of energy?"

"No!" his adoring followers shouted their reply. They had flocked to Richmond from Henry's native hills of Piedmont of central Virginia and Kentucky. Nearly half of Kentucky's 100,000 settlers were Virginia transplants who depended on Henry to protect their interests. Farmers, hunters, and trappers in tasseled buckskins, rifles on their shoulders, knives in their belts—all surged into town to hear him.

"Is this tame relinquishment of rights worthy of freeman?" he called out.

"*No!*" came the cry from gallery.

"The new form of government," he roared, "will oppress and ruin the people!"

It was vintage Henry. Not a soul breathed as the crowd watched his hawk-like face snap from side to side, peering into their hearts and souls.

"Liberty!" he shouted. "The greatest of all earthly blessings. Give us that precious jewel and you may take everything else!"[2]

Henry hoped to talk the convention into submission, speaking three and as many as five times a day on seventeen of the convention's twenty-two days—usually the first to rise from his seat after the opening gavel and the last to speak before the day's adjournment. On the ninth day, however, as Henry's acolytes waited for their hero to rise and speak, a tall, powerfully built young man in disheveled clothes untangled his lanky limbs and stood, demanding recognition from the chair for his maiden address:

"Permit me to attend to what the honorable gentleman has said," his deep country drawl echoed through the hall. As one, then another, and another of his listeners gasped at his daring, the young man accused Virginia's revered champion of liberty of nothing less than hypocrisy and—far worse:

"Tyranny!"

The young man charged that when Patrick Henry was governor, he had ordered the summary execution of a man—without a trial!

The audience buzzed with surprise.

"What has become of the worthy member's maxims?" the young man demanded in tones as eloquent as those of Henry himself.

He has expounded on the necessity of due attention to certain maxims—from which a free people ought never to depart. . . . A strict observance of justice and public faith, and a steady adherence to virtue. . . . Would to heaven that these principles had been observed under his government![3]

Pointing an accusing finger at Henry, the young man called up the name of Josiah Philips, a Tory laborer accused of "arson and murder" in southeastern Virginia in 1777. Then-Governor Henry had told the General Assembly to issue "a bill of attainder" that would convict Philips "of high treason and suffer the pains of death . . . without the usual forms and procedures of the courts of law."[4]

Little wonder, the young man sneered, that Patrick Henry opposed a constitution that specifically outlawed bills of attainder.

Henry paled under the barrage of accusations and revelations.

Can we pretend to the enjoyment of political freedom when we are told that a man has been, by an act of assembly, struck out of existence, without a trial by jury—without examination—without being confronted with his accusers and witnesses—without the benefits of the law of the land? What has become of the worthy member's maxims?

"We, Sir, idolize democracy!" the young man scolded Henry. "The supporters of the Constitution claim the title of being firm friends of liberty and the rights of mankind! I differ in opinion from the worthy gentleman. I think the virtue and talents of the members of the general government will tend to the security, instead of the destruction of our liberty."[5]

Stunned by the attack on their beloved Henry, delegates began rethinking their opposition to central government. In the course of the next ten days John Marshall—for that was the young man's name—joined with James Madison and other constitutionalists in coaxing a majority of delegates to vote for ratification of the Constitution and creation of a new nation: the United States of America.

Although Marshall left the convention intending to return to private life and practice law, he "found the hostility to the [federal] government so strong . . . as to require from its friends all the support they could give it."[6]

The lifelong conflict that ensued between Marshall and the enemies of the federal government—among them his cousin Thomas Jefferson—would eventually provoke the US Civil War. Ironically, almost all the heroes and villains in the conflict were—like John Marshall himself—patriots who believed they were acting in the best interests of the nation and its people.

&⁓

LIKE PATRICK HENRY, JOHN MARSHALL EMERGED ON THE NATIONAL political stage from the obscurity of a log cabin on the edge of Virginia's wilderness. Born forty miles southwest of Alexandria in Fauquier County on September 24, 1755, he was the first of fifteen children of Thomas and Mary Marshall. His father could claim only the most undistinguished Welsh lineage that vanished into history before one of them emerged from the forest near the Potomac River and carved a modest 200-acre farm from the woods of Westmoreland County—near Wakefield and George Washington's birthplace.

As a boy, farmer Marshall's son Thomas and the young Washington became steadfast friends. Thomas Marshall went to a formal school for a about year, before Washington—by then a skilled surveyor—asked Marshall to join him on a surveying expedition into the wilderness sponsored by Britain's Lord Fairfax. Fairfax had ordered all his lands surveyed—some 5 million acres, stretching over Virginia's Northern Neck (see map,

The earliest known portrait of John Marshall shows him having retained many features of his youth—even at forty-three. A hero in the American Revolutionary War, he served in the front lines at the battles of Brandywine and Monmouth and survived the bitter winter at Valley Forge. (FROM *THE LIFE OF JOHN MARSHALL*, BY ALBERT J. BEVERIDGE, VOL. I: FRONTISPIECE)

page 43), a thick finger of land between the Potomac and Rappahannock Rivers, whose geological roots stretched from the eastern slopes of the Blue Ridge Mountains to Chesapeake Bay.

Before he returned from his epic journey Marshall had learned one of the most lucrative crafts in America: surveying. His new skill earned him a position as agent for Lord Fairfax and would eventually allow him to acquire more than 200,000 acres of prime Virginia and Kentucky lands of his own and provide his family with untold wealth for generations.

When his first son John was born, Thomas Marshall leased about three hundred acres at the foot of the Blue Ridge Mountains in a small valley called "The Hollow," where he built a two-room cabin and farmed

John Marshall's childhood home at "The Hollow" in Virginia's Blue Ridge Mountains.
About thirty feet long, its two rooms downstairs were an all-purpose "great room,"
with a stone hearth for cooking, and a master bedroom for the Marshall parents and
an infant. Older children slept upstairs in one of the two rooms of the half-story loft.
(FROM *THE LIFE OF JOHN MARSHALL*, BY ALBERT J. BEVERIDGE, VOL. I:30)

enough land to feed his family. Typical of settler homes in Virginia's wilderness, the Marshall house had two rooms on the ground floor—one of them a "great" room with the hearth for cooking and heating, the other a master bedroom for Thomas, his wife, and, as often as not, a newborn. Older children slept in the half-story loft above, clustered about the chimney for warmth.

Though largely self-taught, Thomas Marshall was well educated for a frontiersman, and his status as agent for Lord Fairfax gave him enough influence to win election to the House of Burgesses, then county sheriff, and finally, chief vestryman. With no school nearby, Thomas Marshall and his wife took charge of their children's education themselves.

"My father," John Marshall explained, "possessed scarcely any fortune, and had received a very limited education, but was a man to whom nature had been bountiful and had assiduously improved her gifts. He superintended my education and gave me an early taste for history and for poetry."[7]

John Marshall's mother, Mary, claimed a more illustrious lineage than did her husband. Descended from Henry Randolph, one of Virginia's earliest English settlers, her extended family included Peyton Randolph, who became first President of the Continental Congress; Edmund Randolph, who became a governor of Virginia and first attorney general of the United States; and Thomas Jefferson. Although John Marshall and Thomas Jefferson would become bitter political foes, they were nonetheless second cousins.

Like Marshall's father, Jefferson's father, Peter, had been a farmer from a family of little consequence until he learned surveying and staked out lands in the Virginia wilderness that gained enormous value by the time his son Thomas was born. As a youngster, Thomas Jefferson was no scholar, but the loss of his father in 1757 when the boy turned fourteen changed him dramatically. Tom and his younger brother inherited an estate of 7,500 acres, more than sixty slaves, twenty-five horses, seventy head of cattle, and two hundred hogs. Tom became an insatiable reader, went on to attend College of William and Mary, and studied law under the brilliant Virginia attorney George Wythe, a signer of the Declaration of Independence who would later train John Marshall.

When John Marshall turned fourteen, his father sent him to a proper school.

"There being no grammar school in the part of the country in which my father resided," John Marshall explained, "I was sent about one hundred miles from home to be placed under the tuition of Reverend Archibald Campbell, a clergyman of great respectability." Although brutal itinerant teachers ran many rural schools, Marshall's teacher was a gentle, superbly learned Scotsman who taught history, Latin, French, higher mathematics, and the Scriptures. Among his other students was James Monroe, then a precocious eleven-year-old who lived on his father's small farm five miles from school. He immediately befriended Marshall.

"Twenty-five students only were admitted into Campbell's academy," Monroe recalled years later, "but so high was its character that youths were sent to it from the more distant parts of the then-colony."[8] Despite a three-year age difference, Marshall and Monroe formed what grew into a close, lifelong friendship. Marshall often accompanied Monroe home after school to spend the night—each carrying "books under one arm and a musket slung over his shoulder," shooting small game along the way to put extra meat on the Monroe family dinner table.[9]

Marshall studied at Campbell's school for a year, then returned home, where a new pastor at the Marshall family church—another Scotsman—tutored the family's children in exchange for room and board, a common practice in early America.

"He remained in the family one year," Marshall reminisced, "at the expiration of which I had commenced reading Horace and Livy. I continued my studies with no other aid than my dictionary. My father superintended the English part of my education, and to his care I am indebted for anything valuable which I may have acquired in my youth. He was my only intelligent companion and was both a watchful parent and affectionate instructive friend."[10]

When John Marshall turned eighteen, his father had amassed enough wealth to buy a 1,700-acre farm at Oak Hill, an elevation a few miles east of "The Hollow," where he built what, for the frontier, was a lavish home. A two-story structure, thirty-by-thirty-three feet, it housed seven rooms, four downstairs and three above, with one of the upstairs rooms a fifteen-by-twenty-foot expanse—large enough to serve as a classroom for the huge flock of Marshall children.*

By then John Marshall was flirting with manhood, and his father gave him an appropriate—and important—set of books: Sir William Blackstone's *Commentaries on the Laws of England*.[11] A four-volume masterpiece on "the rights of persons and things, of private and public wrongs," it was the most influential eighteenth-century study of British laws, and Thomas Marshall had obtained it both for his own use as a community

---

*The area surrounding Oak Hill now comprises the town of Marshall, Virginia, about forty miles due west of Arlington.

leader and for his son, whom he hoped might enter the law. It proved a turning point for the boy, who realized, "I was destined for the bar."[12]

The warmth and affection that his father lavished on his son the boy eagerly passed on to his younger brothers and sisters—just a few at first, then, six, eight, ten, and, finally, fourteen: Eliza, the oldest girl, born in 1756, a year after John; Mary, the following year; Thomas in 1761; James Markham, in 1764; Lucy, 1768; Alexander Keith in 1770; Louis in 1773— and on and on. Isolated as they were, they necessarily turned to their big brother as mentor, schoolmaster, forest guide, trusted friend, and mediator, and he joyfully embraced each of those roles.

The Marshalls had not settled at Oak Hill very long when Boston's notorious "Tea Party" sparked riots and disorders along the East Coast— in New York, Philadelphia, Charleston, and elsewhere. Parliament responded by shutting Boston down with martial law.

"The controversy between Great Britain and her colonies," Marshall recalled, "assumed so serious an aspect as almost to monopolize the attention of young and old. I engaged in it with all the zeal and enthusiasm which belonged to my age and devoted more time to studying military exercises and political essays than the classics."[13]

In February 1775 British troops tightened their stranglehold on Boston, and Patrick Henry called Virginia and the rest of the nation to arms with his legendary appeal to Virginia's House of Delegates:

Our brethren are already in the field! Why stand we here idle? . . .

I know not what course others may take, but as for me, give me liberty, or give me death.[14]

Henry's call inspired Thomas Marshall to enlist as a major in the militia of neighboring Culpeper County, whose troops marched under pennants that pictured a coiled rattlesnake hissing, "Don't tread on me." Refusing to remain behind, eighteen-year-old John Marshall enlisted as an ordinary soldier and chased after his father on the road to war.

On April 19, 1775, open warfare broke out in Massachusetts when British troops marched from Boston to Lexington to arrest rebel leaders

John Hancock and Samuel Adams. After a brief encounter that left eight American defenders dead and ten wounded on Lexington Green, the British continued to nearby Concord to seize rebel gunpowder stores.

By evening the next day 4,000 farmers—so-called Minutemen—had flocked in from the surrounding country. After positioning themselves behind stone walls that lined the road, they set off a steady rain of musket fire that sent British troops racing back toward Boston in panic. By the end of the day, nearly 150 British troops lay dead or wounded, while the farmers suffered 49 dead and 42 wounded.

On April 23 the Massachusetts Provincial Congress voted to raise an army to fight the British, and within a month Rhode Island, Connecticut, and New Hampshire agreed to send 9,500 men to join the 4,000 Massachusetts Minutemen laying siege to British-held Boston. In June Massachusetts delegate John Adams proposed to the Continental Congress in Philadelphia that it adopt Patriot forces surrounding Boston as a Continental Army. In a stroke of genius to wed North and South, he moved to name Virginia's Colonel George Washington commander-in-chief of the largely northern forces, and the states agreed to unite in the fight against British rule.

In Virginia, Royal Governor Lord Dunmore fled the capital of Williamsburg and boarded a warship off Norfolk to direct a campaign of terror against Virginia's civilian population. Squadrons of British marines staged hit-and-run raids on coastal towns and plantations, plundering supplies and carrying off slaves with promises of freedom if they fought for Britain.

Major Thomas Marshall led 500 Culpeper Minutemen, including his son John, in a joint attack on Norfolk with 900 Virginia regulars. "In a few days," his son recounted, "we were ordered to march into the lower country for the purpose of defending it against a small regular and predatory force commanded by Lord Dunmore."[15]

As Thomas Marshall's battalion reached the "Great Bridge" outside Norfolk, he dispatched a trusted slave to Dunmore's Norfolk headquarters. Disguised as a runaway, Marshall's slave convinced Dunmore that

Patriot troop strength was far less than it actually was. Confident of having superior numbers, Dunmore sent only 200 regulars and 300 blacks and Tory volunteers to attack the Virginians.

The slaughter that followed left half the badly outnumbered British attackers and their commanding officer dead, without a single American casualty. Although Dunmore and his surviving troops managed to row to safety on the British frigates in the river, the encounter left him so outraged that he ordered his ships to fire on the Norfolk waterfront, and on January 1, 1776, he sent marines ashore to set the town ablaze.

"I was in the action at the Great Bridge and in Norfolk when it was set on fire by a detachment from the British ships," John Marshall related. Cannon blasts shook the earth, he said, as mobs of British marines surged through town, flinging torches through every ground-floor window, sparing only the homes of self-proclaimed Tories. When nightfall silenced the cannons and the British marines returned to their ships, 6,000 survivors huddled about campfires in nearby forests, all of them left homeless in the dead of winter.

Infuriated by the British atrocity, Culpeper Minutemen returned to town to burn the remaining Tory houses. As Dunmore's ships pulled away, villagers in other towns along Virginia's shoreline trembled in fear as they awaited the same fate.

In March 1776 the British army evacuated Boston, ceding the city and the rest of New England to the Americans, and Massachusetts declared independence from Britain. On June 29 Virginia followed suit, and five days later the Continental Congress approved a Declaration of Independence written largely by Thomas Jefferson, who borrowed concepts and phrases from the seventeenth-century British philosopher John Locke.[16]

On July 4, 1776, President of Congress John Hancock appended his bold signature to the document in Philadelphia. By then Patrick Henry had taken an oath as first governor of the free and independent Commonwealth of Virginia and, as one of his first acts, he merged county militias into a single Army of Virginia. What had been the Culpeper

Militia dispersed into nameless regiments, and John and Thomas Marshall marched northward in separate regiments to support General Washington's Continental Army—the father now a colonel, the son a junior officer. Both joined thousands of other Americans of every age from every state in what would be the fiercest and bloodiest battles of the war.

"In July 1776, I was appointed first lieutenant in the 11th Virginia Regiment" Marshall explained. "I had grown up at a time when a love of union and resistance to Great Britain were identical. I carried these sentiments into the army where I found myself with brave men from different states who were risking life and everything valuable in a common cause . . . and where I was confirmed in the habit of considering America my country and Congress as my government."[17]

With Boston and much of eastern New England in Patriot hands, Washington moved his army from Boston to seize control of New York and its deep-water harbor and direct access to the Atlantic. British General William Howe, however, had the same idea, and Howe transported the 10,000 British troops evacuated from Boston to Staten Island, where they landed unopposed. Ten days later 150 British transports sailed into New York Bay with 20,000 more troops, including 9,000 Hessian mercenaries. The huge expeditionary force stormed ashore in Brooklyn, overrunning 5,000 American defenders, killing 1,500 and capturing the American army's entire meat supply. Only a thick fog allowed survivors to escape after dark across the East River to New York Island (Manhattan) on August 29, but the British did not delay their pursuit. Washington ordered his men to retreat northward toward the Westchester County mainland, hoping to meet up with Thomas Marshall's Virginians, then approaching New York.

Before the Virginia reinforcements arrived, however, the British outflanked the Americans and all-but-surrounded Washington's force in Harlem Heights. Sensing the danger to his commander-in-chief, twenty-two-year-old Lieutenant Colonel Aaron Burr ordered his New Yorkers to attack one of the British flanks. Burr was the grandson of the revered American churchman Jonathan Edwards. He had lost both his parents and all four grandparents when he was only two and went to live with an aunt and uncle in a clan of about twenty children, including his older sister. A brilliant scholar at thirteen, he enrolled at the College of New Jersey, which his father had helped found at Princeton. After graduating at sixteen, he enlisted and served courageously in the Battle of Long Island.

As Burr prepared to charge into the British flank, Marshall's Virginians arrived almost miraculously to reinforce Burr's onslaught, and together they forced the British to pull back and allow Washington and 5,000 troops to escape capture.

"We all agreed to trust to his conduct and courage," a sergeant-major recalled his service with Burr, "and he did not disappoint us, for he effected a retreat with the whole brigade, and I do not think we lost more than thirty men. . . . Colonel Burr was foremost and most active where there was danger, and his conduct, without considering his extreme youth, was afterwards a constant subject of praise, and admiration, and gratitude."[18] Major Theodore Sedgwick, of Massachusetts, later a Speaker of the US House of Representatives, was even more effusive in praise of Burr's heroics, writing to the young man, "You know, my dear Burr, I love you. . . . Pamela [Sedgwick's wife] desires me to tell that she loves you."[19]

Burr's heroic charge into British lines allowed Washington's combined force to make an orderly retreat to northern Manhattan and the Harlem River crossing to Westchester. When they reached White Plains, however, the British were waiting with a massive assault that sent the Americans fleeing in disarray. While some moved northward into the Hudson River Highlands, Washington led a contingent of about 5,000 in full flight across the Hudson to New Jersey.

Wintry winds enveloped the Northeast earlier than usual in 1776, and with the British in close pursuit, Washington and his men staggered westward through sheets of icy rains toward the Delaware River, barely reaching safety on the opposite bank in Pennsylvania. By early December desertions had reduced his army to only slightly more than 3,000 men—among them remnants of Thomas Marshall's 3rd Virginia Regiment and John Marshall's 11th Virginia. Sickness had left 500 of Thomas

Marshall's 700 men unfit for duty. Only he and four other officers stood ready to lead, among them John Marshall's boyhood friend James Monroe, who had abandoned his studies at College of William and Mary to enlist in the Revolution.

The retreat across New Jersey, Monroe recalled later, "will be forever celebrated in the annals of our country for the patient suffering, the unshaken firmness, and gallantry of this small band . . . and the great and good qualities of its commander. . . . [Washington] was always near the enemy, and his countenance and manner made an impression on me which time can never efface. A deportment so firm, so dignified, so exalted, but yet so modest and composed, I have never seen in any other person."[20]

The British advance left New York and most of New Jersey in British hands. With enemy troops almost in sight of the American rebel capital at Philadelphia, Congress fled for Baltimore on December 12 and, all but conceding defeat in the struggle for independence, began debating terms of capitulation. The American Revolution seemed at an end.

As the Continental Congress considered peace overtures to end the Revolution, Washington planned a quick, dramatic strike to save it. In the dead of night on December 25 he and 2,400 troops, including John Marshall's Virginians, boarded small boats and rowed through a blinding snowstorm across the ice-choked Delaware River.

At eight the next morning they reached the east bank of the Delaware, near Trenton, New Jersey, and found the 1,400-man Hessian garrison still abed, dissuaded by the storm from posting their usual patrol. Shocked awake by the reality of their plight, the terrified Germans raced out into the snow in night clothes to secure cannon emplacements at the head of King Street and repel the approaching Americans. Before they could get there, Virginia captain William Washington, a distant cousin of the commander-in-chief, and his eighteen-year-old lieutenant, James Monroe, charged through a hail of rifle fire and seized the weapons. Both fell wounded but held fast until Washington's troops fought their way up King Street and forced the Hessians—1,100 strong—to surrender.

While a quick-thinking surgeon tended to their wounds, Washington commended both his cousin and Monroe, whom he promoted on the spot to captain.

Washington's victory set off a wave of euphoria that temporarily bolstered troop morale and public support for the Revolution. The new year saw army ranks swell instead of shrink, and a subsequent Washington victory at Princeton left western New Jersey in Patriot hands. Congress returned to Philadelphia, and Washington moved his Continental Army into Pennsylvania to protect the capital from British attack.

"In May 1777," John Marshall recalled, "I was promoted to the rank of captain. I was in the skirmish at Iron Hill where the light infantry was engaged and in the battles of Brandywine, Germantown, and Monmouth."[21]

Although Iron Hill proved less significant, Brandywine, Germantown, and Monmouth emerged as three of the bloodiest, most important battles of the war. In mid-July 1777 General Howe sailed from New York into Chesapeake Bay with 15,000 troops, who landed on the northernmost shore at Head of Elk (now Elkton), Maryland, and began to march toward the American capital at Philadelphia.

In a disastrous miscalculation George Washington massed his forces on the Philadelphia side of the Brandywine Creek at Chadd's Ford, where, on September 11, the two sides opened fire. Throughout the day the battle raged with increasing intensity. Washington concentrated his fire power at the center of what appeared to be the main British thrust, but British General Lord Cornwallis quietly slipped away to the northwest with 8,000 British and Hessian troops. They crossed the Brandywine at its narrowest point, far from the battle at Chadd's Ford, then looped around and behind the American army's right flank and threatened to encircle Washington's entire army.

The Battle of Brandywine quickly turned into a rout, with American troops fleeing in panic and suffering more than 1,000 dead or wounded and more than 300 taken prisoner. Colonel Thomas Marshall, his son John, and the rest of the Virginia troops were in the thick of the fighting, with Colonel Marshall twice thrown to the ground when his horses were shot from under him. Bounding onto riderless mounts, he saw Virginia's commanding General William Woodford fall wounded, assumed command of the regiment himself, and held off the British advance long enough for Washington's army to escape entrapment. Decorated for his bravery, Thomas Marshall won promotion to general and the gift of a ceremonial sword from the Virginia Assembly.

As Congress fled westward to Lancaster, Howe and his troops marched into Philadelphia, establishing his main encampment near the northwestern edge of the city in Germantown. Rather than allow the British to sweep westward, Washington made a bold move on the night of October 3, sending two separate columns along what seemed to be parallel roads to Germantown for a two-pronged attack on the British. Before he gave the order to advance, he mounted his magnificent white horse and "rode through every brigade of his army," according to John Marshall, "delivering in person his orders . . . exhorting his troops to rely principally on the bayonet and encouraging them by the steady firmness of his countenance as well as by his words to a vigorous performance of their duty."[22]

Again, however, Washington miscalculated badly. One of the roads to Germantown followed a long serpentine course, while the other was a straighter, shorter approach. The column on the shorter road penetrated the streets of Germantown long before its twin column arrived. Faced with an impenetrable wall of British fire and no support from the second column, the advance party of Americans retreated.

Just then, however, a dense fog rolled over the area, and retreating troops ran into their own second column, which mistook them for enemy soldiers and fired. Caught between American and British fire, the trapped column suffered 200 dead, 600 wounded, and 400 taken prisoner. John Marshall suffered a wound in his hand but returned safely to camp, where his mate from Parson Campbell's woodlands school, Captain James Monroe, dressed his injury.

As November snows began to fly, Washington ordered his troops to repair to winter quarters twenty miles northwest of Philadelphia at Valley

Forge, an elevated wooded plateau that a small force could readily defend against a larger enemy. From the bluffs facing east, sentries could warn of a British approach from Germantown, while gentle slopes to the west offered an avenue of quick retreat.

Before the last of Washington's troops arrived at their mountain-top encampment, however, cries of dismay echoed across through the surrounding forest as the troops realized the area had no springs. The nearest source of water was at the foot of the mountain, near the forge that gave the valley its name. Washington nonetheless ordered the troops to raise a small city of log huts, and Captains Marshall and Monroe chose to share one and spend winter together.

The choice of Valley Forge proved a macabre climax to what had been eighteen months of military setbacks for George Washington and his hapless Continental Army. Isolated from every major source of supply, his men ran out of essentials in less than a month of what became the most bitter American winter in memory. By Christmas desertions, disease, starvation, thirst, and exposure to subzero temperatures reduced Washington's Continental Army of 11,000 men to fewer than 5,000. Some froze to death; most of those who survived were too weak to fight. When Quartermaster General Thomas Mifflin failed to respond to Washington's orders for supplies, the commander-in-chief appealed to Congress for help.

Congress, however, all but ignored his requests, with some member states apparently losing interest in the Revolution. Thirty-five-year-old Thomas Jefferson, Washington's fellow Virginian, shocked Washington by resigning from Congress and returning home to the hills of central Virginia. After signing the Declaration of Independence and joining in the collective pledge to sacrifice "our lives, our fortunes and our sacred honor," Jefferson failed to risk any of those assets and abandoned the Revolution. "The situation of my domestic affairs," he mewled, "renders it indispensably necessary that I should solicit the substitution of some other person."[23]

Washington was irate. "Where is Mason, Whyte, Jefferson?" the commander-in-chief cried out in anger to his close friend Benjamin Harrison, a delegate in Virginia's House. They had helped write the Declaration of Independence, inspired young men across the land to charge into battle, but when they themselves heard the cannons roar, they fled the slaughter they had helped provoke. Fifty-six had signed the Declaration of Independence: nine died in battle, five were captured by the British, and many, such as John Adams, who didn't or couldn't fight, risked death simply by remaining in Congress to raise arms, ammunition, military supplies and money for Washington's Continental Army.

Except Jefferson!

Gentleman Tom had fled the war to his Palladian villa atop a mountain near Charlottesville, Virginia, where he sipped his favorite wines, bowed his beloved violin, and read philosophy. To augment his musical and intellectual solitude, he culled nearby prisoner-of-war camps for the companionship of musically and intellectually gifted Hessian officers—enemy commanders who had fought American troops until their defeat at the Battle of Saratoga. He formed an intimate friendship—and chamber music group—with Baron de Geismer, a Hessian general and talented violinist. Baron Jean Louis de Unger,[24] a young scientist with a passion for philosophy, proved a gifted conversationalist.

"I am alarmed," Washington raged, "and wish to see my countrymen roused. Idleness, dissipation and extravagance . . . and an insatiable thirst for riches seem to have got the better of every other consideration and every order of men."[25]

Jefferson cited financial considerations to justify his decision to remain beyond the fray: "My estate is a large one . . . upwards of ten thousand acres of valuable land on the navigable parts of the James River and two hundred Negroes and not a shilling out of it is or ever was under any encumbrance for debt."[26] In contrast, Washington had left a 20,000-acre plantation at Mount Vernon, Virginia, to fight in the war.

At the end of 1777 Washington and his troops grew desperate for supplies. With Congress lacking powers to tax the states or the people, Washington wrote directly to each state governor pleading for aid.

"It is not easy to give you a just and accurate idea of the sufferings of the troops," Washington lamented to his old friend Governor Patrick

Henry, of Virginia. "I fear I shall wound your feelings by telling you that on the 23rd [of December] I had in camp not less than 2,898 men unfit for duty by reason of their being bare foot and otherwise naked. . . . I cannot but hope that every measure will be pursued . . . to keep them supplied from time to time. No pains, no efforts can be too great for this purpose. The articles of shoes, stockings, blankets demand the most particular attention."[27]

John Marshall was as appalled as his commander: "The inability of Congress and the failure of the states to comply with requisitions rendered our resistance less efficient than it might have been," Marshall complained.[28] "Happily, the real condition of Washington was not well understood by [British General] Sir William Howe, and the characteristic attention of that officer to the lives and comfort of his own troops saved the American army."[29]

The gregarious, fun-loving Marshall had a big hand in lifting troop morale at Valley Forge, injecting a spirit of optimism wherever he could. "He was an excellent companion and idolized by the soldiers and his brother officers, whose gloomy hours were enlivened by his inexhaustible fund of anecdote," wrote Reverend Philip Slaughter. "John Marshall was the best tempered man I ever knew."[30]

In April 1778 George Washington elicited a chorus of cheers by announcing that France had recognized American independence and would send troops and military supplies to support the Continental Army. As summer approached, the impending arrival of the French forced the British to evacuate Philadelphia and consolidate their forces in New York.

As the long British wagon train moved northward through New Jersey's blistering summer heat, Washington's forces followed, harassing the rear. After a week exhausted Redcoats encamped at Monmouth Courthouse (now Freehold, New Jersey). Six miles behind, Washington ordered his troops to attack the British rear guard, sending English-born General Charles Lee toward the center of the British line with four thousand troops. As Lee advanced, two smaller American forces sliced into the British flanks, one under French Major General Lafayette, the other led by Pennsylvania's Brigadier General "Mad" Anthony Wayne and John Marshall's 11th Virginia.

Washington held the main army in reserve, and after Lee's attack was to begin, he sent his fiery twenty-three-year-old aide, Lieutenant Colonel Alexander Hamilton, to reconnoiter. Hamilton had temporarily abandoned college in New York City to enlist in the war. He displayed such brilliance and heroism in action at New York, Trenton, Brandywine, and Germantown that Washington made him his personal aide—all but adopting the boy when he learned of his harsh, near-tragic background.

Born out of wedlock to an itinerant Scottish trader on the Caribbean Island of Nevis, Hamilton was orphaned at twelve, worked as a clerk for an island merchant, and so impressed his employer with his hard work and intelligence that the merchant paid for Hamilton's journey to New York. A cousin there paid for his education at King's College (later, Columbia University), and he was on his way to a degree when the Revolutionary War began.

As Hamilton loped toward the battle lines, he was astonished to find Lee's force retreating in chaos, and he galloped back to report to Washington. Infuriated by Hamilton's report, the commander-in-chief spurred his great white horse into Lee's camp, shouting "till the leaves shook on the trees."[31] He ordered Lee to the rear, calling the Englishman a coward. Taking command himself, Washington rode into the maelstrom of retreating troops, his mount rearing right, then left, herding the men into line. Amidst a chorus of blood-curdling shrieks of wounded men and horses, the commander's call rang out: "Stand fast, my boys! The southern troops are advancing to support you!"[32]

"General Washington was never greater in battle," declared the awe-struck young French General Gilbert de Lafayette. "His presence stopped the retreat; his strategy secured the victory. His stately appearance on horseback, his calm, dignified courage . . . provoked a wave of enthusiasm among the troops."[33]

As Washington called to his men, Hamilton led a frantic assault into the center of enemy lines, while James Monroe and the 3rd Virginia under

General George Washington atop his great steed halting the retreat of American troops at the Battle of Monmouth Courthouse (New Jersey). After calling to his troops to stand and fight, he turned the tide of battle, and the British retreated. (LIBRARY OF CONGRESS)

Colonel Thomas Marshall attacked on the left. Brigadier General "Mad" Anthony Wayne lived up to his sobriquet with an insane charge into the British right flank with John Marshall's 11th Virginia. The British tried to pull back from the onslaught only to be met by a company of Americans led by Lieutenant Colonel Aaron Burr Jr. Like Marshall, Monroe, and Hamilton, Burr had survived the brutal winter at Valley Forge before following Washington into the jaws of combat at Monmouth.

"It should be remembered," Burr wrote on the eve of battle to the aunt who had raised him as a son, "we are engaged in . . . the most important revolution that ever took place. . . . Fire or the sword has scarce left a trace among us. We may truly be called a favored people."[34]

They were all there under the suffocating New Jersey sun: the heroic Men of Monmouth—Burr, Hamilton, Marshall, Monroe—wielding their terrible swift swords against what Thomas Jefferson had assured them was "absolute tyranny." They were a disparate group: Marshall and Monroe—farm boys from the Virginia woods; Burr—a minister's son and Princeton scholar; Hamilton—the bastard son of a bankrupt itinerant Scot trader from an obscure Caribbean island.

All charged as one with comrades from Massachusetts and New Hampshire, Connecticut, Rhode Island, New York and Delaware, New Jersey and Maryland, Pennsylvania, Virginia, the Carolinas and Georgia. Their common quest and common sufferings had brought them together in the dust and dirt of a bloody hell and turned them into brothers. For the first time in the history of the Americas—perhaps the world—a large, heterogeneous band of men and boys had shed national, regional, and religious differences to merge as one new people: Americans all!

Or so they believed at the moment.

Before Washington's men could press their advantage, darkness fell on the field of battle and ended the day's fighting. As Washington and his exhausted troops slept, the British quietly slipped away to Sandy Hook, a spit of land on the northeastern New Jersey shore at the entrance to New York Bay. Transports carried them to New York and deprived the Americans of a clear-cut victory, but Washington nonetheless boasted that "their trip through the Jerseys has cost them [the British] at least 2,000 of their best troops in killed, wounded, prisoners, and deserters. We had 60 men killed—132 wounded and about 130 missing, some of whom I suppose may yet come in."[35]

Energized by the fighting at Monmouth, Marshall and Monroe sought more action, but enlistment terms of their troops had expired. Their men were returning home, and neither officer had replacements to lead into battle. Nor were there any battles to fight. Washington planned to await the French army's arrival before engaging the British again, and he moved his forces through northern New Jersey to the west bank of the Hudson River opposite Manhattan to contain British forces on the island while awaiting the French. Monroe took a post as an aide to the general staff, while Marshall volunteered for a special attack that General "Mad" Anthony Wayne was planning in the Hudson Highlands, about fifty miles up-river from New York.

The British had seized two rocky points that jutted into the water on opposite sides of the river and provided landings for a ferry connection. Wayne organized a small corps of 1,350 elite officers and troops for a quick strike to seize Stony Point on the western side of the River. He chose Captain John Marshall as one of the officers to lead the strike.

On June 15, 1779, after the silent night had cloaked their movements, Wayne and his raiders, including Marshall, were ready to scale the steep rock cliffs of Stony Point. Armed with bayonets and hunting knives, they hoped to assault sentries at the top and capture the British garrison while most of the enemy still slept.

"This will not reach your eye, until the writer is no more," Wayne scribbled at the foot of the cliffs in a note to his brother-in-law. "Attend to the education of my little son & daughter."[36] In his heart General Wayne knew the expedition was certain suicide.

CHAPTER 2

Commotions

As Marshall and the other troops clambered over the cliff tops into the British camp at Stony Point, New York, a prearranged signal set off a barrage from General "Mad" Anthony Wayne's artillery, which had quietly rolled into the forest behind the British. The bursts of shell fire drew attention away from the raiders, and, after only twenty-five minutes, Marshall and his men had secured the fort and taken 500 British prisoners at a cost of only 15 American lives. Twenty British soldiers died, with 83 Americans and 60 British wounded.

The victory proved of no value, however. At the ferry base across the river from Stony Point, the British repelled a similar assault and left the two landings in the hands of opposing forces—unusable by either.

A month later, in August 1779, Marshall volunteered for what would prove his last engagement of the war. He joined Virginia General Henry "Light-Horse Harry" Lee in another night assault—this one on a British fort at Paulus Hook (now Jersey City), on the Hudson River opposite lower Manhattan. The Americans took 158 British prisoners and captured the last British military emplacement in northern New Jersey.

As the Continental Army moved to winter quarters in Morristown, New Jersey, at the end of 1779 Washington learned of British plans to invade Virginia. Thomas Jefferson had succeeded Patrick Henry as governor in June 1779 after Henry had completed his third successive term and was constitutionally ineligible to succeed himself. Washington urged Jefferson to install *chevaux-de-frise** defenses at the mouths of navigable state rivers to prevent British ships from sailing upstream. He also asked Jefferson in the strongest terms to step up military recruiting efforts. Most Virginia troops had returned home after their three-year commitments, and the state's officers—Marshall, Monroe, and the rest— were left without men to defend the state. Convinced that citizens would, like the Massachusetts Minutemen, stream from their homes en masse to repel invaders, Jefferson "totally disbelieved" Washington's warnings.

"Peace is not far off," Jefferson all but scoffed at Washington. "The English cannot hold out long, because all the world is against them."[1]

As a precaution, though, the governor ordered the capital moved fifty miles upstream from Williamsburg to Richmond and stored all state papers, archives, and other records in a shabby-looking forge outside the new capital.

With no infantrymen to command himself, Marshall took a leave of absence to visit his father, who commanded an artillery regiment in Yorktown. To his joy, he learned that the officer corps included two of his brothers, Thomas Jr., and James Markham, both captains. Adding even more pleasure to his imminent family reunion were four, beautiful, unmarried young ladies who lived across the road from his father's headquarters—the four daughters of state councilor Jacquelin Ambler. Targets of longing looks from every lonely officer in camp, the girls were the youngest descendants of an old and noble Huguenot family that had fled France after the St. Bartholomew's Day Massacre of Protestants in 1572 during the French wars of religion.

The first of the Amblers arrived in Virginia in 1672 with much of their fortune intact—only to see it largely disappear in the looting and destruction of the Revolutionary War. Still socially and politically

---

*Timbers embedded in the river bed at an angle facing downstream. Tied together by a network of wires with their ends shaped into sharp spikes, they prevented enemy ships from sailing upstream.

influential after the Revolution, Ambler's most valuable assets were his daughters, whose beauty, charm, and education, he hoped, would compensate for the absence of dowries. A close friend of Thomas Marshall, Ambler planned a ball to present his daughters to society after he learned that, in addition to Colonel Marshall's two other sons and a gaggle of other eligible young officers, the young hero Captain John Marshall was coming to visit.

"Our expectations were raised to the highest pitch," Eliza Ambler, the oldest Ambler daughter, wrote of John Marshall's anticipated arrival. "We had been accustomed to hear him spoken of by all as a very *paragon*. . . . The eldest of fifteen children, devoted from his earliest years to his younger brothers and sisters, he was almost idolized by them, and every line received from him was read with rapture."[2]

The John Marshall who finally staggered into town, however, left the Ambler girls aghast. Instead of the sword-wielding Adonis in shining armor they had conjured in their imaginations, the young man they saw was a filthy, emaciated, unshaven, unkempt vagabond—an elongated skeleton in tatters. He and his comrades had walked from the northern battlefields, sleeping in the open along the way, seldom stopping for anything but the most basic needs.

"I lost all desire of becoming agreeable in his eyes," Eliza Ambler shuddered, "when I beheld his awkward figure, unpolished manners, and total negligence of person."[3]

Not, however, Eliza's youngest sister, fourteen-year-old Mary Ambler, whom her family and friends called "Polly." Too young to go to the ball, Polly had never even taken dancing lessons, but, intent on glimpsing the fabled Captain John Marshall, she ignored the admonitions of her older sister and sneaked into the ballroom. When she and John saw each other, they fell in love.

"She with a glance divined his character," Polly's sister explained, "and understood how to appreciate it. . . . [She] resolved to set her cap at him . . . and at the first introduction he became devoted to her."[4]

John Marshall would treasure every minute of those first moments with Polly the rest of his life: "The ball at Yorktown . . . the dinner on fish at your house the next day . . . the very welcome reception you gave me . . . our little tiffs and makings up . . . and all the thousand indescribable but deeply affecting instances of your affection or coldness which constituted for a time the happiness or misery of my life."[5]

Marshall became a daily visitor to the Ambler home, reading poetry to the girls and gradually winning over the entire family. "Beneath the slovenly garb there dwelt a heart complete with every virtue," Polly's oldest sister Eliza conceded later.

> From the moment he loved my sister he became truly a brother to me (a blessing which before I had never known). . . . During the short stay he made with us, our whole family became attached to him. . . . We felt a love for him that can never cease; and how could it have been otherwise when there was no circumstance, however trivial, in which we were concerned that was not his care.[6]

As the first days of 1780 passed and Governor Jefferson did nothing to enlist new recruits, John Marshall's father set out with sons Thomas Jr. and James Markham for Kentucky, then still part of Virginia. With land the most valuable resource at the time, Virginia had set aside thousands of acres in Kentucky's wilderness as bounties for service in the Revolutionary War, with grants based on rank and length of service. To claim ownership, however, recipients had to survey and stake out their properties—a difficult and costly, time-consuming adventure that left many returning soldiers so intimidated by the enormity of the task that they willingly sold their bounty rights to speculators for pennies on the dollar.

As a Revolutionary War general, Thomas Marshall claimed almost 110,000 acres of bounty lands for himself, while his sons, as captains, could each add at least 4,000 acres more to family holdings. Before they left, the Marshalls bought warrants at prices well below their face values for thousands more acres from other veterans and built their holdings in Kentucky alone to 152,229 acres.

The road to Kentucky was more trail than road. Carved from the wilderness by Daniel Boone, "Boone's Trace" began west of Richmond,

A signer of the Declaration of Independence, Judge George Wythe became a legendary law professor at College of William and Mary, preparing, among others, Thomas Jefferson, John Marshall, and George Washington's nephew Bushrod Washington for the law. (LIBRARY OF CONGRESS)

south of the Shenandoah Valley, sliced through the Cumberland Gap, and turned north into central Kentucky, before splitting: a western fork led to Louisville and a northern fork into the fertile bluegrass country in Fayette Country, which included Lexington. Thomas Marshall sought— and won—appointment as chief surveyor for both Fayette County and the town of Lexington.

John Marshall, meanwhile, extended his leave from the army to study law at College of William and Mary under the legendary George Wythe, who had trained Governor Jefferson. Wythe was teaching nearly forty other students when Marshall enrolled—among them George Washington's favorite nephew, Bushrod Washington, and Spencer Roane, who would soon marry one of Patrick Henry's daughters.

A signer of the Declaration of Independence, Wythe was Virginia's most renowned lawyer and legal scholar—and designer of a unique American curriculum that expanded the usual study of textbooks with a monthly moot court for students to act as attorneys before a jury of professors. He also organized students into a mock legislature to write and debate laws, with Wythe acting as "speaker" and preparing each to enter government and lead his state.

John Marshall completed his studies in August 1780 and had no sooner won admission to the Virginia bar that autumn when Benedict Arnold, who had switched sides in the war, sailed from New York for Chesapeake Bay with a fleet of twenty-seven ships carrying 1,600 British troops. His fleet sailed across the bay and up the James River unimpeded because of Jefferson's failure to install *chevaux-de-frise*. Caught unprepared, Jefferson and other Virginia officials fled Richmond toward the hills of Charlottesville, where Jefferson had built an incongruously pretentious home he called "Monticello" ("little mountain" in Italian).

"Such terror and confusion, you have no idea of," Ambler's daughter Eliza wrote the night of Arnold's arrival. "Governor, Council, everybody scampering . . . "

> How dreadful the idea of an enemy passing through such a country as ours committing enormities that fill the mind with horror and returning exultantly without meeting one impediment to discourage them. . . . But this is not more laughable than . . . our illustrious Governor, who they say took neither rest nor food for man or horse until he reached [his] Mountain.[7]

Arnold and his men burned much of Richmond, including the forge where Jefferson had stored Virginia's records and official history.

With Jefferson unable or unwilling to defend the state, Washington sent the young French Major General Lafayette with 1,000 regulars to Richmond. Lord Cornwallis, however, rode in from the south with 7,000 troops to seize and hold the state capital and send Lafayette and his men in full flight northward. General "Mad" Anthony Wayne waited at the Pennsylvania border with 1,300 Pennsylvanians to replenish, reclothe, re-arm, and reinforce Lafayette's men before counterattacking the British. Far from his sources of supply in Chesapeake Bay off Yorktown, Cornwallis had no choice but retreat.

In the spring of 1781, as Governor Jefferson's second one-year term in office neared its end, Virginia's House of Delegates, led by Patrick Henry, took up a motion to impeach Jefferson and call on General Washington to take command of all Virginia forces. Jefferson pleaded with Washington that only a few days remained before the end of his term, after which he pledged his "retirement to a private station . . . relinquishing [his office] to abler hands."[8]

Adding to Jefferson's public humiliation as governor was a devastating personal loss: his daughter Lucy Elizabeth—not yet two years old—had died. Nor was that the last blow he was to suffer. Lucy's death left Jefferson's wife so weak physically and so shattered emotionally that less than five months after her daughter's death Martha Jefferson followed her daughter to the grave, leaving Jefferson with three surviving young daughters to raise by himself.

On June 3, 1781, Thomas Jefferson ceded the governorship to General Thomas Nelson without explanation. Forty years later Jefferson was still unwilling to explain his conduct as governor. His autobiography revealed nothing:

> From a belief that, under the pressure of the invasion under which we were then laboring, the public would have more confidence in a military chief, and that the military commander, being invested with the civil power also, both might be wielded with more energy, promptitude and effect for the defense of the state, I resigned the administration at the end of my second year, and General Nelson was appointed to succeed me.[9]

John Marshall and James Monroe both hoped the new governor would change the recruitment picture, but they soon learned that "the militia in the field was officer'd and . . . that [they] could procure none whatever."[10]

Two months later, on the night of October 14, 1781, Alexander Hamilton and the Marquis de Lafayette—both close friends and battlefield comrades of Marshall and Monroe at Monmouth—led the heroic charge through enemy redoubts at Yorktown. On October 17 Lord Cornwallis, the British commander, proposed "a cessation of hostilities" and, two days later, signed the articles of capitulation that ended fighting in America. John Marshall rode home to Oak Hill, where neighbors elected him to the Virginia House of Delegates and sent him back to Richmond and the arms of his beloved Polly Ambler.

When Marshall took his seat in the spring of 1782, his friend James Monroe had also won election to the legislature. The two would now serve their country together in peace as they had in war—this time alongside such legendary Virginians as Patrick Henry, George Mason, Richard Henry Lee, and James Madison.

Their wartime heroics made Marshall and Monroe instant celebrities, while Marshall's romance with Polly Ambler and close ties to the rest of the Ambler family gave Richmond's gossip mills more than enough fodder. Both young men won immediate acceptance by legislators, who gave the young heroes prime committee appointments as well as invitations to important social functions.

From the first, Marshall championed veterans' rights, demanding an end to state seizures of properties owned by former soldiers unable to pay property taxes. "I partook largely of the sufferings and feelings of the army and brought with me into civilian life an ardent devotion to its interests," Marshall explained. He grew convinced, however, that state politics lay behind the sufferings of the army and its veterans "and that no safe and permanent remedy could be found but in a more efficient and better organized general [federal] government."[11]

By the end of Marshall's first year in the legislature the sufferings of the army had grown unbearable. Without power to levy taxes, the Confederation Congress was bankrupt and unable to pay the troops, many of whom roamed the countryside pillaging farms for food and clothing. In Newburgh, New York, where Washington's Continental Army lay encamped after Yorktown, an unsigned leaflet urged officers to take up arms and march against Congress.

"My God," Washington shuddered at what he termed a call to treason. He ordered officers to assemble and read the letter to them. He then acknowledged the hardships officers and troops had faced but called the letter "something so shocking that humanity revolts at the idea." He reminded them, "I have never left your side one moment" and pledged his name and honor that "you may command my services . . . in the attainment of complete justice for all your toils and dangers."[12]

Although Washington's appeal ended the mutiny in Newburgh, troops encamped in Lancaster, Pennsylvania, did not hear his message. Enraged over government failure to pay them, they marched to Philadelphia, their numbers increasing to more than 500 as they reached the doors of Congress to extract justice—and money. As rifle barrels shattered windows and took aim, congressmen fled the hall and the city, crossing the Delaware River to New Jersey. Congress reconvened in Princeton on June 24 and met there on and off until October, when it moved to more spacious quarters in Annapolis, Maryland, and ultimately New York City, far from any mutinous troop encampments.

Congress was still meeting in Annapolis when word arrived that the British had recognized American independence and ended the Revolutionary War. Washington rode to Annapolis, resigned his commission, and returned to private life, and the army disbanded.

"At length then the military career of the greatest man on earth is closed," John Marshall wrote to his friend Monroe. By then the House of Delegates had elected Monroe to the Confederation Congress as one of Virginia's representatives. Recalling the hardships he and Monroe had shared with Washington at Valley Forge and elsewhere, Marshall was overcome by emotion:

> May happiness attend him wherever he goes. May he long enjoy those blessings he has secured his country. When I speak or think of that superior man, my heart overflows with gratitude. May he ever experience from his countrymen those attentions which such sentiments of themselves produce.[13]

John Marshall's wife "Polly"—Mary Ambler Marshall—in a drawing by her oldest son Thomas Marshall. (FROM *THE LIFE OF JOHN MARSHALL*, BY ALBERT J. BEVERIDGE, VOL. I:168.)

On January 3, 1783, John Marshall married Polly Ambler. The bride was seventeen, appropriately shy; the groom slightly more than ten years older. After paying the parson, he confessed to one of his sisters-in-law that he had "but one solitary guinea left."[14] It was fortunate that Polly's cousin John Ambler was one of the state's richest young men, with a country estate that served as a picture-book setting for the wedding and wedding reception—and enough cash to lend John Marshall the money to begin married life.

Marshall's marriage and his service in the legislature made it more convenient to make Richmond his permanent home, and he and Polly rented a small, two-room cottage. Rather than travel north to Oak Hill to run for reelection every year, he gave up his seat in the legislature after his first term and opened an office in Richmond to practice full-time law. Among his first clients was his friend James Monroe, whose service in Congress—and romance with beautiful Elizabeth Kortright—now kept him in New York most of the year. He entrusted Marshall with management of his bounty lands in Kentucky and his affairs in Richmond.

Life in New York proved costly, however, and Monroe soon ran out of cash and sent a messenger to Marshall for more.

"I wish it was possible to relieve your wants," Marshall replied, "but it is impossible. . . . There is not one shilling [in your account], and the keeper of it could not borrow one. . . . I am pressed warmly by Ege [a Richmond merchant] for money, and your old landlady Mrs. Shera begins now to be a little clamorous. I shall be obliged, I apprehend, to negotiate your warrants at a discount."[15]

Marshall eventually dipped into his own pocket for enough money to send Monroe for his immediate needs, then changed the substance of his letter to lighter fare: "The excessive cold weather [here] has operated like magic on our youth," he reported. "They feel the necessity of artificial heat and quite wearied with lying alone, they are all treading the broad road to matrimony."[16]

At the time Richmond was little more than a frontier town of about 1,200 people on the edge of the wilderness. The streets were still dirt roads, and walkways were little more than elongated dumping grounds for ashes. St. John's Church, where Patrick Henry had delivered his "liberty-or-death" oration, was the town's only church and the only building of consequence. A state house of sorts looked more like a warehouse than the home of the state legislature and court. Several hundred wooden houses dotted the surrounding hills, but most were little more than shacks that shook with every gust of wind and struggled to stay upright when a six-horse transport wagon rumbled by.

The town had one tavern—Farmicola—a sizable two-story inn that doubled as Richmond's men's club, where Marshall was a consistent loser at whist but a popular conversationalist and drinking companion. The upstairs at Farmicola housed beds for visitors who crowded into

Richmond when the House of Delegates was in session. The downstairs welcomed "generals, colonels, captains, senators, assemblymen, judges, doctors, clerks, and crowds of gentlemen of every weight and caliber and every hue of dress sitting altogether about the fire, drinking, smoking, singing, and talking ribaldry."[17]

On July 24, 1784, Polly gave birth to the Marshalls' first child, whom they named Thomas, for John's father. Three weeks before the boy's birth Marshall had purchased a slave for V£90 (Virginia pounds) to relieve Polly of some household chores. After Thomas was born, he bought two more slaves for only V£30, the equivalent of two months' rent, and relieved Polly of all the rest of her household chores.

Late in 1785 Polly elated her husband with news that she was pregnant with their second child, and he in turn surprised her with news that he had taken a major case called *Hite v. Fairfax*, which, if he won, would make him one of America's wealthiest men.

Hite v. Fairfax traced its origins to 1649, when King Charles II of England granted a group of noblemen 5 million acres on Virginia's Northern Neck, the northernmost of three eastern Virginia peninsulas that reached into Chesapeake Bay. Bounded by the Potomac River on the north and the Rappahannock River on the south, Virginia's Northern Neck (see map, page 43) stretched inland to the Blue Ridge Mountains, hundreds of miles to the west. By the early eighteenth century one man in England—Lord Fairfax—had acquired the entire Northern Neck.

When Virginia's colonial government ran out of money in the early 1730s, it seized and sold lands of absentee owners who had failed to build homes on their properties and showed no intention of settling there. Among the lands seized were tens of thousands of acres of vacant Fairfax lands, including a 54,000-acre parcel that it sold to a speculator who resold it to Jost Hite, the owner of a gristmill near Germantown, Pennsylvania. Although Hite held a bill of sale for the 54,000 acres, Lord Fairfax still held the deed and legal title.

In 1735, when Lord Fairfax learned what Virginia was doing to his grant, he sailed for Virginia as fast as Atlantic winds permitted to survey and stake out his lands and build homes on them before Virginia seized

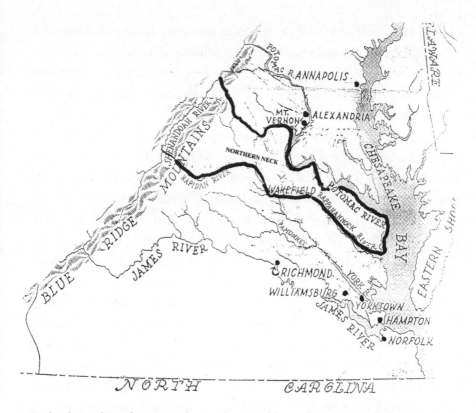

England's Lord Fairfax acquired a royal grant of five million acres, including all of Virginia's Northern Neck. Bounded by the Potomac River on the north and the Rappahannock to the south, the Northern Neck stretched from the slopes of the Blue Ridge to Chesapeake Bay. The Marshall family would eventually gain possession of more than 200,000 acres of the Fairfax Manor Lands on the Blue Ridge, where Lord Fairfax built his mountain home.

everything he owned. Among his surveyors were George Washington and Thomas Marshall, who surveyed about 215,000 acres, removing them from the pool of unclaimed wilderness the state could claim.

Lord Fairfax built a palatial home he called Belvoir, near George Washington's Mount Vernon. He built a second simpler house—a hunting lodge he called Leeds Manor—on the eastern slope of the Blue Ridge Mountains near the South Branch of the Potomac River. Named for his native English home at Leeds Castle in Kent, Leeds Manor stood on the

54,000 acres that Hite had bought and included the land at Oak Hill, where Thomas Marshall would later build his family home.

By 1785 Lord Fairfax and Jost Hite were long dead, but potential fortunes awaited their heirs from the sale of the lands if they could prove ownership. Hite's descendants held his original bill of sale from the Virginia government, but a descendant of Lord Fairfax, the Reverend Denny Martin Fairfax, held the original deed in England. Hite's heirs demanded that Denny Fairfax surrender the deed, but Fairfax refused, arguing that Virginia had seized and sold the Fairfax lands illegally.

In 1785 Hite's heirs sued, and Denny Fairfax turned to Thomas Marshall, who had surveyed much of the land. Marshall, in turn, referred Fairfax to his son John Marshall, who saw an opportunity for the Marshall family to profit by buying the original deed to the Fairfax Manor lands themselves. He sent his younger brother James Markham Marshall to Britain to negotiate with Denny Fairfax, who agreed to sell the deed for £20,000 (about $1.5 million in today's US dollars), or two shillings an acre—about 40 percent below market prices for Virginia lands. For the Marshalls to consummate the sale, however, John Marshall would have to defend Denny Fairfax's title to the lands against Hite family claims.

Beginning in 1786, the next eight years would see *Hite v. Fairfax* consume every legal skill at John Marshall's command in four federal courts, including the US Supreme Court. If he won the case, however, it promised him fame as an attorney and both him and his family untold wealth from the resale of the lands, whose value had appreciated dramatically.

In 1786 Marshall reaped a windfall when his cousin Edmund Randolph won election as governor of Virginia. After taking his oath, the governor retired from his private law practice and directed all his clients to his favorite young cousin John Marshall. The acquisition of Governor Randolph's practice catapulted Marshall to the top of his profession in Virginia, which, despite the growth of New York, was still the nation's largest, wealthiest, and most populated state.

"My extensive acquaintance in the army was also of great service to me," Marshall noted in his autobiography. "My numerous military friends, who were dispersed over the state, took great interest in my favor, and I was more successful than I had reason to expect."[18]

On June 15 of the same year Polly added to her husband's joy by giving birth to the Marshalls' second child, whom they named Rebecca, after Polly's mother. Unfortunately baby Rebecca died after only five days, plunging Polly into a deep depression that only intensified in September, when a miscarriage claimed another Marshall offspring.

Thomas Jefferson's daughter Martha—a mean-spirited gossip—wrote her father that "Mrs. Marshall, once Miss Ambler, is insane. The loss of two children is thought to have occasioned it."[19]

At the end of 1786 John Marshall bought his first home in Richmond, where, in December 1787, Polly gave birth to their second son, whom they named Jacquelin Ambler Marshall after Polly's father. The multiple childbirths and the miscarriage, however, took a crippling toll on Polly's emotional and physical health—much as similar losses had affected her mother and sisters. She emerged a lifelong semi-invalid who needed a full-time personal caretaker—and a husband close to home to assume responsibilities normally performed by a wife. He embraced the role with good humor, however, growing more joyful and loving toward his wife. A huge bear of a man, Marshall cherished taking the fragile Polly in his arms and cooing poetic professions of his love. The more responsibilities he assumed in life, the happier he seemed and the more time he found to take on more.

"His exemplary tenderness to our unfortunate sister," Polly's older sister Eliza told friends, "is without parallel. . . . Early after her marriage, she became prey to an extreme nervous affliction . . . but this only served to increase his care and tenderness."

> He is always and under every circumstance as devoted to her as at the moment of their first being married. His never failing cheerfulness and good humor are a perpetual source of delight to all connected with him and, I have not a doubt, have been the means of prolonging the life of her to whom he is so tenderly devoted.[20]

Helping Marshall prolong Polly's life and relieving him of many household burdens was Robin Spurlock, an evidently brilliant young man. Spurlock was a slave who had appeared among John Marshall's wedding presents and, as Polly grew weaker, stepped in and gradually took charge of the entire Marshall household.

Marshall's father and two brothers, meanwhile, had accumulated about 230,000 acres in Kentucky. After setting aside fertile lands to settle and farm themselves, they converted the rest of their holdings into great wealth by dividing them into tracts for sale to land-hungry migrants streaming across the Appalachians. Although many were Europeans seeking opportunities in the New World, thousands of others were American Tories who had seen their holdings plundered and confiscated in the East and now sought to rebuild their lives in the West—often under assumed new names.

By the mid-1780s Thomas Marshall realized he would never return East, and he transferred his magnificent 824-acre Oak Hill property to his son John. John cherished his boyhood home and immediately expanded it to nearly 1,100 acres by purchasing an adjacent 260-acre property. Although he would use it only sporadically at first, it soon proved a valuable second home for him and Polly, who found the cool mountain breezes of the Blue Ridge a welcome escape from Richmond's blistering summer heat.

While Thomas Marshall and his sons were amassing fortunes in Kentucky, the vast majority of Revolutionary War veterans in the East remained mired in poverty. Most were farmers on small barren plots that seldom yielded enough to feed a family, let alone pay crushing property taxes that state governments imposed after the war to pay for public services the British government had provided before independence. Although many veterans had received warrants for western bounty lands, few had Thomas Marshall's skills, time, or money to exploit their holdings. Most gladly accepted cash offers from speculators, who bought rights to thousands of acres for a few pennies on the dollar and left veterans with little to show for their military service—but a few pennies.

When John Marshall turned eighteen in 1773, his father Thomas had accumulated enough wealth to buy a 1,700-acre farm and build this home at Oak Hill. The seven-room house measured thirty by thirty-three feet, with one of the three rooms upstairs serving as a classroom for the fifteen Marshall children. (FROM THE LIFE OF JOHN MARSHALL, BY ALBERT J. BEVERIDGE, VOL. I: 64)

Unable to pay property taxes, thousands of farmers fell victim to government seizures of their homes—and few could appeal. Most courts were in coastal cities—Boston, New York, and such. By the time a farmer in rural Massachusetts or New York traveled the long, rutted roads to a far-off court, the judge had already declared him in default and sent a sheriff to seize his property. Farmers saw their lands and homes confiscated and their livestock and personal possessions—including tools of their trade—auctioned at prices too low to clear their debts. Hysterical wives and terrified children watched helplessly as sheriffs' deputies dragged farmers off to debtors' prisons, where they languished indefinitely—unable to earn money to pay their debts and without tools to do so even if they won their freedom.

By 1786—five years after Yorktown—enraged farmers across the East took up pitchforks and rifles to protect their properties, firing at sheriffs who ventured too near. Reassembling their wartime companies, some set fire to debtors prisons, courthouses, and offices of county clerks. In western Massachusetts former captain Daniel Shays, a destitute farmer struggling to hold onto his property, organized an army of 500 other farmers and marched to Springfield. Shouting their battle cry of "Close down the courts!" they shut down the state supreme court before marching on the federal arsenal to arm themselves with more powerful weapons. Their battle cries echoed across the state, provoking farmers to march on courthouses in Cambridge, Concord, Worcester, Northampton, Taunton, and Great Barrington—and shut them down.

"The commotions . . . have risen in Massachusetts to an alarming height," Virginia's congressional delegate Henry "Light-Horse Harry" Lee wrote to Washington from the Confederation capital in New York. "After various insults to government, by stopping the courts of justice etc., the insurgents have taken possession of the town of Springfield. . . . This event produces much suggestion as to its causes. Some attribute it to the weight of taxes and the decay of commerce . . . others, to British councils."[21]

The farmer uprising in Massachusetts soon spread to other states. New Hampshire farmers marched to the state capital at Exeter, surrounded the legislature, and demanded forgiveness of all debts, return of all seized properties to former owners, and equitable distribution of property. A mob of farmers in Maryland burned down the Charles County courthouse, while farmers in Virginia burned down the King William County and New Kent County courthouses, east and north of Richmond.

"All is gloom in the eastern states," John Marshall fretted to former brigadier general James Wilkinson, an enigmatic figure whom Marshall had known at Valley Forge. Wilkinson had resigned from the army after joining a failed plot to oust Washington as Continental Army commander. After the war Wilkinson had settled in Kentucky and was on his way to New Orleans on an ill-defined mission for Kentucky planters and needed a passport to travel into Spanish territory. He turned to the influential lawyer John Marshall, and although Marshall was unable to help, he sent Wilkinson a chatty letter with his views on Shays's rebellion.

"These violent, I fear bloody, dissentions," Marshall commented, "cast a deep shade over that bright prospect which the revolution in America and the establishment of our free governments had opened to the votaries of liberty throughout the globe. . . . I fear that these have truth on their side who say that man is incapable of governing himself. I fear we may live to see another revolution."[22]

CHAPTER 3

"*We, Sir, Idolize Democracy!*"

THE CHAOS CREATED BY FARMER REBELLIONS IN 1786 PARALYZED STATE legislators in Massachusetts, New York, Virginia, and elsewhere with fear.

"This long session has not produced a single bill of public importance," John Marshall complained in Virginia. "It is surprising that gentlemen of character cannot dismiss their private animosities but will bring them in the assembly."[1]

James Madison, one of Virginia's delegates to the Confederation Congress, agreed. "Nothing can exceed the confusion which reigns . . . indeed runs through all of our public affairs and must continue as long as the present mode of legislating continues." He wrote to his friend and mentor Thomas Jefferson, predicting that the Virginia legislature's conduct would "soon bring our laws and our legislature into contempt among all orders of citizens."[2]

No more able than the state legislatures to cope with the spreading chaos, the Confederation Congress urged its presiding officer, Revolutionary War hero Henry "Light-Horse Harry" Lee, to appeal to his friend George Washington, who remained the most prominent living symbol of national unity.

"A majority of the people of Massachusetts is in opposition to the government," Lee explained to his former commander-in-chief, "and their leaders *avow* the *subversion* of it to be their object together with the abolition of debts, the division of property and reunion with Great Britain."

> In all the eastern states, the same temper prevails. . . . The malcontents are in close connection with Vermont, and that district . . . is in negotiation with the Governor of Canada. My dear General, we are all in dire apprehension that a beginning of anarchy . . . has approached and have no means to stop the dreadful work.[3]

Lee proposed calling a convention of state leaders to permit Congress to act "with more energy, effect, and vigor."[4] To everyone's amazement, even Patrick Henry, Virginia's patron saint of state sovereignty, agreed. Henry predicted that "ruin is inevitable unless something is done to give Congress a compulsory process on delinquent states."[5]

Learning of Henry's declaration, Washington grew optimistic: "Notwithstanding the jealous and contracted temper which seems to prevail in some of the states, I cannot but hope and believe that the good sense of the people will ultimately get the better of their prejudices."[6]

As popular dissatisfaction with government swelled, a surge in land speculation added to national disarray by provoking territorial disputes between states, which the Revolution had left independent and sovereign. Although all had joined the loose-knit Confederation of American States, the Articles of Confederation created no central authority and left its congress nothing more than a forum in which to exchange views. It had no powers to tax, raise an army, or assume any other responsibilities of a domestic government.

Like Europe's nations, American states were ready to attack each other at the slightest provocation. New York and New Hampshire were edging toward war over conflicting claims to lands in Vermont; both Virginia and Pennsylvania claimed sovereignty over lands in present-day western Pennsylvania and Kentucky; Massachusetts claimed all of western New York; and Connecticut prepared to send its militia into Pennsylvania after Pennsylvania militiamen fired on Connecticut farmers who had settled on vacant lands in the Wyoming Valley of northeastern Pennsylvania.

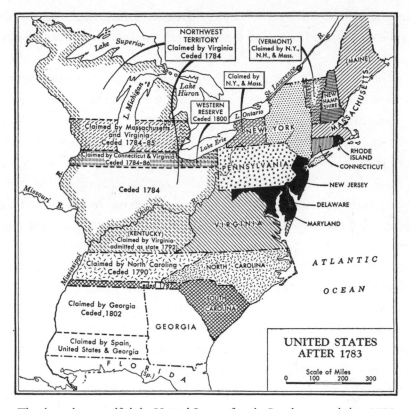

The chaos that engulfed the United States after the Revolution ended in 1783 is evident in the cross-hatched areas depicting conflicting territorial claims of the thirteen sovereign states. Adding to the chaos were British and Spanish troops encamped outside the dark boundary line, ready to attack. The map shows Virginia as the nation's largest, wealthiest, and most heavily populated state—and enough political power to name four of the first five Presidents.

In addition to territorial disputes, economic disputes embroiled six states. Maryland and Virginia each claimed its border lay across the Potomac River on the opposite shoreline, thus giving each the right to collect fees and duties from ships traveling the waterway. Farther north, states with deep-water ports such as Philadelphia, New York, and Boston were bleeding the economies of neighboring states with heavy duties on imports that passed through their harbors on their way to inland destinations. "New Jersey, placed between Philadelphia and New York, is like a cask tapped at both ends," James Madison complained, "and North Carolina, between Virginia and South Carolina seems a patient bleeding at both arms."[7]

With Congress impotent and New York too distant, delegates from far-off southern states appeared only intermittently at the Confederation Congress after it fled Philadelphia. A few states even stopped appointing delegates. When Congress did meet, its members often had little in common; they barely understood each other's words, let alone each other's thinking—especially on the issue of slavery. Without money or means to raise it, Congress stopped repaying principal and interest on foreign debts, disbanded American naval operations, and reduced the army to a mere eighty privates.[8]

Secretary at War Henry Knox, who had been a major general and chief of the artillery in the Revolutionary War, warned Washington that "different states have . . . views that sooner or later must involve the country in all the horrors of civil war. . . . We are entirely destitute of those traits which should stamp us *one* nation, and the Constitution of Congress [Articles of Confederation] does not promise any alteration."[9]

John Marshall agreed that "everything has been mixed . . . we have been united in some respects, separate in others. We have acted as one people for some purposes, as distinct societies for others, separate in others."[10]

In fact, George Washington had already responded to the crisis, but with little fanfare. Hoping to use common commercial interests to unite a few states, he invited representatives of Maryland and Virginia to his plantation at Mount Vernon to end their economic war by establishing a joint shipping channel in Chesapeake Bay and the Potomac River. Washington's presence encouraged his guests to outdo one another with concessions, adopting uniform commercial regulations and even a uniform currency. In effect, they established an economic union.

The potential economic benefits of their union became so evident that Pennsylvania and Delaware joined, and before long, Virginia leaders urged all states to participate in a conference to unify interstate and foreign commerce regulations, eliminate interstate trade restrictions, and facilitate establishment of trade agreements with foreign nations.

By early 1787, after twelve of the thirteen states agreed to participate in what they assumed was an economic conference, Congress issued an official, if vaguely worded, call to the states to convene "for the sole and express purpose of revising the Articles of Confederation . . . [and] render the federal constitution adequate to the exigencies of government and the preservation of the union."[11]

Only Rhode Island refused—three times. Rhode Island's Atlantic ports saved shippers in the South and the West Indies days of sailing around Cape Cod to reach New England via Boston Harbor. Rhode Island's government was not about to share a penny of profits reaped from those who took advantage of the state's coastal gateway.

By early 1787 Boston's merchant-bankers had organized a private 3,000-man army under Revolutionary War General Benjamin Lincoln to march to western Massachusetts to confront the Shaysite force, which had swelled to 1,500 men. The troops from Boston reached Springfield in late January and repelled the Shaysites, leaving 4 farmers dead and 20 wounded. A few days later, on February 4, Lincoln's army crushed the rebellion with a surprise attack that left 30 more farmers wounded, 150 taken prisoner, and the rest in flight northward across the border to independent Vermont. Marshall was elated by "the prospect of reestablishing order and good government in Massachusetts.

"I think their government will now stand more firmly," he told friends, "provided some examples are made to impress on the minds of the people a conviction that punishment will surely follow an attempt to subvert the laws and government of the commonwealth."[12]

In defeat, however, the Shaysites scored a resounding victory for Massachusetts farmers, who flocked to the polls as never before and turned Governor James Bowdoin and three-quarters of the state legislature out of office. Governor-elect John Hancock pledged amnesty for Shays and his followers, and the new, pro-farmer legislature acceded to most Shaysite demands. It exempted clothing, household possessions, and tools of trade from seizure in debt proceedings and allowed imprisoned debtors to return to work by taking a pauper's oath that they had no income. In a symbolic gesture, Governor Hancock cut his own salary and convinced the legislature to declare a tax holiday for a year and reduce property taxes thereafter.

Just as the shots fired at Lexington had echoed in London's Parliament, the shots fired at Springfield reverberated in Congress and many state capitols, even jolting some state-rights advocates into realizing the only way to forestall the spread of anarchy was by strengthening the central government.

"It is indispensable," Washington had warned Congress and the American people when he resigned his commission after the war, "that there should be lodged somewhere a Supreme Power to regulate and govern the general concerns of the Confederated Republic, without which the Union cannot be of long duration."

> There must be a faithful and pointed compliance on the part of every state
> with the demands of Congress . . . that whatever measures have a tendency
> to dissolve the Union . . . ought to be considered as hostile to the liberty
> and independency of America and the authors treated accordingly.[13]

Washington now pressed state leaders to act together to save the nation in peace as they had in war. "There are errors in our national government," he railed at New York's John Jay, who served as secretary for foreign affairs in the Confederation Congress. "Something must be done!"[14]

On May 17, 1787, the first delegates appeared in Philadelphia to revise the Articles of Confederation—the tissue-thin document that had served as a constitution since the end of the revolution. Although more than seventy delegates had won election, only fifty-five showed up, and they elected George Washington President of the convention. Despite Washington's pleas to Patrick Henry that he attend, the Virginia patriot so opposed creation of a strong central government that he refused to go to the convention.

Besides Washington, the Virginia House of Delegates elected Governor Edmund Randolph, John Blair, James Madison, George Wythe, and George Mason, whose plantation and manor, Gunston Hall, lay near

Washington's Mount Vernon. Although both Marshall and Monroe had hoped to serve, the House of Delegates considered them too young and without seniority. In contrast, New York saw fit to name the young Alexander Hamilton as one of its three delegates.

For the first time in their lives the three wartime comrades—all members of that elite band of heroic Men of Monmouth—now differed on how to govern their new nation. Marshall and Hamilton, still under the influence of their old commander-in-chief, embraced Washington's concept of a strong federal government. Monroe had fallen under the spell of his law instructor Thomas Jefferson, who stood with Patrick Henry in espousing state sovereignty in domestic affairs.

Over the next four months—124 days in all—delegates to the Constitutional Convention staged a coup d'état. Instead of revising the Articles of Confederation as instructed by Congress, they discarded it in favor of a new constitution that created a new and powerful federal government. Of the forty-two delegates still in attendance when the convention ended, three refused to sign, leaving the 4,500-word finished document with only thirty-nine signatures—scarcely representative of "We the People" who, the preamble insists, created the seven articles of the document.

The first three articles defined the shape and powers of the three branches of government—the national legislature, the executive, and federal judiciary—as well as the methods of selection and qualifications for service (and removal) in each. Article I gave Congress the most powers, *inter alia*, powers to tax the people, levy duties, borrow money, regulate foreign and interstate commerce, maintain a standing army and navy, declare war, and "make all laws . . . necessary and proper" for exercising its powers. It placed no limit on the number of terms legislators could serve if reelected.

Article II gave limited powers to a President, who was to be commander-in-chief of the military and serve indefinitely if reelected. The President would nominate ambassadors, federal judges, and heads of executive departments and negotiate treaties. The states lost all rights to deal with foreign nations.

Article III created a federal judiciary with an indefinite number of lower courts, to be determined by Congress, and one Supreme Court with powers to hear appeals from lower courts.

Article IV forced the states to recognize each other's laws and give all citizens rights of citizenship in every state. The same article also provided for admission of new states and guaranteed "a republican form of government" in every state.

Article V provided for amending the Constitution, and Article VI ranked laws by category, with the Constitution and US laws and treaties ranking highest as "the supreme law of the land." State laws ranked next, and local laws ranked lowest, with little or no consequence for the rest of the nation.

For the Constitution to take effect and permit establishment of a new federal government, Article VII required approval by ratification conventions in nine states, and for it to take effect in any given state, it would have to win approval by a popularly elected convention in that state.

The Constitution was admittedly a compromise between different interest groups and geographic regions of the new nation, each with conflicting interests: farmers vs. bankers, big states vs. little states, North vs. South, East vs. West, slave holders vs. abolitionists, and so forth.

Each wanted rights or powers that deprived others of some rights and powers. States with large populations sought proportionate representation, outraging the states with small populations. Small states argued that three states with the largest populations—Virginia, Pennsylvania, and Massachusetts—would outvote all other states combined and control the nation.

Small states demanded one vote per state, as in the Confederation Congress, but the heavily populated states complained that eight states with a total population smaller than Virginia's alone would be able to dictate to the majority of the American people.

Delegates compromised by creating a bicameral legislature, with a lower house based on proportionate representation and an upper house in which each state would cast two votes. Instead of unfettered majority rule, as in a democracy, the compromise created a republican government that protected the rights of the minority to block legislation it deemed oppressive. Nonetheless, the Constitution vested more powers in the lower house—the House of Representatives—than in any other branch of government, including the upper house, or Senate. As the only branch of government elected directly by "We the People,"* the House had exclusive powers to originate government tax laws and spending measures, to impeach (indict) federal officials (including the President) for "high crimes and misdemeanors," and to elect a President of the United States if the Electoral College failed to do so. The House would, in fact, elect two of the first six Presidents.

In the end every state won a little and lost a little. No state won everything, and, except for white adult male property owners, the vast majority of "We the People" obtained few if any benefits. In most states women and children remained chattel, most blacks remained slaves, and most poor whites remained indentured or without properties of their own and, like women and blacks, unable to vote or hold public office. To keep the South in the Union, the North agreed to prevent the new federal government from interfering with the slave trade for twenty years.

"This Constitution has been formed without the knowledge or idea of the people," Virginia's George Mason complained as the convention neared its end. "It is improper to say to the people, 'Take this or nothing.'" Mason went on to cite Patrick Henry's repeated demands for another, second convention "to know more of the sense of the people and . . . provide a system more consonant to it. I would sooner chop off my right hand than put it to the Constitution as it now stands," Mason raged.[15]

After seeing a copy of the Constitution, Henry echoed Mason's sentiments.

"What right had they to say, *We, the People*?" Henry demanded to know. "My political curiosity . . . leads me to ask who authorized them

---

*Two senators each would be named by state legislatures until 1917.

to speak the language of *We, the People.* . . . The people gave them no power to use their name."[16]

The Constitution was curious in many ways, creating an executive, or President, with few specified powers: it declared the President commander-in-chief of the armed forces but denied him the power to raise troops or send them into action. Only Congress could raise an army or declare war, thus leaving a peacetime President as commander-in-chief of no one and powers to do nothing. The Constitution obligated the President to "take care that the laws be faithfully executed," but gave him no law enforcement arm or powers to arrest or punish miscreants.

Even more curious, the Constitution created a nonelective federal judiciary whose members would serve for life and a Supreme Court with few enumerated powers. An appellate court with almost no original jurisdiction, it would try cases without juries, thus denying respondents a right guaranteed in the English-speaking world since 1215 when King John signed the Magna Carta at Runnymede, England.

In addition to denying citizens the right to trial by jury in the highest court, the Constitution failed to include a bill of rights to protect civil liberties such as freedom of speech, freedom of religious choice, freedom of the press, rights of assembly, and rights to redress of grievances.

"The Constitution is not free from imperfections," Washington admitted, "but there are as few radical defects in it as could well be expected considering . . . the diversity of interests that are to be attended to. As a constitutional door is opened for future amendments and alterations, I think it would be wise in the people to accept what is offered."[17]

New York's Alexander Hamilton agreed, arguing against any immediate amendments to the Constitution as written. By enumerating government powers, he argued, the Constitution automatically left all else outside the government's jurisdiction. "Why declare that things should not be done which there is no power to do?" the hero of Monmouth and Yorktown asked. "Why should it be said that the liberty of the press shall not be restrained when no power is given by which restrictions may be imposed?"[18]

A hero in battles at Trenton, Monmouth, and Yorktown, Alexander Hamilton was General George Washington's closest aide-de-camp in the Revolutionary War and wrote fifty-one of the eighty-five Federalist essays that proved instrumental in ratification of the Constitution. He would go on to serve in Washington's cabinet as the nation's first Secretary of Treasury. (LIBRARY OF CONGRESS)

For the new constitution to take effect, each state had to call a popularly elected ratification convention, and at least nine states would have to vote in its favor. But without Virginia—America's largest, richest, and most heavily populated state—the new nation would be relatively powerless, and, as John Marshall conceded, a majority of Virginians, led by their popular former governor Patrick Henry, "were in the opposition."[19]

"As this government stands," Patrick Henry had avowed after reading the Constitution, "I despise and abhor it. . . . I speak as one poor individual—but when I speak, I speak the language of thousands."[20]

By February 1788 six states had ratified—Delaware, Pennsylvania, New Jersey, Georgia, Connecticut, and Massachusetts. The states with the least land and fewest people—Delaware, New Jersey, and Connecticut—favored ratification to win military protection from the large army a central government would afford. Sparsely settled Georgia—beset by Indian raids from Spanish-held Florida—also needed protection of a strong federal force. Powerful banking interests in Pennsylvania and trading interests in Massachusetts had controlled majorities in the ratification conventions of those two states and ignored popular opposition to ratification.

When Virginia's 170 delegates met at their ratification convention in June 1788, Maryland and South Carolina had become the seventh and eighth states to adopt the new Constitution. Virginia sent most of its great figures to Richmond for the convention—Henry, Madison, Randolph, Mason, Lee, Wythe. The most notable absentee was Washington, who had presided over the Constitutional Convention and felt Virginians should decide on ratification without his direct interference.

Also missing was Thomas Jefferson, whom the Confederation Congress had sent to Paris as American minister to France. Despite his distance from home, Jefferson tried to influence the convention by writing regularly to his protégés James Madison and James Monroe.

"Were I in America," he wrote, "I would advocate it [ratification] till nine [states] should have adopted it and then as warmly take the other side to convince the other four that they ought not to come into it until the declaration of rights be annexed to it."[21]

As the two most prominent young leaders in the state, Marshall and Monroe easily won election to Virginia's ratification convention. Marshall's winning personality and the proximity of his home to the convention site made his parlor a popular social center for delegates of all political persuasions.

For the first time in their lives, however, the two friends Marshall and Monroe—brothers in battle at Monmouth—opposed each other. In

Monroe's first confrontation with his friend, he accused Marshall's constitutionalists of failing to secure individual liberties. "We have struggled too long to bring about this revolution," Monroe declared. "We have fought and bled freely to accomplish it." He did not oppose strengthening central government, he said, but he bridled at ratifying a document that excluded a bill of rights.

"How are we secured in the trial by jury?" he asked.

> Unless we qualified their exercise by securing this, might they not regulate it otherwise? As it is with trial by jury so with the liberty of conscience; that of the press would soon follow. Like all the state constitutions, the federal constitution should define the powers given to government and define the mode in which they shall be exercised.[22]

Monroe went on to list his five principal objections to the Constitution: the federal government's powers to tax people directly without their consent; the absence of a bill of rights to guarantee individual freedoms; the absence of presidential term limits; the opportunity for collusion between the President and Congress to oppress the people; and treaty-making powers that might undermine the interests of a particular region of the nation.

"I shall always believe," Monroe went on, "that the exercise of direct taxation by one body over the very extensive territory contained within the bounds of the United States will terminate either in anarchy and a dissolution of government or a subversion of liberty."[23]

John Marshall shot up from his seat to challenge his friend. Known for disheveled clothes that flapped about like tattered sails, Marshall unveiled a new persona as he stood—a new jacket, vest, elegant linen shirt, new pants and shoes, and silk stockings. While delegates often milled about and chatted as others spoke, Marshall's deep, mellifluous voice commanded everyone's attention:

"The friends of the Constitution are as tenacious of liberty as its enemies," Marshall challenged Monroe. "What are the objects of the national government?" he asked rhetorically. "To protect the United States and promote the general welfare!"

Protection in time of war is one of its primary objects. Until mankind shall cease to have avarice and ambition, wars shall arise. There must be men and money to protect us. How are armies to be raised? Must we not have money for that purpose? But the honorable gentleman says that we need not be afraid of war.

Marshall paused to let his sarcasm sink in before raising his voice at his friend:

"Look at history!

"How were the liberties of the frontiers to be preserved by an impotent central government? Could they . . . be secured by retaining that weak Government?

"No!"[24] he bellowed in answer to his own question.

As Monroe shied under Marshall's withering attack, James Madison— the author of many provisions in the Constitution—reinforced Marshall's argument:

"Congress ought to have the power to provide for the execution of the laws, suppress insurrections, and repel invasions," Madison reiterated Marshall's assertions. "Without a general controlling power to call forth the strength of the Union, to repel invasions, the country might be overrun and conquered by foreign enemies."[25]

Too many delegates nodded in agreement for Patrick Henry to remain still any longer.

Although Marshall's oratory had bludgeoned his friend Monroe, Monroe was, by his own admission, a less-than-gifted public speaker. Seeing Monroe's distress, Patrick Henry, whom some called America's "Demosthenes," rose to put the upstart Marshall in his place. All eyes fixed on the great patriot—the legendary "Trumpet of the Revolution." Picking up Monroe's theme, he looked at the gallery filled with Kentuckians in tasseled deerskin shirts and coonskin hats:

"Why?" he paused.

"Why do we love this trial by jury?" Henry's mountain twang rang through the hall.

*Patrick Henry, the iconic patriot who called
America to arms, bitterly opposed ratification of
the Constitution. A champion of the Constitution,
young John Marshall won notoriety debating Henry
at the Virginia ratification convention, where he
accused the former governor of tyranny during his
term in office.* (Library of Congress)

Because it prevents the hand of oppression from cutting yours off! They
may call anything rebellion and deprive you of a fair trial. . . . Something
must be done to preserve your liberty and mine. The rights of conscience,
trial by jury, liberty of the press, all your immunities and franchises, all pretensions to human rights and privileges are rendered insecure, if not lost.[26]

"Is the relinquishment of trial by jury and liberty of the press necessary for your liberty?" he cried out.

"*No!*" the buckskins in the gallery answered. Presiding officer George
Wythe gaveled them to order.

Henry insisted that the Confederation of American States deserved
"the highest encomium:

It carried us through a long and dangerous war: It rendered us victorious in that bloody conflict with a powerful nation: It has secured us territory greater than any European monarch possesses. . . . To obtain the most splendid prize you did not consolidate. . . . The genius of Virginia landed you on the shore of freedom.

"Consider what you are about to do before you part with this [Confederation]," he pleaded.[27] "This [new] government . . . will destroy state governments and swallow the liberties of the people . . . your President may easily become King. . . . Congress will have an unlimited, unbounded command over the soul of this commonwealth." Assailing congressional powers with power to pass any laws it deemed "necessary and proper," Henry mocked what he called the absurdity of adopting this system and relying on the chance of getting it amended afterward.

"I should take that man to be a lunatic who should favor adoption of a government avowedly defective in hopes of having it amended afterwards."[28]

If Henry cowed Marshall, the young attorney did not show it. Indeed, he all but sprang from his seat to bark back at Henry:

"The supporters of the Constitution claim the title of being firm friends of liberty and the rights of mankind," the former soldier cried out. "We, Sir, idolize democracy!

"I differ in opinion from the worthy gentleman. I think that the virtue and talents of the general government will tend to the security instead of the destruction of our liberty." Citing the very powers he would one day assert, Marshall declared that if Congress passed a law "not warranted by any of the powers enumerated, it would be considered by the judges as an infringement of the Constitution.

"They would declare it void!"[29]

Marshall scoffed at Henry's contention that the Atlantic Ocean eliminated the causes of war by separating the nation from Europe.

"Sir," he looked Henry in the eyes, "I say the sea makes them neighbors to us."

Does not our naval weakness invite an attack on our commerce? May not the Algerines seize our vessels? Cannot they and every other predatory or maritime nation pillage our ships and destroy our commerce? . . . If anything be necessary, it must be to call forth the strength of the Union when we may be attacked or when the general purposes of America require it.[30]

"The Confederation," Marshall went on, "has nominal powers, but no means to carry them into effect. . . . I defy you to produce a single instance where requisitions on the several individual states composing a confederacy have been honestly complied with. . . . Our own experience shows the contrary."[31]

Marshall all but shouted that the instability of Congress and the failure of the states to comply with Washington's requisitions had emasculated Patriot military strength in the Revolutionary War. He called it "improper" to compare taxing powers under the new Constitution with those of Parliament:

"We *were not* represented in Parliament. Here we *are* represented!"

As Henry's anger at the young man's insolence festered, Virginia's war hero General Henry Lee added more fire power to Marshall's assault with a reference to Henry's failure to serve in the war.

"I have had a different experience from the Honorable Gentleman," Lee smiled at Henry condescendingly. "It was my fortune to be a soldier of my country."

In the discharge of my duty . . . I saw what the Honorable Gentleman did not see: Our men fighting with the troops of the King. . . . I have seen incontrovertible evidence that [state] militia cannot always be relied upon. Let the Gentleman recollect the action of Guilford [North Carolina]. The American regular troops behaved there with the most gallant intrepidity. What did the militia do? The greatest numbers of them fled.[32]

But it was the diminutive James Madison who delivered the most effective argument against Patrick Henry and the antifederalists by emphasizing the strict limits the Constitution imposed on the new federal government. Barely five feet tall, Madison suffered chronic intestinal problems and "a constitutional liability to sudden attacks, somewhat resembling epilepsy."[33] Too frail and sickly for military service, he had spent three years of the war in Congress and led the unsuccessful struggle for interstate unity and congressional powers to levy taxes for national defense.

His head bent down and all but invisible to most of the delegates, Madison read in short feeble bursts from notes inside his hat—"so low that his exordium could not be heard distinctly," according to one delegate. Madison argued that the Constitution did not grant the new national government any powers beyond those spelled out in the document.

"The powers of the federal government are enumerated," his voice squeaked. "It has . . . defined and limited objects, beyond which it cannot extend its jurisdiction. . . . Congress ought to have the power to provide for the execution of the laws, suppress insurrections, and repel invasions. Without a general controlling power to call forth the strength of the Union to repel invasions, the country might be overrun and conquered by foreign enemies."[34] He repeated Washington's argument that Article V gave opponents of the Constitution the right to amend it.

Marshall then reminded the convention that "all delegated powers are liable to be abused." He said the opponents of the Constitution were making "a recommendation of anarchy" and that the friends of the Constitution were "tenacious of liberty [and] wish to give no power that will endanger it."[35]

On June 24, as storm clouds gathered across the horizon, Henry came to the hall to make a last, desperate stand against the constitutionalists by raising an explosive issue that all had pondered but dared not address:

"May they not pronounce all slaves free?" Henry demanded to know.

As slaveholders gasped and looks of horror spread across the hall, Henry stared directly at Madison and, without giving the shaken little Federalist a chance to respond, he answered his own question. In words that echoed across the South for the next seventy-five years—words that would justify secession and civil war— Henry warned Virginians that the new government would abolish slavery.

They have the power in clear unequivocal terms and will clearly and certainly exercise it! As much as I deplore slavery . . . prudence forbids abolition. . . . The majority of Congress is in the North, and the slaves are to the South. In this situation, I see a great deal of the property of Virginia in jeopardy.[36]

As angry shouts spewed from the gallery, torrential rain pounded the roof, lightning blazed across the sky, thunder shook the building. Henry took advantage of the drama, lifting his voice in a crescendo and calling on God's wrath to punish the authors of the Constitution:

"He [Madison] tells you of important blessings, which he imagines will result to us and mankind in general from the adoption of this system," Henry argued. "I see the awful immensity of the dangers with which it is pregnant.

"I see it!" he cried out.

"I feel it!"

He spread wide his arms and looked to the heavens, playing the scene like the veteran actor he was. The storm had turned day into night; each bolt of lightning struck closer to the frightened delegates.

"Our own happiness alone is not affected by the event," Henry's voice boomed after a lightning bolt had crashed near the hall. "All nations are interested in the determination. We have it in our power to secure the happiness of one half of the human race. Its adoption may involve the misery of the other hemispheres."[37]

Unnerved by the power of the storm and Henry's prophecies of doom, some delegates left the hall, shuddering at the dangers Henry had linked to ratification. When the convention adjourned for the day, the Constitution that John Marshall favored so strongly seemed doomed. The chaos of the Confederation was about to explode into widespread interstate wars over conflicting territorial claims.

CHAPTER 4

Quoits Was the Game

WHEN VIRGINIA'S RATIFICATION CONVENTION RESUMED THE NEXT MORNING, some spectators claimed Henry had summoned "black arts" to call lightning from the heavens on his antagonists the previous day. Whether he had or not proved immaterial. James Madison summoned a few black arts of his own, albeit political rather than meteorological.

Collaring a handful of moderate antifederalists, Madison pledged to work for passage of a bill of rights in the First Congress if they agreed to support ratification. He and Marshall convinced enough delegates to switch their votes to produce an eighty-nine to seventy-nine victory for ratification.

Although delegates believed their votes had made Virginia the decisive ninth state to ratify the Constitution, New Hampshire had actually ratified it a few days earlier. Together the two states ended the chaos of the Confederation and created the world's newest nation—the United States of America.

From the moment of its birth, however, the new nation found itself engulfed in as much chaos as the old. Many opponents of ratification refused to accept the will of the majority, and before the ink had dried on the new Constitution, they set out to shred the document and overturn the new government.

"I had grown up," Marshall explained his vote for ratification, "when 'United we stand, divided we fall' was the maxim of every orthodox American. And I imbibed these sentiments so thoroughly that they constituted a part of my being."[1]

Many others, however, felt differently. To his distress, Marshall's closest friend, James Monroe, had voted against ratification and now pledged to overturn it or reshape it with amendments. The two heroic soldiers who had stood together in battle to win the nation's independence now stood at odds in peace as Americans tried forming a new government.

Both Monroe and Marshall reaped rewards from their convention efforts, however. Although Monroe lost the debate, he won election to the new US Senate when Henry's antifederalists rallied enough votes to win both Virginia seats in the new upper chamber. Federalists, meanwhile, heaped ample rewards on John Marshall for his stand in favor of ratification. The state's wealthiest planters—federalists all—entrusted him with their legal portfolios, and when the presidential election sent George Washington to the nation's new capital in New York City, he too gave Marshall control of his legal affairs in Virginia.

With more than 300 clients, all together generating over £1,500 a year, Marshall became the state's most prominent and wealthiest lawyer. Even College of William and Mary retained him as its attorney, and in the fall, after the convention, he invested some of his newfound wealth in two adjacent half-acre lots in Richmond, where he built a stately, two-and-one-half-story Federal-style brick home.

Built in the upscale "Court End" district near the elegant new state Capitol and courthouse, Marshall's house boasted nine rooms, including a paneled dining room where he began hosting monthly "lawyers' dinners"—acclaimed stag affairs for his Richmond colleagues and any notables passing through town. Like most grand homes, small outbuildings stood behind the Marshall home to house the kitchen, laundry, stable, slave quarters, and a "necessary."*

---

*Wealthy homeowners built kitchens and other, similar facilities in outbuildings to prevent damage to the main house in the event of kitchen fires.

John Marshall's success practicing law allowed him to buy two adjacent, half-acre lots near the state capitol in Richmond and build this stately, two-and-one-half-story, Federal-style brick home. (LIBRARY OF CONGRESS)

Although Marshall owned thousands of acres of raw land elsewhere in Virginia, he had lacked interest in farming and, therefore, owned only a handful of slaves—all of them household help. With Polly too fragile after two miscarriages and the deaths of three infant children,* Marshall gave his slaves relative autonomy—and, indeed, depended on them—to manage housekeeping and other household chores and tend to grocery shopping. Robin Spurlock, the slave Marshall had received as a wedding gift, proved so talented a manager that Marshall made him head slave, or de facto *major domo*. By choice, Robin stayed with Marshall the rest of his life, and other Marshall slaves remained in the family long after emancipation. "Robin Spurlock, who dressed after the same fashion as his master . . . regarded his master as the greatest man in the world and

---

* Rebecca after five days, Mary Ann at two and one-half years, and John James, four months.

By 1800, Richmond had grown from a frontier town of about 1,200 people to the South's most beautiful state capital, dominated by the classical Capitol on the distant hill. (FROM *THE LIFE OF JOHN MARSHALL*, BY ALBERT J. BEVERIDGE, VOL. I:184.)

himself as the next," according to one Marshall acquaintance. "He stood at the head of the colored aristocracy of Richmond."[2]

Marshall gave Spurlock relatively free rein to come and go and encouraged his assumption of leadership in Richmond's black community. Spurlock, in turn, enlisted Marshall's help in winning freedom for illegally enslaved African Indian children. Treaties between the Indians and both the Virginia and US governments had established a rule of maternal descent, designating interracial children of Indian mothers as Indians and, therefore, free—even if their fathers were slaves. Slave owners, however, routinely violated the treaty, and as Spurlock discovered such violations, he reported them to Marshall.

Despite their political differences, Marshall's friend James Monroe often joined him in courtroom forays to win freedom for Richmond's illegally enslaved interracial men, women, and children. Shocked by rampant injustices to blacks, Marshall became a champion of equal justice under the law in Richmond. In one case he won a governor's pardon for a free black woman sentenced to die for killing a white intruder who had broken into her home and assaulted her.

Marshall's fame spread far beyond Richmond after he convinced Patrick Henry to forgive and forget their differences at Virginia's ratification convention and join as cocounsel in two dramatic cases that gripped the nation and won Marshall international acclaim.

Commonwealth v. Randolph was the first case they handled together—a grisly tale of adultery and infanticide. Richard Randolph—one of the prominent Virginia Randolphs—went on trial for fathering a child by his wife's unmarried sister Nancy, then suffocating the newborn and dumping it on a pile of broken shingles for slaves to burn some distance behind the mansion. Spattered blood stained the walls and floors throughout the house—Nancy's room, the stairs, and elsewhere. Slaves said they had heard agonizing screams during the night.

After Richard Randolph surrendered to the sheriff, John Marshall prepared the case for trial but let Patrick Henry, the nation's most celebrated courtroom orator, examine witnesses. Together Henry and Marshall formed the most brilliant legal team in American history at the time, working so well in tandem that they became lifelong friends.

"He was a learned lawyer," Marshall spoke of Henry with reverence years later, "a most accurate thinker and a profound reasoner."[3]

Magistrates called seventeen witnesses, but Henry made quick work of them: none had actually seen a crime committed; none had seen a dead baby; there was no *corpus delicti*. None could even prove that Nancy had been pregnant.

One claimed he saw Nancy in Randolph's embrace, and Nancy's aunt, Mary Cary Page, a notorious neighborhood gossip, said she had peeked through a crack in Nancy's bedroom door while Nancy was undressing and thought, "Nancy's belly seemed plump."

Henry nodded his head thoughtfully, then stared at the floor . . . and stared . . . and stared . . .

"Which eye did you peek with?" he asked suddenly.

As the courtroom exploded with laughter, Henry shook his head. "Great God! Deliver us from eavesdroppers," he smiled.[4]

After Henry ended his theatrics, Marshall closed with a straightforward argument, calling Randolph's embrace a simple display of caring for an ailing sister-in-law. Her friends and relatives had all differed on whether she had even been pregnant, he pointed out, and he presented many possible causes for her weight gain.

Without leaving their seats to consider their verdict, the sixteen magistrates agreed and dismissed the case.

The courtroom erupted in cheers—for Randolph, of course, but also for what all agreed had been a brilliant performance by the two great lawyers. Decades later Nancy revealed she had miscarried a stillborn fetus, fathered not by her brother-in-law but a lover who had died before they could marry and legitimize the infant's birth.

In their second case the sensational Marshall-Henry team took on one of the most important cases either legal giant would ever handle—and the only case Marshall would ever personally plead before the US Supreme Court.

Best known as the "British Debts Case," *Ware v. Hylton* involved thousands of claims by British merchants for about £5 million in unpaid pre–Revolutionary War debts incurred by former American clients—*plus* £2 million in interest.

Among the 30,000 American debtors, half were Virginians—10 percent of the state's adult white male population. They included President George Washington, who owed British merchants £3,999 for prewar purchases—plus £1,600 interest—and Patrick Henry himself, who owed £972 plus interest. Most had assumed the Revolution would wipe out their debts to British creditors, but the Treaty of Paris of 1783 that ended the war specifically required American subjects to repay such debts and gave British merchants the right to sue in American courts to recover what Americans owed them.

Virginia (and a few other states), however, had complicated matters during the Revolution by ordering Americans to deposit moneys they owed British creditors into the state treasury, thus allowing each state, in effect, to use British funds to pay for its wartime expenses. If the court ruled in favor of the British merchants, therefore, many Virginians faced paying their debts a second time—clearly unjust, but no more so than depriving British merchants of the moneys due them. The Constitution had made all treaties with foreign governments "the supreme law of the land," however, and declared judges in every state "bound thereby," thus giving British merchants an evident advantage.

With thousands of Americans—and many Britons—anxiously awaiting the outcome, Henry moved into John Marshall's home in Richmond, and on November 23, 1791, the two lawyers strode arm in arm to court to hear lawyers for British merchants present clear-cut, irrefutable arguments. Marshall was ready, however. He had fashioned a defense that Henry converted into his inimitable courtroom theater, rising slowly, clad in drab black homespun, contorting his face to that of a suffering martyr.

Looking older than his fifty-five years, Henry apologized to the court for his infirmities. He swayed a bit, as if losing his balance, then caught himself before uttering hoarsely, mournfully,

> I stand here, may it please your honors, to support, according to my power, that side of the question which respects the American debtor. I beg leave to beseech the patience of this honorable court; because the subject is very great and important.[5]

He went on for three consecutive days, his voice growing stronger with each phrase until it boomed accusatory charges at the heart of the British Empire: Even if failure to pay the alleged debts had inadvertently violated the Treaty of Paris, Henry argued, Britain had made such a violation moot by its own gross violations of the Treaty. The British had seized American cargo ships on the high seas, impressed American seamen, and refused to evacuate forts in American territory along the northern and western frontiers. Britain had plundered American assets of far greater value than the debts British merchants were trying to collect.

How, he then asked, would the British have treated Americans had England won the war? As spectators rose and cursed the British lawyers, he answered his own question:

> In the wars of the revolution which have taken place in that island, life, fortune, goods, debts, and everything were confiscated. . . . Every possible punishment has been inflicted on suffering humanity that it could endure.[6]

In contrast to many of his cases, Henry relied on more than theatrics and oratory. He cited renowned British legal authorities who asserted that creditors had always risked forfeiture of debts incurred in revolutions. He then described revolutions in Britain in 1715 and 1745 to demonstrate that if the British government had defeated the Americans, "the most horrid forfeitures, confiscations, and attainders would have been pronounced against us." Indeed, had the British caught Patrick Henry himself, they would have hung him without trial as a traitor, then drawn and quartered his lifeless body.

"Would not our men have shared the fate of the people of Ireland?" he demanded. "What confiscations and punishments were inflicted in Scotland? The plains of Culloden and the neighboring gibbets would show you."

> Had we been subdued, would not every right have been wrested from us? Hungry Germans, blood-thirsty Indians, and nations of another color would have been let loose upon us. Sir, if you had seen . . . the simple but tranquil felicity of helpless unoffending women and children, in little log huts on the frontiers . . . the objects of the most shocking barbarity . . . by British warfare and Indian butchery. . . . Would it not be absurd for us to save their debts, while they should burn, hang, and destroy?[7]

With Christmas approaching in1791, the court reserved decision and adjourned for the holidays. It would not issue a ruling until June 7, when it rejected the Marshall-Henry argument that a breach of a treaty by either side automatically nullifies the entire treaty.

The court sustained their other arguments, however, awarding their client—and, by implication, all Virginia debtors—full credit for the amount he had paid into Virginia's state treasury. It ruled that he now owed British creditors only the difference between that amount and the original debt.

Virginians—and, indeed, all Americans—cheered the decision, which rescued some 30,000 American debtors from financial disaster. American and British legal scholars for years thereafter cited the Henry-Marshall case as an historic legal triumph that was both just and equitable to creditors and debtors.

After a series of negotiations that followed the decision, the US government agreed to pay the British government £600,000 to settle the issue—a mere 12 percent of the original British claims of £4,930,000. In the end American debtors escaped without paying an extra penny from their collective pockets.

Marshall's courtroom victories added to his national and even international celebrity. He won election as Richmond's representative to the Virginia House of Delegates, the governor appointed him colonel of the Richmond Regiment of the Virginia militia, and the Grand Lodge of Ancient Free and Accepted Masons of Virginia elevated him to deputy grand master. Political foes as well as friends embraced the fun-loving attorney, regularly inviting him to dinners and late nights of cards or billiards, but the hilarity and laughter of his life away from home contrasted sharply with the gloom that emanated from Polly's sickroom. To his distress, the slightest sound—even a child's barely audible whimper—provoked his wife's tremors and tears.

Marshall so enjoyed his outside social life that he decided to unite the friends he liked most in a new men's social club—Richmond's first. Variously called the Quoits Club, or Barbecue Club, it limited membership to thirty elected members, among them the city's leading merchants, political leaders, and professional men—and three *ex officio* members, the governor, the city's Episcopalian bishop, and its Presbyterian minister, John Buchanan. The club met every Saturday afternoon from May to November at Pastor Buchanan's farm outside Richmond, where they feasted on barbecued pig, among other comestibles. Club members elected Marshall and attorney John Wickham to cater the meals during the first season because of their reputations as *bons vivants*.

"Quoits was the game," recalled one member, "and toddy, punch and mint julep to wash down a plain substantial dinner, without wines or desert. Among the most skillful in throwing the quoit was Judge Marshall,* even in advanced years, and it delighted his competitors as much as himself to see him ring the peg."[8] Drinking from tumblers, however, saw them consume so much that Pastor Buchanon warned, "Those who drink from tumblers on the table may become tumblers under the table."[9]

Marshall did not let quoits interfere with his responsibilities at home, though. As one colleague put it, Marshall was "exactly what a wife, a child, a brother, and a friend would desire."[10]

By then George Washington was well into his second year as the nation's first President. He had spent much of his first year making appointments to the new government—110 in all. He tried to enlist the thirty-four-year-old hero of Monmouth, John Marshall:

> I have the pleasure to inform you that you are appointed [Attorney] of the District [of Virginia] and your Commission is enclosed. . . . The high importance of the Judicial System in our national government made it an indispensable duty to select such characters to fill the several offices in it as would discharge their respective trusts with honor to themselves and advantage to their country.[11]

Although it was the highest honor of Marshall's legal career, he astonished Washington by refusing.

"I thank you, sir, very sincerely for the honor which I feel is done me," Marshall wrote to his former commander-in-chief, "and I beg leave to declare that it is with real regret I decline accepting an office which has to me been rendered highly valuable by the hand which bestowed it." Few

---

*Like horseshoes, quoits required players to ring a peg with an iron ring or a ring made of thick, stiff rope.

ever dared reject a Washington request, let alone appointment, but Marshall said "sessions of the federal and state courts being at the same time in different places, an attendance in the one becomes incompatible with the duties of an attorney in the other."[12]

In fact, Marshall didn't want the job. He had served as Virginia's acting attorney general for a while and had disliked prosecuting every defendant according to the letter of the law—regardless of how justified the defendant was in violating the law or how unjust the law.

But Marshall's most important reason for rejecting the President's appointment was Polly, who was pregnant for the sixth time, and their two surviving sons, Thomas, five, and Jacquelin Ambler, two, needed strong parental oversight that Polly, even at her strongest, was unable to provide. She had already miscarried twice, and their first daughter, Rebecca, had died after five days. Marshall needed to remain close to home.

He had also just won election to Virginia's General Assembly—a satisfying if undemanding job that required only a few weeks a year at the capitol in Richmond, a few steps from home. Making his life even simpler and more pleasant, the Assembly and court met in the same building, allowing him to attend legislative sessions, walk home for midday dinner, and return to appear at the bar in the afternoon. A week after Marshall had rejected the President's appointment, he took his oath as a member of Virginia's General Assembly, and on November 24, 1789, Polly gave birth to a daughter, Mary Ann.

It was Robin Spurlock, his head slave, who inspired one of the first laws Marshall sponsored in the Virginia Assembly, making it a crime to sell free persons as slaves. Passed by an impressive majority, the Marshall-Spurlock bill prevented enslavement of children of freeborn women fathered by enslaved fathers.*

---

*In the codicil to his will, dated August 13, 1832, Marshall emancipated "my faithful servant Robin," bequeathing him fifty dollars, or one hundred dollars "in the event of his going to Liberia. . . . Should it be found impracticable to liberate him consistently with the law and his own inclination, I desire that he may choose his master among my sons, or if he prefer my daughter" (JM *Papers*, 12:198).

Another reason Marshall rejected Washington's appointment was the continuing *Hite v. Fairfax* case, which was still making its way through Virginia's court system. The outcome would determine the fate of the entire Marshall clan's enormous land holdings in Virginia. He simply could not and would not allow personal political advancement divert his attention from that case and the interests of the rest of the Marshall family.

Marshall's rejection of a presidential appointment, however, annoyed Washington. The President had already suffered unexpected rebuffs by men who, like Marshall, had served him loyally during the Revolution and who, he hoped, would serve just as loyally in his new government. He was badly mistaken. Many of his wartime aides who acquiesced to his martial battlefield commands bristled at his often brusque personality in civilian life, and some who stayed to serve him did so only because of lust for power.

Although his former artillery commander Henry Knox of Massachusetts agreed to be secretary at war, Philadelphia's Robert Morris had turned down the post of treasury secretary, while New York's John Jay refused appointment as secretary of state.

Morris had been in charge of government finances during the war, but his own finances had suffered so badly that he needed to return to private life to rebuild his fortune. Jay had headed foreign affairs under the confederation and authored five of the *Federalist* essays that made so compelling an argument for constitutional ratification, but he had no inclination to serve as a mere extension of Washington's overarching persona. Jay revered the President but had his eye on the US Supreme Court, where he would be free to act independently, and Washington finally named him the nation's first Chief Justice.

For treasury secretary Washington turned next to the young lawyer Alexander Hamilton—one of the heroic Men of Monmouth who had been a courageous officer throughout the Revolutionary War and one of Washington's most trusted aides-de-camp.

Twenty-three years younger than the President, Hamilton studied law after the war and married into a politically powerful family with strong ties to New York's business and banking communities. A passionate advocate of the Constitution, Hamilton had written fifty-one of the eighty-five *Federalist* essays and proved himself as proficient in politics as he had been in the military, maneuvering his way into the top ranks of the new Federalist Party at both the state and national levels.

After Jay refused to lead the foreign service, Washington asked his fellow Virginian Thomas Jefferson to take the job. Jefferson was in his fifth year as America's minister plenipotentiary in Paris—an appointee of the Confederation Congress. Except for Benjamin Franklin, who was too old for the job, and John Adams, who was now vice president, no one had more experience in foreign affairs than Jefferson.

Nonetheless, Washington had some misgivings. Eleven years younger than the President, Jefferson had, to his credit, supported Henry's famous call to arms against British rule before winning election to the Continental Congress and coauthoring the Declaration of Independence. But he not only failed to serve in the war; he made disastrous—indeed, some thought, treasonous—decisions as governor of Virginia. He had ignored Washington's orders to defend the state's waterways, opening the way for British troops to sail up the James River unimpeded and burn Richmond, then march across the state ravaging some of the richest farms and plantations.

Adding to Washington's reluctance was Jefferson's resistance to ratification of the Constitution. His stance immediately put him at loggerheads with Alexander Hamilton. Each had radically different visions of the presidential structure they would have to swear to help Washington build. Hamilton mistrusted the political intelligence of ordinary citizens and their ability to govern; he believed in a strong, national government that conformed in many ways to Plato's *Republic*, with both voting and public service restricted to a highly educated, propertied elite, led by a powerful chief executive.

Jefferson, in contrast, distrusted government—especially a centralized national government. He had cheered Paris mobs that stormed the Bastille prison in Paris and forced the French monarch to cede powers to a

Appointed the nation's first Secretary of State by President George Washington, Thomas Jefferson immediately crossed swords with Treasury Secretary Alexander Hamilton and threw Washington's cabinet into chaos. (LIBRARY OF CONGRESS)

popularly elected national assembly. Like Patrick Henry, Jefferson held a naive belief in the goodness of man and espoused Jean-Jacques Rousseau's embrace of the common man's right to govern himself, free from government intrusion. The opening words of Rousseau's *Le Contrat Social* (*The Social Contact*) had stunned the world in 1762 with a revolutionary new sociopolitical concept: *Man was born free and everywhere he is in chains.*[13]

Both Hamilton and Washington saw anarchy as the inevitable result of Rousseau's and Jefferson's visions of society, but Jefferson exalted anarchy as "proof that the people have liberty. . . . I hold it that a little rebellion now and then is a good thing. . . . The tree of liberty must be refreshed from time to time with the blood of patriots and tyrants."[14]

From the first, Hamilton and Jefferson mistrusted and disliked each other—with good reason. Both sought to influence Washington's policies; both lusted for power and eyed the Presidency if and when Washington relinquished it.

The first break between the two came when Hamilton praised certain aspects of Britain's constitutional monarchy. Jefferson lashed out, accusing Hamilton of being a monarchist when, in fact, Hamilton had been primary author of the *Federalist* essays in support of republican government and the very Constitution that Jefferson now pledged to uphold.

Jefferson's remarks infuriated Hamilton, who, unlike Jefferson, did not own and had never owned slaves. In fact, he had joined Aaron Burr Jr., his former comrade in arms at Monmouth, to lead the struggle to free slaves in New York State. An active member of the New York Manumission Society, Hamilton called slavery "repugnant to humanity . . . inconsistent with the liberality and justice which should distinguish a free and enlightened people."[15]

In contrast, Jefferson owned about 200 slaves, calling them inferior to whites. While publicly embracing populism, he lived off slavery at his isolated mountain home while tarring Hamilton and northern Federalists as aristocrats.

The outbreak of the French Revolution only added to Hamilton-Jefferson differences. During Jefferson's last days as American minister to France, Parisian mobs had stormed the Bastille prison, then raged through the streets massacring friends and foes alike.

"The liberty of the whole earth was depending on the issue," Jefferson exulted. "Rather than it should have failed, I would have seen half the earth desolated."[16] Later, he added, "If the happiness of the mass of the people can be secured at the expense of a little tempest now and then, or even a little blood, it will be a precious purchase. *Malo libertum periculosum quam quietam servitutem.* [I prefer dangerous liberty to quiet servitude.]"[17]

Jefferson's enthusiasm for French violence disgusted Washington, Hamilton, and other American leaders. Washington warned that "little irritation would be necessary to blow up the spark of discontent into a flame that might not easily be quenched."[18] Hamilton called radical leaders of the French Revolution "assassins reeking with the blood of murdered fellow citizens."[19] Vice President Adams said the French revolutionaries "make murder itself as indifferent as shooting a plover."[20]

While Anglophiles and Francophiles in America's capital debated the benefits and evils of the French Revolution, sleepy Richmond and other inland towns were far more concerned with property rights, state rights, and other domestic issues. For the Marshalls, their concerns were even more personal: in February 1792 Polly gave birth to another boy, John James—only to watch him die in June—and two months later, in August, the Marshalls lost their thirty-month-old daughter, Mary Ann.

John Marshall all but abandoned his law practice during those first eight fateful months of the year to be near Polly's bedside and care for their two surviving boys, eight-year-old Thomas and five-year-old Jacquelin Ambler. They needed his constant attention—as did Polly—and he decided the time had come to sell his practice, abandon public service, move to the peaceful Blue Ridge, and let chaos consume the rest of the nation.

And it did.

CHAPTER 5

The Great Divide

FROM THE MOMENT HE ENTERED PRESIDENT WASHINGTON'S CABINET in March 1790, Thomas Jefferson suffered badly in confrontations with the glib and gifted New York lawyer Alexander Hamilton. Hamilton was a street fighter. Orphaned and often forced to survive on his wits as a child, he developed a quick tongue that made him a far more effective lawyer than the soft-spoken Jefferson. Although Virginia's young lawyers like John Marshall considered Jefferson one of the state's "ablest men and soundest lawyers,"[1] Jefferson nonetheless personified Hamilton's impression of the typically lethargic Virginia gentleman, raised in a cradle, gently rocked by slaves who hummed him to sleep on his father's tobacco plantation.

Hamilton's heroism as a Revolutionary War officer further embarrassed and embittered Jefferson. While Hamilton charged into enemy lines with John Marshall, James Monroe, and Aaron Burr at Trenton and Monmouth, gentleman Tom Jefferson sat by the fire in his mountain-top mansion in central Virginia, playing his violin, sipping fine French wines, and never firing a shot at the enemy. An admitted failure as Virginia's wartime governor, Jefferson entered George Washington's cabinet smarting from taunts of cowardice, while Hamilton collected accolades from his fellow New Yorkers for his wartime heroism. Seething with envy, Jefferson tried to undermine the low-born hero's reputation.

"Hamilton . . . would be a phenomenon," Jefferson sneered to his acolyte James Madison, "if the courage of which he has the reputation in military occasions were genuine."[2]

As Washington's first term progressed, the President expressed growing weariness with the burdens of office and whetted both Hamilton's and Jefferson's appetite for power. Raw ambition tinctured their competing visions of government and turned the two men into irrational adversaries. Each nourished the embryos of a divisive two-party system, with Hamilton organizing supporters under the banner of federalism and support for strong, centralized government. In contrast, Jefferson supporters feared centralized government. Calling themselves "Republicans" or, in some cases, "Democrat Republicans," they espoused state sovereignty. Hamilton fed northern hatred for the South with warnings that slave labor was not only immoral, it would undermine the northern economy, which depended on workers paid by the piece. Jefferson whipped up southern hatred for the North with warnings that Federalists planned to strip states of their sovereignty, establish a monarchy, and, worst of all, impoverish the South by abolishing slavery and letting blacks roam free to slaughter their former white tormentors.

In Richmond John Marshall steered clear of national politics. Though a Federalist at heart and a member of the Virginia state assembly, he had been sincere in turning down the President's appointment as Virginia's district attorney. He loved private practice and the close ties it allowed him to maintain to his home, his wife, his children, and his friends. He built an enormous, thriving practice and remained a doting husband and father. At the same time he was an active state legislator and an equally active competitor at quoits. To his joy, assembly membership required little more time or effort than quoits.

To promote his presidential ambitions, Jefferson enlisted his friend James Madison to help organize "Democratic Clubs" in major cities while paying newspaper editors to smear Hamilton's character. One pseudonymous article charged that Hamilton was an illegitimate child—that his mother had not divorced her first husband when she entered into a common-law relationship with Alexander's father and gave birth to their son. To further tar Hamilton, the article noted the high incidence of illegitimate mixed-race children in the West Indies.

Hamilton retaliated by accusing Jefferson of subverting "principles of good government" by fostering disorder and opposition to taxes. He labeled Jefferson a danger "to the union, peace, and happiness of the country." When Jefferson accused Hamilton of preparing "a change from the present republican form of government to that of a monarchy,"[3] Hamilton responded angrily that he, not Jefferson, had authored the *Federalist* essays that ensured ratification of the Constitution. Hamilton asserted that he was "affectionately attached to the republican theory. I desire above all things to see the quality of political rights, exclusive of all hereditary distinction."[4]

Visibly annoyed by the public feud, Washington scolded Jefferson: "I believe it will be difficult, if not impracticable to manage the reins of government or to keep the parts of it together . . . if . . . one pulls this way and another that, before the utility of the thing is fairly tried. It must inevitably be torn asunder, and, in my opinion, the fairest prospect of happiness and prosperity that ever was presented to man will be lost—perhaps forever!"[5]

Washington's reelection to the presidency in December 1792 combined with the Christmas holidays to calm cabinet chaos for a while, but the public execution on the guillotine of French King Louis XVI in January 1793 renewed the sniping, with Hamilton calling the execution "horrid and disgusting" and Jefferson all but rejoicing.

"We are not expected to be transported from despotism to liberty in a feather bed," Jefferson smiled.[6]

Washington was too appalled by events in France to comment, but he turned noticeably cold toward Jefferson and kept a bust of the French king prominently displayed in his office—for all to see as they entered and left.

On February 1, 1793, France declared war on Britain, Holland, and Spain and further divided Washington's cabinet. Under the Franco-American treaty of alliance in 1778, each nation had pledged to help the other repel attacks by foreign enemies, and France now demanded that the United States join her at war against Britain—much as she had joined Americans in their War of Independence against Britain.

"Nothing should be spared on our part to attach France to us," Jefferson told the President as he urged sending American armed forces to join the French.[7]

Outraged by Jefferson's embrace of French revolutionaries "wading through seas of blood," Hamilton argued against American participation in the war, calling it self-destructive. Britain, he said, was America's most important trading partner and source of government revenues. To war on the side of France against Britain, Hamilton asserted, was not only economically suicidal; it was morally indefensible.

"When I contemplate the horrid . . . massacres," he raged, "I am glad to believe there is no real resemblance between what was the cause of America and what is the cause of France."[8] Hamilton urged Washington to strengthen ties to Britain, arguing that the treaty with France was a *defensive* alliance against attack on either nation by a third party. Britain had not attacked France; France had been the aggressor, declaring war on England when England had been at peace.

Washington agreed that France had embarked on an offensive, not defensive, war—that the Franco-American treaty did not apply. He also agreed on the economic sense of rapprochement with England. With the United States all but defenseless—with only a token army and no navy— the President knew he could not risk war with England, or any other nation, for that matter.

More than annoyed by the resumption of the Jefferson-Hamilton feud over foreign affairs, Washington again scolded Jefferson: "It behooves the government of this country," the President warned his secretary of state, "to use every means in its power to prevent the citizens . . . from embroiling us with either of these powers [England or France] by endeavoring to maintain a strict neutrality. I therefore require that you will . . . [take] such measures as shall be deemed most likely to effect this desirable purpose . . . without delay."[9]

As the Franco-English war gained momentum, groups gathered outside printers' offices to read the newspapers—or hear them read by the more literate of their number. Half sided passionately with their ancestral motherland, while others demanded—just as passionately—that the American government support its Revolutionary War ally and go to war against her former oppressor England. To enhance newspaper sales, the press fanned the flames of war, with some editors demanding a break with France, while others assailed Anglophiles as monarchists and traitors. What began as street-corner debates deteriorated into fights that spread down alleys and avenues in major cities and exploded into bursts of street brawls.

President Washington pleaded for national unity, saying it would be "unwise in the extreme . . . to involve ourselves in the contests of European nations."[10] Newspaper editors all but ignored him, knowing that the uglier and more widespread the riots, the more newspapers they would sell.

Richmond was not immune. "A great majority of the American people deems it criminal to remain unconcerned spectators of a conflict between their ancient enemy [Britain] and republican France," John Marshall wrote in Richmond's *Virginia Gazette and General Advertiser* under the pseudonym *Gracchus.** Recalling the Franco-American alliance during the Revolutionary War, Marshall declared, "The attachment to France is warm and universal. . . . Few things would more disgust the people with their government than a belief that it opposed the general wish and was unfriendly to our favored ally."[11]

In an effort to calm the presses and the nation, Washington proposed issuing a formal proclamation of neutrality—only to set the simmering cabinet chaos aboil again. Jefferson argued that the Constitution gave the President no power to issue proclamations and that the Constitution

---

*Most Americans signed letters and essays to periodicals with pseudonyms—primarily to avoid challenges to duels, but also to avoid libel suits and to avoid alienating friends and family. Gracchus was a Roman tribune who championed social, political, and judicial reform.

reserved the power to declare war to Congress. A declaration of neutrality, he said, was a declaration *not* to go to war and, therefore, within the purview of congressional, not presidential, authority. As the President grumbled, Hamilton retorted that presidential powers stretched well beyond strict constitutional wording. Scoffing at Jefferson's semantics over the term "neutrality," Hamilton suggested that the President simply eliminate the word from his final proclamation.

Putting aside his pro-French sentiments, John Marshall joined other Richmond leaders in rallying behind the President and echoing Hamilton's words that "it is in the interest of the United States . . . to maintain a strict neutrality towards the belligerent powers of Europe."[12]

Before Washington could decide on the final language of his proclamation, Citizen Edmond-Charles-Edouard Genet, the French Republic's new minister plenipotentiary (ambassador) to the United States, sailed into Charleston, South Carolina, with more fuel for the nation's political inferno. He carried two sets of instructions from the French revolutionary government, an official set and a second set of secret orders.[13]

His official instructions ordered him to seek *passive* American cooperation under the Franco-American treaties of 1778 for mutual defense. In effect, he was to convince Washington to let the French navy bring captured ships and cargoes into American ports for auction and/or refitting as French naval vessels. He was also to persuade the American government to pay enough of its war debts to France to allow him to purchase badly needed American foodstuffs to ease the famine in France.

Genet's second set of secret instructions, however, ordered him to pursue other, more nefarious goals: he was to spread chaos across the continent—to organize *three* armies to "liberate" Louisiana, capture the rich Mexican silver mines, and seize the Floridas from Spain. He was also to organize and launch a fleet of privateers to prey on British shipping. If Washington's government refused to cooperate, he was to exploit pro-French ferment to foment revolution, topple the American government, and convert the United States into a French puppet state. Once under French control, the United States would become part of a

French-controlled North American federation of Canada, Florida, Louisiana, and the French West Indies.

Pro-French newspapers headlined Genet's arrival and whipped up mass hysteria that engulfed daily life in Boston, New York, Philadelphia, Charleston, and other cities. Reinventing themselves as revolutionary egalitarians, self-styled Francophiles addressed each other as "Citizen" and "Citess" (for women) and shot angry stares or insults at those who used "monarchist" forms of address such as "Mister," "Sir," or "Madam." The title "Reverend" was "not only anti-republican, but blasphemous," according to the *New-York Journal*.[14] The *Boston Gazette* asserted that "every friend of the Rights of Man in America will constantly feel an *attachment* for their French *brethren*. . . . France is contending the cause of both EUROPE and AMERICA, and GOD grant her success."[15]

Fearing the British would see the United States as a French ally and draw the nation into war, Washington threw off constitutional restraints and, on April 22, issued a formal neutrality proclamation. With Hamilton's help he avoided a possible constitutional flap over the word "neutrality" and declared the United States *at peace*—with Britain, France, and all other combatants. He pledged to engage in "conduct friendly and impartial toward [all] the belligerent powers." He enjoined Americans "from all acts and proceedings inconsistent with the duties of a friendly nation toward those at war," including "any hostilities on the seas." He barred American ships from carrying "any of those articles deemed contraband by the modern usage of nations."[16]

Genet tried offsetting the effects of Washington's Neutrality Proclamation by buying boldfaced newspaper advertisements that called on "Friends of France" to ignore the President and enlist in the French service to fight the British.

"Does not patriotism call upon us to assist France?" his advertisements asked. "As Sons of Freedom, would it not become our character to lend some assistance to a nation combating to secure their liberty?"[17]

To support his advertisements, Genet organized a network of agents to enlist Americans in a French war to recapture Canada, Louisiana, and the rest of the North American empire that France had lost in 1763.[18] Within weeks French agents had organized a fleet of American privateers to prey on British shipping offshore and a network of nearly forty so-called Democratic Societies across the United States that merged into local political groups formed to support Jefferson's presidential ambitions.

By mid-April 1793 Genet's plans were complete.

"I have prepared the revolution of New Orleans and Canada," he wrote to the French foreign minister in Paris. "I have destroyed the maritime commerce of the English in these waters."[19] Washington, he predicted, would have no choice but to support him with additional troops, weapons, and funds or resign in favor of the Francophile Jefferson.

With his privateers marauding British ships along the coast, Genet left Charleston for Philadelphia in a coach and four on what grew into a triumphal procession. Jefferson's Democratic Clubs heralded Genet's approach to each town as a Second Coming. Church bells tolled his arrival, cannons boomed, and French flags flapped in the wind in what Genet called a succession of civic festivals.

"The arrival and conduct of Mr. Genet excited great sensation throughout the southern states," Marshall explained with evident mixed feelings as Genet approached Richmond.

> We were all strongly attached to France—scarcely any man more strongly than myself. I sincerely believed human liberty to depend in a great measure on the success of the French revolution. My partiality to France, however, did not . . . render me insensible to the danger of permitting a foreign minister to mingle himself in the management of our affairs and to intrude himself between our government and people.[20]

Marshall organized a meeting of city and state leaders in Richmond to rally support for the President and the Neutrality Proclamation.

"Ever since . . . the voice of your country induced you to abandon the retirement you loved," Marshall addressed the President, "your conduct has been uniformly calculated to promote [our] happiness and welfare.

And in no instance has this been more remarkable . . . than in your Proclamation respecting the neutrality of the United States. As genuine Americans . . . we cannot refrain from expressing our pleasure in its adoption."

Then, in a harsh rebuke to Jefferson, Marshall declared,

> We recollect too well the calamities of war not to use our best endeavors to restrain any wicked citizen . . . who, disregarding his own duty and the happiness of the United States, in violation of the law of the land and the wish of the people, shall dare to gratify his paltry passions at the risk of his country's welfare.[21]

In a political maneuver that startled Jefferson more than the resolution itself, John Marshall recruited College of William and Mary law professor George Wythe to chair the Richmond conference and sign the resolution supporting Washington's Neutrality Proclamation. The sixty-seven-year-old judge had trained both Marshall and Jefferson in the law, and though a Federalist, he remained a Jefferson intimate.

Although Genet never saw the Marshall resolution, Marshall's friend Senator James Monroe did, and he responded with heat.

Writing under the pseudonym *Agricola*,* Monroe called those at Marshall's Richmond conference "enemies of the French Revolution, who are likewise notoriously the partisans for monarchy." Monroe's wartime friendship with Lafayette—formed at Brandywine, Valley Forge, and Monmouth—had turned him into so confirmed a Francophile that he questioned Marshall's "attachment to the equal rights of mankind." Monroe charged Marshall with trying "to bring about a more intimate connection with Britain."[22]

Marshall returned fire with a barrage of sarcasm and vitriol: "When a gentleman . . . who seems not to be impelled by the mere vanity of

---

*Anti-British to the core at the time, Monroe chose the pseudonym Agricola, the Roman general who led the Roman conquest of Britain.

becoming an author, presses forward with a bold venture on the conduct of his fellow citizens, his charge demands our consideration."[23]

Writing under the pseudonym *Aristides** Marshall castigated Agricola (Monroe) for subordinating his love of country to party zeal and affection for a foreign nation.

The citizens of Richmond, Marshall declared, had convened for two purposes: "The one, approving the conduct of the President of the United States toward the belligerent powers of Europe; the other declaring a detestation and abhorrence of any interference whatever of a foreign nation or minister with our political contests or internal government."

> Can the American exist who, like Agricola . . . could witness . . . efforts to create divisions among us and opposition to our government without feeling himself . . . degraded and insulted? Weigh, I beseech you, the consequences of a foreign minister . . . appealing to the people from the constitutional decisions of their government. If one foreign minister can make the appeal, what shall restrain every other from making it?[24]

Marshall argued that the nation was at peace with all of Europe's warring nations and had treaties with them all—none either offensive or defensive. "They place us in a state of perfect neutrality . . . and until it shall be the will of Congress to dissolve them, it is the duty of the Supreme Executive of the United States to observe them."[25]

Undeterred by Marshall's cold reception in Richmond, Genet continued his triumphal procession northward toward the American capital of Philadelphia. While he was en route his privateers captured more than eighty British merchant vessels—many inside American territorial waters—and sailed them into American ports to be sold by French consuls. Without arms, customs officials from Hamilton's Treasury Department could only stand along the waterfront and watch helplessly.

---

*Aristides the Just, as he was known, was an Athenian statesman and heroic general in the defense of Athens in the Persian War.

News of Genet's triumphal procession widened the already bitter divisions in the cabinet and provoked a frenzy of fear in the national capital of Philadelphia that Genet's approach might herald a French invasion. Washington was irate, warning that Genet's activities might provoke Britain into declaring war on the United States. Jefferson tried calming the President, defending Genet's activities:

"It is impossible for anything to be more affectionate, more magnanimous, than the purport of his mission," Jefferson cooed before leaving the presidential mansion to greet Genet.

When Genet arrived at the outskirts of Philadelphia, 500 coaches of ardent Francophiles waited to escort him into the city. Thousands rushed into the streets to cheer and march—and discard all pretenses of neutrality or loyalty to the President. An estimated 5,000 supporters rallied outside Genet's hotel and set off demonstrations that raged through the night into the next day—and the next—and the next.

John Adams described "the terrorism excited by Genet . . . 10,000 people in the streets of Philadelphia, day after day, threatened to drag Washington out of his house and effect a revolution in the government or compel it to declare war in favor of the French Revolution and against England." Adams said he "judged it prudent and necessary to order chests of arms from the war office" to protect his house.[26]

When Jefferson met Genet, he embraced the Frenchman as a friend and confidant and all but conspired with him to drag the United States into another war with Britain before escorting him to the Presidential mansion to present his credentials to Washington.[27]

In a near-treasonous action Jefferson gave Genet's confederate André Michaux, a French botanist, a letter of introduction to Governor Isaac Shelby of Kentucky, implying federal government approval of Genet's efforts to raise an army in the West.

When the President learned of the letter, he erupted in anger, raging at Genet and accusing Jefferson of disloyalty for supporting Genet. After the President questioned Jefferson's allegiance to the nation, the secretary of state offered to resign, but the President demanded that Jefferson remain until the end-of-the-year government recess.

Citizen Edmond-Charles-Edouard Genet, the first minister plenipotentiary to the United States from the French revolutionary regime, presents his credentials to President George Washington in the Executive Mansion, Philadelphia, as Secretary of State Thomas Jefferson looks on. (LIBRARY OF CONGRESS)

In Virginia Marshall and other state officials rallied behind the President and ordered the state militia to seize all privateers and their cargoes entering Virginia ports. Virginia prepared for war with France.

Adding to the turmoil generated by Genet's arrival in Philadelphia was the sudden appearance of the French fleet sailing into Delaware Bay from the Antilles. Genet raced to the waterfront and ordered gangways lowered, allowing French seamen to pour into the streets and join the Jacobin mobs.

"The town is one continuous scene of riot," the British consul wrote to his foreign minister in London. "The French seamen range the streets by night and by day, armed with cutlasses and commit the most daring outrages. Genet seems ready to raise the tricolor and proclaim himself proconsul. President Washington is unable to enforce any measures in opposition."[28]

As pro-French mobs raged through the city's streets demanding Washington's head, Genet sent the President an ultimatum "in the name of France"—to call Congress into a special session to choose between neutrality and war. He predicted that Americans would support him and "demonstrate . . . that their future is ultimately bound with France."[29]

Without a law enforcement arm, President Washington watched helplessly as his young American republic began to collapse. In Richmond, however, Washington's friend Governor Henry "Light-Horse Harry" Lee ordered defenses reinforced at Norfolk and called up the Virginia militia to defend the port against invasion. Aware of John Marshall's heroics on the battlefield, he appointed Marshall brigadier general and gave him command of the second brigade.

"We fear—and not without reason—a war," John Marshall warned his friend Virginia attorney general Archibald Stuart. "The man does not live who wishes for peace more than I do, but the outrages committed upon us are beyond human bearing. Pray Heaven we may weather the storm."[30]

CHAPTER 6

The Two Happiest
People on Earth

"Is Genet to set the acts of this government at defiance with impunity?" Washington raged at Jefferson. "What must the world think of such conduct, and of the government . . . submitting to it? We are an independent nation! We will not be dictated to by the politics of any nation under heaven!"[1]

On July 31 Washington ordered Jefferson to draw up a demand for Genet's recall, but Genet ignored Jefferson and the President by boarding a French warship and sailing to New York with the French fleet for refitting. In Richmond Governor Lee ordered Marshall and his men to march to Smithfield, on the James River, where the notorious privateer/pirate captain John Sinclair and a group of French sympathizers were outfitting the *Unicorn* with cannons to attack British shipping offshore. On July 23 Marshall reached Smithfield, surrounded Sinclair's house and seized thirteen cannons and a store of small arms before approaching the river's edge, where they surprised Sinclair and his men, who surrendered the ship without resistance.

Genet, meanwhile, arrived in New York on August 15, where a sea of French flags and huge crowds along the waterfront cheered him with songs of the French Revolution.

Oui, ça ira, ça ira, ça ira;
Les aristos á la lanterne;
Oui ça ira, ça ira, ça ira;
Les aristos on les pendera.*

Within a few days, however, the chant diminished, and one by one, the church bells ceased ringing. On August 15, 1793, an eerie silence enveloped the ship, and when Genet emerged topside and looked over the rail, he found the waterfront deserted. He disembarked and walked toward the inn where he had been lodging. A servant awaited, his bag packed to leave. Genet demanded an explanation. The answer struck like a dagger:

"Yellow fever, *Monsieur*."

Yellow fever had swept into the city and sent all but the very poor fleeing for their lives into the country.

"The coolest and the firmest minds," John Adams recalled later, "have given their opinions to me that nothing but the yellow fever . . . could have saved the United States from a fatal revolution of government."[2]

The pro-French Jefferson resigned as secretary of state at the end of the year, and a new French government, angry over Genet's alienation of the Washington administration, recalled him. His replacement sailed from France with an arrest warrant. Genet insisted the incoming ship carried a guillotine on board to execute him once it left American waters to return to France.

The tearful envoy pleaded for political asylum, and Washington allowed the Frenchman who had threatened the foundations of American government to remain. In the year that followed, he became an American citizen, married New York Governor George Clinton's daughter, and retired to obscurity as a Long Island farmer near New York City.**

---

*Yes, it'll do; yes, it'll do; yes, it'll do; the aristocrats hanging high on the gallows; yes, etc.; we'll hang them all.

** One of Genet's great grandsons, Edmond Charles Clinton Genet, was the first American aviator killed in World War I in the skies over France with the Lafayette Escadrille, a group of American fliers who volunteered to fight with the allies before the United States formally entered the war.

Washington replaced Jefferson with Attorney General Edmund Randolph, the former governor of Virginia and a cousin of both Jefferson and Marshall. Federalist attorney William Bradford of Philadelphia took over as attorney general.

The departures of Jefferson and Genet calmed the chaos in Washington's cabinet and on America's streets long enough to give Washington's Neutrality Proclamation a chance to take hold. As neutral American ships ferried ever-increasing cargoes to France and Britain, American shipbuilders, merchants, craftsmen, and farmers reaped the benefits of increased prosperity and a sudden spike in the *re*-export trade. With Britain and France attacking and sinking each other's cargo ships, merchants in the British and French West Indies shipped their Europe-bound cargoes to the United States first, then re-exported them to Europe on ships flying the neutral American flag. More than 50 percent of the sugar, coffee, spirits, cocoa, indigo, pepper, and spices from the West Indies now traveled to the United States for transfer onto neutral American vessels bound for Europe. With the economic boom, shipbuilders expanded the American merchant fleet to more than 5,000 vessels, putting so many Americans to work that dissatisfaction with the federal government and the Washington administration all but vanished.

Just as the nation was sailing smoothly through profitable neutral waters, however, the British government stunned allies and enemies alike by blockading French waters and ordering its navy to seize *all ships* bound for France and the French West Indies—neutral or not. Still worse, it designated *all goods* bound for France as contraband: corn, wheat, flour—anything that might help sustain France or the French people. In the months that followed, the British made a mockery of Washington's Neutrality Proclamation by seizing more than 250 American vessels.

Facing national humiliation or war, Washington's political instincts devised a dual policy that combined bravado with wisdom: bravado, to placate war hawks in Congress and the American public and give pause to British policy makers, and wisdom, to further what he considered the best interests of the nation. He called on the nation to gear for war, asking Congress to raise an army of 15,000 and state governors to ready 80,000 militiamen. Virginia Governor Henry Lee had already put his state militia on alert, and Brigadier General John Marshall deployed his second brigade to protect the capital city of Richmond.[3]

While American war hawks flapped their wings, Washington coaxed the Federalist Anglophile, Chief Justice John Jay, to go to England to seek an understanding and rapprochement with the British government. To calm French fears that Jay would negotiate an Anglo-American alliance against France, Washington sent the outspoken Republican Francophile, Senator James Monroe, to France as minister plenipotentiary, with instructions to broaden Franco-American trade.

Before Monroe could sail, however, he and several Senate colleagues stumbled onto a scandal of sex and misuse of government funds that threatened the Washington administration and the Federalist Party with collapse.

In 1791 James Reynolds, a professional confidence man and speculator who had specialized in bilking veterans of bounty lands, found a way to blackmail Treasury Secretary Alexander Hamilton after Hamilton succumbed to the flirtations of Reynolds's wife. Playing the outraged husband, Reynolds demanded—and Hamilton paid—$1,000 and gave Reynolds a low-level Treasury Department post. Arrested shortly thereafter for embezzling Treasury funds, Reynolds went to jail.

After a congressional clerk reported Hamilton's ties to Reynolds, Congress appointed a committee of three to investigate. Two were Federalists—Speaker of the House Frederick Muhlenberg, an ordained Lutheran minister from Pennsylvania,* and Virginia Representative Abraham Venable. The third committee member was Antifederalist James Monroe, who had fought beside Hamilton in the Revolutionary War.

When the committee confronted Hamilton on December 15, 1792, the usually icy Treasury secretary uncharacteristically dissolved in tears and confessed to a sordid relationship—not with the Reynolds but with

---

*The first Speaker of the US House of Representatives, Muhlenberg was the son of Heinrich Melchior Muhlenberg, a German immigrant and patriarch of the Lutheran Church in America.

Reynolds's wife. Far from misappropriating government funds, Hamilton had spent his own money for Mrs. Reynolds's services and bribes to her husband to keep silent about the affair. Convinced that Hamilton had been a victim of blackmail and that "the affair had no relation to official duties," the Congressmen declared the explanation "entirely satisfactory."[4] Monroe then offered to safeguard the dossier of the investigation but sent it to Hamilton's avowed enemy, Republican leader Thomas Jefferson. Shortly afterward whispers in political circles asserted that Monroe had irrefutable proof of Hamilton's collusion with Reynolds to misuse government funds.

As Jay and Monroe sailed off to their separate destinations overseas, Congress reinforced the President's Neutrality Proclamation by passing a Neutrality Act forbidding US citizens to enlist in the service of a foreign nation and banning the refitting of foreign warships in American ports.

Beyond the confines of the Capitol, however, few Americans paid attention to the Neutrality Act. Jefferson had retreated to his aerie in Charlottesville, Virginia, and Genet disappeared in his cabbage patch in Long Island's vegetable fields. But the Democratic Societies they had organized acquired lives of their own, inciting chaos wherever they could.

Depending on the temper of local citizens, club leaders howled for local self-rule, universal white-male suffrage, restoration of state sovereignty, violent overthrow of the federal government, or any other disruptive cause they could contemplate. In Richmond the Democratic Society hurled hate-filled criticisms at Washington, Governor Lee, and Marshall, whose seizure of the *Unicorn* had set off howls of protest among French sympathizers in Richmond.

"My constant effort," Marshall explained, "was to show that the conduct of our government respecting its foreign relations were just . . . and that our independence was brought into real danger by the overgrown and inordinate influence of France."[5]

The influence of Democratic Societies reached far beyond Virginia, however. Leaflets promised American protesters in South Carolina, Kentucky, Pennsylvania, New York, and elsewhere support from the French revolutionary government:

"France has been called to lead a gigantic revolution and worldwide up-rising to liberate the oppressed peoples of the world," proclaimed Jacques Pierre Brissot de Warville, a mediocre journalist-turned-pamphleteer who thought himself a prophet and clawed his way to leadership among French revolutionaries. "All Europe will be Gallicized, communized, and Jacobinized," he promised, and American Democratic Societies extended his pledge to include North America.[6]

At the time American farmers were chafing under a two-year-old federal whiskey tax on distilled liquors. The tax infuriated farmers west of the Appalachians, where almost every farm had a still to convert grain into whiskey. The absence of roads across the rugged Appalachians made it impossible to transport grain in bulk by wagon to eastern markets. By converting grain into whiskey, they could pour the fruit of their labors into jugs and barrels that mules could easily carry on the narrow mountain trails. Faced with what they called confiscation of their profits, many refused to pay the whiskey tax, and when collectors threatened to seize their properties, the farmers met them with pitchforks, tar and feathers, and gunfire.

Refusing to see the logic behind farmer discontent, President Washington called whiskey tax protests "the first *formidable* fruit of the Democratic Societies." He blamed Genet for having "brought the eggs of these venomous reptiles to our shores."[7]

Protests reached a climax at dawn on July 16, 1794, when a mob near Pittsburgh burned the homes of the whiskey-tax collector and the US marshal, forcing them to flee with their families. Remaining tax collectors in the area either followed or publicly resigned their commissions; the flow of tax revenues to the federal treasury from western Pennsylvania—an area with about 77,000 people and some 5,000 stills—came to a halt. Farmers in Kentucky, Virginia, Georgia, and the Carolinas quickly followed suit.

In Philadelphia Attorney General William Bradford declared Pennsylvania tax protests part of a "plan for weakening and perhaps overthrowing the general government." Secretary of War Knox urged the President to send "a superabundant force" to crush the rebels.[8]

Washington agreed, then scrawled his name across a proclamation and ordered Treasury Secretary Hamilton to raise an army of 13,000 if the westerners refused to yield. Governor Lee ordered John Marshall, still a brigadier general, to lead the Virginia militia to Pennsylvania and join Hamilton's army. Marshall, however, had also become the state's acting attorney general and was prosecuting several critical cases. Governor Lee, therefore, took Marshall's place as commander of the Virginia force.

On October 20 Washington ordered his combined forces to march on Pittsburgh, but when they arrived, the rebels had vanished. America's first revolution against constitutional rule ended without a shot being fired.

PRESIDENT WASHINGTON'S LAST FULL YEAR IN OFFICE BEGAN WITH the resignation of his old friend Secretary of War Henry Knox. A beloved intimate of Washington since the beginning of the Revolutionary War, he cited the infirmities of advancing age for his decision. The President sent Knox his "regrets at parting with (perhaps never more to meet) the few intimates whom I love; among these be assured you are one."[9]

No sooner had Knox left his cabinet than Treasury Secretary Hamilton stunned the President by announcing that he too was resigning. As with Knox, the loss of Hamilton was an emotional as well as political blow. Washington had all but adopted the orphaned youngster after the boy's heroics at the Battle of Trenton twenty years earlier. A surrogate son, he had served as Washington's most trusted aide during and after the war. He had led the charge at Yorktown, then masterminded Washington administration fiscal policies that converted the United States from an impoverished debtor nation to a land of opportunity and prosperity. He was irreplaceable.

Although Hamilton did not disclose the "urgent motives" that impelled his departure, whispers of his infidelity at home had grown more audible around the capital. With his effectiveness threatened, he decided to return to New York to prepare for inevitable public exposure and spare

Washington the pain and embarrassment of his presence in the presidential family.

Hamilton had no intention of relinquishing political power, however, and before leaving, he urged the President to fill cabinet vacancies with Hamilton allies. Washington thereupon appointed Postmaster General Timothy Pickering as secretary of war and Comptroller of the Treasury Oliver Wolcott Jr. as secretary of the Treasury. Pickering was a Harvard-educated Massachusetts lawyer who had served Washington as adjutant general in 1777 before becoming quartermaster general for the rest of the Revolution. He was a loyal federalist, had strongly backed ratification, and, like Hamilton, was an ardent Anglophile. Wolcott was the son of Connecticut's governor and a devoted Hamilton loyalist. Only Secretary of State Edmund Randolph, an avowed Francophile, remained in the cabinet to try to offset the influence of Hamilton's Anglophiles.

Soon after his appointment as Treasury secretary, however, Wolcott cut short Randolph's career by giving Pickering a copy of a letter purportedly written by Randolph to the outgoing French minister, soliciting bribes to further French interests. Pickering showed it to Washington and accused the former Virginia governor of treason.

The letter and Pickering's accusation staggered Washington. He had known and trusted Randolph for years—considered him a close personal friend. A wealthy plantation owner like Washington and a cousin of both Thomas Jefferson and John Marshall, Randolph came from one of Virginia's oldest and most distinguished families. He had been Washington's aide-de-camp in Cambridge at the beginning of the Revolutionary War in 1775. A dozen years later he had supported Washington in the struggle for ratification of the Constitution. Washington all but broke down in tears as he confronted Randolph with the letter and demanded Randolph's resignation.

Adding to Washington's despair over the departures of Randolph, Hamilton, and Knox was the death of Attorney General William Bradford in August. In only eight months the President had lost the four most important members of his cabinet.

To fill the post of attorney general for the remaining months of the administration, Washington turned to his own lawyer, John Marshall, but Marshall only added to the President's despair by refusing the appointment. The Fairfax Manor Lands case—and the wealth it promised his family—still required his attention, as did his children and his ailing wife, Polly. Nothing in the world—no honors, powers, or emoluments—matched the value of his home and family. When he and Polly were together, he claimed, they became "the two happiest people on earth."[10]

After Marshall refused to join Washington's administration, the President faced rejections by two of his Supreme Court appointees. Even Patrick Henry refused, pleading a desperately ill wife and eight children to support along with "loss of crops and consequent derangement of my finances and . . . my own health."[11]

At a loss for a replacement, Washington turned to former Treasury Secretary Hamilton for help: "Aid me, I pray you, with your sentiments. What am I to do for a Secretary of State? Mr. Marshall . . . has declined the office of attorney general and I am pretty certain would accept no other. I ask frankly and with solicitude and shall receive kindly any sentiments you may express."[12]

On Hamilton's advice, Washington elevated Pickering to the powerful post of secretary of state, then named the pliant James McHenry secretary of war.

With Pickering, McHenry, and Wolcott in the three most important cabinet posts, Hamilton suddenly had more influence on government in early 1795 than when he actually sat in the cabinet. Only Virginia's Charles Lee, the younger brother of Governor Henry Lee, acted and thought independently of Hamilton, but as attorney general, he had little influence on policy. The attorney general's function then was to act as the President's lawyer and legal adviser—not as a policy maker.

Washington had no sooner installed his new cabinet when a barrage of criticism exploded over the Capitol and rioters poured into the streets calling for Washington's resignation. Until then the Senate had been debating terms of the Jay Treaty in secret, but one or more Republicans with ties to Jefferson leaked details of the treaty to the Republican press. Bold headlines vilified John Jay—and his presidential patron: Jay had failed to negotiate an end to British depredations against American shipping and the cruel impressment of American crewmen.

"The whole country was agitated with that question," John Marshall recalled later to his friend Associate Justice Joseph Story. "The commotion began at Boston and seemed to rush through the Union with a rapidity and violence which set human reason and common sense at defiance."[13]

Southerners grew particularly irate when they learned that the northerner Jay had failed to win compensation for the loss of slaves the British had lured away during the Revolution. Indeed, the only concessions Jay won from the British were withdrawal of their troops from the Northwest Territory and resumption of limited American trade with Britain and the West Indies. They agreed to let a joint commission settle financial claims of British and American citizens against each other.

Jefferson pounced, firing a barrage of angry letters to Republican allies describing Jay's treaty as a "monument of folly or venality" and labeling it "Hamilton's Treaty."

"I have always found," he wrote to Mann Page, a Virginia attorney and Republican political leader, "that rogues would be uppermost, and . . . rising above the swinish multitude, always contrive to nestle themselves into the places of power and profit."

> These rogues set out with stealing the people's good opinion and then steal from them the right of withdrawing it by contriving laws and associations against the power of the people themselves.[14]

Jay had, of course, hoped to win concessions on both the impressment and slave issues but found Britain with no incentive to yield on either question. Aside from sheer economic and military power, British warships had crushed the French fleet in a critical naval battle and seized full command of Atlantic waters, with no need to cede anything to any nation on earth.

When the terms of the Jay Treaty became public in March 1795, southern legislatures with Republican majorities instructed their senators in Philadelphia to reject it. Elections were still under way in Virginia, however, and Richmond's Federalists hoped to win an Assembly majority to support the Jay Treaty by putting such popular figures as John Marshall on their list of candidates. Marshall's wife, Polly, was pregnant again, however, and he refused to leave home to campaign. To his relief, she gave birth in September to another daughter, Mary, whom they nicknamed Polly. After Polly's birth, John Marshall learned that, through no effort of his own, he had won the election, ensuring a Federalist majority in the Virginia Assembly and election of Federalists as the state's US senators.[*]

"I was well satisfied at being again in the assembly," Marshall admitted.[15]

Jefferson, however, responded bitterly to Marshall's election victory, noting that "Marshall will be able to embarrass the Republican Party a good deal. . . . His lax lounging manners have made him popular with the bulk of the people of Richmond, and a profound hypocrisy [has made him popular] with many thinking men of our country."[16]

In June 1795 the Federalist majority engendered by the Virginia elections ensured ratification of the Jay Treaty and not only earned Marshall national political attention, it coincidentally earned him and his family untold wealth. In approving the treaty, Congress effectively recognized the legitimacy of pre–Revolutionary War claims by British citizens to lands confiscated by American states and individuals. It thus legitimized Denny Martin Fairfax's claim of ownership of the Fairfax Manor Lands and his right to sell the lands to the Marshalls for the agreed upon £20,000.

Recognizing the Jay Treaty as the law of the land, John Marshall went to Philadelphia in January 1796 to obtain a final Supreme Court ruling in *Hite v. Fairfax*. It was the first time since his marriage more than a dozen years earlier that he separated from his beloved Polly, and he left ridden with anxieties.

---

[*] Until the 1913 ratification of the Seventeenth Amendment allowing popular election of US senators, state legislatures determined each state's senators.

"My Dearest Polly," he wrote after his arrival in Philadelphia,

> After a journey . . . beyond measure tedious . . . I am at length safe at this place. . . . I have not yet heard from my beloved wife and children. You ought not to keep me in suspense about you. . . . Kiss our children and especially our sweet little Poll for me and tell Tom I expect him to attend to his brother and to you. I count on Jacquelin's great improvement before my return. I am, my dearest Polly, your affectionate
> J. Marshall[17]

Press reports of Marshall's eloquent defense of Washington and the Jay Treaty in the Virginia Assembly had preceded him, and, when he arrived in the nation's capital, congressional Federalists embraced him as a new party leader.

"My arguments were spoken of in such extravagant terms as to prepare the Federalists of Congress to receive me with marked attention and favor," he reported. "A Virginian with any sort of reputation who supported the measures of the government was such a *rara avis* that I was received by them all with a degree of kindness which I had not anticipated."[18]

In arguing before the Supreme Court, Marshall's attorneys cited the Anglo-American Treaty of Paris of 1783 that ended the Revolutionary War and banned any American confiscations of British property. The Supreme Court under Chief Justice John Jay agreed, thus denying the property rights of Jost Hite and giving Denny Fairfax clear title and the right to sell the Manor Lands to the Marshall family.

On February 1, 1794, Fairfax drew up a bill of sale, and John Marshall and his brothers had only to raise £20,000 to become owners of 215,000 acres of Virginia's—indeed, America's—most valuable and fertile lands. Fortunately John's older brother James Markham was engaged to Hester Morris, daughter of the famed Philadelphia banker Robert Morris.

Widely hailed at the time as the "Financier of the Revolution," Morris had served as superintendent of finance for the Continental Congress during the Revolutionary War and speculated in land after the war—some of it in Virginia. He had appointed John Marshall his attorney in that state and agreed to pay Marshall's legal fees by financing the Marshall family purchase of the Fairfax Manor Lands.

The property the Marshalls acquired covered twelve counties stretching from the Potomac River in the East across the Blue Ridge Mountains and Shenandoah Valley in the West, north to the Mason-Dixon Line and south to the Rappahannock River (see map, page 43). At a price of less than two shillings an acre, the Marshalls stood to reap upward of four times their investment if they resold the land—about $6 million in today's currency. The sale of land he did not reserve for his own use would earn John Marshall enough wealth to allow him to devote the remainder of his life to public service without financial strain.

News of his son's court victory elated the aging Thomas Marshall, who longed for a family reunion. "The thoughts of seeing you once more," he wrote to his son from Kentucky, "I really believe is a principal means of keeping me alive."

> And I will endeavor to live one more year in hopes of that event. I am told Mr. J. Ambler [Polly Marshall's father] talks of coming out with you. Happy shall I be to see him with you and all my family and friends who may think it worthwhile to ride out to this country to take leave of me before I close my eyes forever.[19]

Marshall's father praised his son for defending Washington and the Jay Treaty. "Next to that of my own family," the Marshall family patriarch declared, "the good of my country and our worthy President is nearest my heart, and the part you take in the present storm gives me much pleasure. Indeed, you never seriously disobliged me in your life. . . . God bless you once more, prays your [father], T. Marshall."

In contrast to John Marshall, Thomas Jefferson kept his eyes focused on the presidency, appealing constantly to public rage over the Jay Treaty. In a letter to his friend Philip Mazzei, an Italian doctor-turned-wine-merchant who had bought a farm near Jefferson's Monticello, the former secretary of state shed all traces of loyalty to the government he had once pledged to serve:

"In place of the noble love of liberty and republican government," Jefferson charged "an Anglican, monarchical, and aristocratical party has sprung up whose avowed object is to draw over us . . . the forms of the British government. . . . All the officers of the government . . . prefer calm despotism to the boisterous sea of liberty."

Spurred by Jefferson, Republicans spread rumors that Vice President Adams would deliver the nation back to the English if he won election and succeeded Washington to the presidency. Jefferson even vilified the man who had once entrusted him with the conduct of the nation's foreign affairs:

"It would give you a fever," Jefferson wrote to Mazzei of Washington and Adams, "were I to name to you the apostates who have gone over to these heresies, men who were Samsons in the field and Solomons in the councils, but who have had their heads shorn by the harlot England."[20]

At Jefferson's behest, the southern Republican minority in the House of Representatives provoked a constitutional crisis aimed at seizing treaty-making powers from the President and Senate by refusing to appropriate funds for the Jay Treaty's joint arbitration commission until Washington submitted all of Jay's documents from the treaty negotiations. Using its control over the purse to "defund" the treaty, the House prepared, in effect, to "Jacobinize" the US government by shifting control of government to the popularly elected branch of the legislature.

Although the Constitution gave the Senate *sole* authority to reject or approve treaties, it gave the House *sole* authority to appropriate funds. By refusing to fund the Jay Treaty, the House threatened to use its funding authority to nullify a treaty—an eventuality that the framers of the Constitution had not intended or envisioned.

In Richmond Marshall sprang to defend the President and the Constitution by calling another public meeting. Warned that he might be "treated rudely," Marshall was "fully prepared not only with the words of the Constitution and the universal practice of nations . . . to show that a commercial treaty [with Britain] was constitutional."

One or two of my cautious friends advised me not to engage in the debate . . . that it would destroy me totally. I had reasons to know that a politician even in times of violent party spirit maintains his respectability by showing his strength and is most safe when he encounters prejudice more fearlessly. There was scarcely an intelligent man in the House who did not yield . . . on the constitutional question.[21]

Infuriated at what he saw as a clear violation of the Constitution by House Republicans, Washington delivered a stern lecture:

Having been a member of the general convention, I have ever entertained but one opinion . . . that the power of making treaties is exclusively vested in the President, by and with the advice and consent of the Senate . . . and that every treaty so made became the law of the land . . . [and] they become obligatory. . . . This construction agrees with the opinions entertained by the state conventions, when they were deliberating on the Constitution. . . . All the papers . . . were laid before the Senate . . . the assent of the House of Representatives is not necessary to the validity of a treaty.

Washington refused to release any documents of the treaty negotiations, saying it would "establish a dangerous precedent. . . . A just compliance with the Constitution . . . forbids compliance with your request."[22]

Only Washington, with his enormous prestige and popularity, could have addressed Congress in such demeaning language. Although he made no threats, he did not have to. Brigadier General John Marshall stood firmly behind Washington with two brigades of Virginia militiamen in the South. And Alexander Hamilton had lined up almost every House Federalist behind the President. Recalcitrant congressmen quickly retreated, fearing political consequences if they refused. In the end Washington crushed the House attempt to defund the Jay Treaty and insert itself into foreign affairs and treaty negotiations, two areas over which he seized full control for himself and all future Presidents.

"I do not know how to thank you," the President wrote in an emotional letter to Alexander Hamilton,

for the trouble you have taken . . . on the request of the House of Representatives for the papers relative to the British treaty . . . to show the im-
propriety of that request. . . . To express again my sincere thanks for the
pains you have been at to investigate the subject, and to assure you, over
and over, of the warmth of my friendship and of the affectionate regard
with which I am . . . G. Washington[23]

Washington's words had no effect on the French revolutionary government, however. Calling the Jay Treaty a violation of the 1778 Franco-
American treaty of amity and commerce, the French government abruptly
ended its alliance with the United States and ordered French ships to
seize American vessels and cargoes bound to and from England. It ordered captured crews and passengers imprisoned, and told its military to
prepare for all-out war and an invasion of North America. In Richmond
Governor Lee put the state militia on alert, and Brigadier General John
Marshall prepared to go to war again.

CHAPTER 7

X, Y, Z

WHILE JOHN MARSHALL PREPARED FOR WAR AGAINST THE FRENCH IN Virginia, his boyhood friend and Revolutionary War comrade James Monroe, the American minister to France, raced about Paris trying to placate French officials and prevent war. He sent strong protests to the State Department and to President Washington that it was "in the interest of America to avoid a rupture with France."[1] Because of the time it took for mail to cross the Atlantic, however, Monroe did not and could not know that Washington had replaced Francophile Edmund Randolph with the avidly Francophobic Timothy Pickering, who embraced all things English and supported the Jay Treaty.

Pickering's first act in office was to purge the State Department of pro-French employees, including Monroe. A few weeks later, on September 1, 1796, the French recalled their minister from the United States, and a week later Monroe received Pickering's letter of recall "owing to [your] misconduct."[2] Astonished by Pickering's accusation, Monroe fired a long, bitter response:

"You charge me . . . with a neglect of duty," raged Marshall's friend. "Permit me to remark that this charge is not more unjust and unexpected than the testimony by which you support it is inapplicable and inconclusive." Monroe charged that the Jay Treaty had given the French

117

government more than ample justification for severing relations with the United States.

"Paris was starving," he wrote, "and our vessels destined for the ports of France were seized and carried into England."

> Do difficulties like these . . . give cause to suspect that I was idle or negligent at my post? . . . But you urge that as I knew this discontent existed, I ought to have encountered and removed it. I do not distinctly comprehend . . . what it was you wish . . . I should have done.[3]

Monroe believed Pickering had deceived him. While his Federalist counterpart in London, John Jay, was undermining Franco-American relations, Monroe had followed his instructions to the letter in Paris. He had established warm, cordial diplomatic relations, promoted peaceful trade in nonmilitary goods, and firmly established America's diplomatic presence in western Europe. He had done his job to perfection.

The original State Department instructions to Monroe had pledged that "Mr. Jay . . . is positively forbidden to weaken the engagements between this country and France,"[4] but Secretary of State Pickering had put partisan politics above national interests and done exactly what Jay had been forbidden to do.

Pickering used Monroe's complaints and favoritism for France to convince Washington to replace him with someone "who will promote not thwart the neutral policy of the government." The President then wrote to John Marshall that "nothing would be more pleasing to me" than for Marshall to go to France, "if only for a few months . . . to explain the views of this government" to the French.

Again Marshall turned down a presidential appointment, this time citing pressures of work but, in fact, refusing to participate even indirectly in the censure of his longtime friend Monroe. Having already introduced some friction into their friendship during their debate over ratification of the Constitution, Marshall had no intention of profiting from Monroe's dismissal from government service. Patrick Henry also refused to replace

A hero of the Revolutionary War, James Monroe had repaired relations with the Jacobin government in France, when the Secretary of State ordered his recall from Paris for "neglect of duty." (LIBRARY OF CONGRESS)

Monroe, and Washington finally appointed South Carolina's Charles Cotesworth Pinckney.[5]

In the spring of 1797 James Monroe and his family sailed for home, with Monroe seething with anger and bitterness. Before leaving, he sent a long and detailed letter to his mentor Jefferson, the guardian of Hamilton's confession to adultery and his letters to Mrs. James Reynolds. Before Monroe's own ship had crossed the Atlantic, James Callender, a Scottish-born pamphleteer and journalist whom Jefferson called "a man of genius," had published the entire Hamilton dossier. Callender said he had done so to respond to "unfounded [Federalist] reproaches on Mr. Monroe."[6]

"We shall presently see," Callender wrote of Hamilton, "this great master of morality, although himself the father of a family, confessing that he had an illicit correspondence with another man's wife." Although the original Senate inquiry had cleared Hamilton of the charge, Callender repeated the libel that, as Treasury secretary, Hamilton had acted with James Reynolds to enrich himself by using privileged information to speculate in government securities.[7]

After Monroe arrived in New York, Hamilton appeared at his door at ten one morning with his brother-in-law John Barker Church. Hamilton was "very much agitated" and blamed Monroe for releasing the dossier. Monroe explained he had left the dossier with a trusted "friend [Jefferson] in Virginia" and was unaware it had been released.

Hamilton did not believe him: "This as your representation is totally false!"

Offended at Hamilton's tone, Monroe snapped back: "Do you say I represented falsely?"—and, without waiting for a reply, declared, "You are a scoundrel!"

Once close comrades on the battlefield, the two Men of Monmouth stood toe to toe:

"I will meet you like a gentleman!" Hamilton barked.

"I am ready; get your pistols!" Monroe snapped.

"I shall!" replied Hamilton, who, like Monroe, had been a crack marksman in the war.

"Gentlemen, gentlemen. Be moderate!" cried Church as he stepped between the two political titans.[8]

"You have been and are actuated by motives towards me malignant and dishonorable!" Hamilton raged.

Monroe shot back: "Why you have adopted this style I know not. If your object is to render this affair a personal one between us . . . I am ever ready to meet."[9]

Monroe called on his friend New York attorney Aaron Burr Jr. to serve as his second. Another of the heroic Men of Monmouth who had fought alongside Monroe and Hamilton, Burr had also served with Monroe in the US Senate. Although an Antifederalist, Burr dined and socialized with

Hamilton and was a cordial professional colleague. Burr sought to be peacemaker between two old friends.

He urged Monroe to send Hamilton a conciliatory letter, and Monroe complied: "Seeing no adequate cause . . . why I should give a challenge to you," Monroe wrote, "I own it was not my intention to give or even provoke one." After delivering Monroe's letter, Burr urged Hamilton to accept Monroe at his word, and Hamilton relented, conceding that "any further step . . . would be improper."[10] Ironically, Burr prevented a duel that might have saved him from confronting Hamilton seven years later—almost to the day.

After abandoning his challenge to Monroe, Hamilton ignored Burr's further advice—and that of his own supporters—to put the Reynolds affair behind him. Instead, he published a pamphlet in which he confessed his sexual relationship with Mrs. Reynolds to the American people but presented incontrovertible proof of his innocence in her husband's malfeasance. Although Hamilton's pamphlet shocked his patron George Washington, it did little to reduce Hamilton's influence among Federalists. With casual winks and smirks about their own sexual dalliances, the men whose appointments Hamilton had engineered in the President's cabinet continued to follow his political directives.

IN SEPTEMBER 1796 GEORGE WASHINGTON WAS NEARING THE END OF his second term in office and sent this announcement to the press:

> The period for a new election . . . to administer the executive government of the United States being not far distant . . . it appears to me proper . . . that I should now apprise you of the resolution I have formed to decline being considered among the number of those out of whom a choice is to be made.[11]

With those words, the President began a memorable farewell message to the nation, saying he would limit his service in office to two terms—a precedent that every succeeding President would follow for 140 years.* Washington sent his message to the *American Daily Advertiser* as a letter to the American people. In it he tried to establish broad precedents for his successors in the conduct of national and foreign affairs.

Warning Americans against "the baneful effects of the spirit of [political] party," he urged binding the nation's regions into "fraternal union." Political parties, he argued, "kindle the animosity of one part [of the nation] against another, foment occasional riot and insurrection . . . open the door to foreign influence and corruption [and] become potent engines by which cunning, ambitious, and unprincipled men . . . subvert the power of the people and usurp for themselves the reins of government."[12]

In foreign affairs Washington warned against "the insidious wiles of foreign influence," which he called "one of the most baneful foes of republican government. . . . The great rule of conduct for us, in regard to foreign nations is in extending our commercial relations to them with as little political connection as possible."[13]

Washington proclaimed what he hoped would be the defining words of America's foreign policy: "'Tis our true policy to steer clear of permanent alliances with any portion of the foreign world."[14]

The French government, however, would have none of it and sent a new minister to America with instructions to ensure election of a pro-French President. When Citizen Pierre-Auguste Adet arrived, he launched a barrage of pseudonymous warnings to the press that only by electing Thomas Jefferson President could the United States avoid war with France.

The Republican *Aurora* led the Adet campaign: "The American nation has been debauched by Washington," avowed owner Benjamin Franklin Bache, Benjamin Franklin's grandson. A fierce opponent of centralized

---

*Franklin D. Roosevelt ran for reelection to a third term in 1939 and won a fourth term four years later. Mounting concern over the lack of presidential term limits provoked enactment of the Twenty-Second Amendment to the Constitution in 1951, limiting the president to no more than two full terms in office.

government, Bache had opposed ratification and sought to stem the growth of federal government authority.

"If ever a nation has suffered from the improper influence of a man," Bache railed, "the American nation has suffered from the influence of Washington. If ever a nation was deceived by a man, the American nation has been deceived by Washington." Calling Washington "the source of all the misfortunes of the country," the *Aurora* replied to the President's farewell address with vitriol:

> If ever there was a period for rejoicing, this is the moment. Every heart in unison with the freedom and happiness of the people ought to beat high with exultation that the name of Washington from this day ceases to give currency to political iniquity and legalized corruption.[15]

The press attacks on Washington combined with the French ambassador's meddling in the election to produce effects exactly opposite to those intended. Most Americans—even political opponents of the President—revered the "Father of Our Country" and bridled at the *Aurora*'s insults. Meanwhile Federalist newspapers condemned the French ambassador for attempting to "wean us from the government and administration of our own choice and make us willing to be governed by such as France shall think best for us—beginning with Jefferson."[16] One Federalist newspaper warned that a Jefferson presidency would be "fatal to our independence now that the interference of a foreign nation in our affairs is no longer disguised."[17]

Voters responded by electing John Adams President and relegating Thomas Jefferson to the obscurity of the vice presidency. New York's Aaron Burr Jr., finished fourth behind Federalist Thomas Pinckney, the younger brother of former South Carolina Governor Charles Cotesworth Pinckney, whom Washington had appointed American emissary to France to replace James Monroe.

At sunrise on February 22, 1797, Washington's last birthday in office, church bells pealed and cannons boomed in the capital of Philadelphia;

President Washington toasts members of his administration at his farewell dinner, on the eve of Vice President John Adam's inauguration as the nation's second President. Adams is seen here in profile seated opposite the President, and Martha Washington is seated at the foot of the table on extreme left. Although Washington's close friend Alexander Hamilton did not attend the dinner, the artist nonetheless depicted him to the President's immediate right, with Secretary of State Pickering to the President's left. (LIBRARY OF CONGRESS)

at noon an endless line of militiamen marched to the music of parading bands. Across the nation flags flew from every perch in every city, town, and village. Americans rejected the harsh words of the *Aurora* and the rest of the opposition press: they had tired of arguments, riots, and chaos continuously disrupting their lives, and they inundated Washington with testimonies of appreciation for his service to the nation.

On the eve of his departure from office the Washingtons entertained for the last time in the presidential residence:

"Ladies and gentlemen," the President raised his glass to the political notables at the table, "this is the last time I shall drink your health as a public man. I do so with sincerity, and wishing you all possible happiness." He then toasted President-elect John Adams, the man who, in the Continental Congress of 1775, had selected Washington to lead the Continental Army. According to one witness, tears ran down the cheeks of those present as they tried to sip from their glasses.[18]

Just before noon on Saturday, March 4, 1797, President Washington walked to Congress Hall in a black suit, a military hat, his hair powdered as usual. Greeted by ear-splitting cheers and applause, he climbed the speaker's platform and took his seat. The new vice president, Thomas Jefferson, loser to Adams in the presidential election, followed without expression and sat between Washington and the Speaker's chair.

President-elect Adams appeared last, sat momentarily in the Speaker's chair, then rose to take the oath of office. None of Jefferson's supporters uttered a word of protest. The presidential structure that Washington had built stood rock solid; the crowd of onlookers was orderly, watching the peaceful transition of elected governments with deep, silent respect, knowing they themselves had raised the new President to power without firing a shot. It was one of the most remarkable moments in world history.

"A solemn scene it was indeed," President Adams wrote to his wife, Abigail, "and it was made affecting to me by the presence of the general, whose countenance was as serene and unclouded as the day. He seemed to me to enjoy a triumph over me. Methought I heard him say, 'Ay! I am fairly out and you fairly in! See which of us will be happiest!'"[19]

To the new President's deep disappointment, however, the smooth transfer of power did little to calm the chaos that seemed to hold the nation—indeed, the world—in its unyielding grip. Within days of taking office Adams learned that the French government had rejected Charles Cotesworth Pinckney's credentials, expelled him from the country as an undesirable alien, and ordered stepped-up attacks on American shipping. Although the bloodbath of the French Terror had ended with the execution of Maximilien Robespierre, the French Revolution gained new momentum with the rise to power of Paul Barras.

America's second President, John Adams, called his inauguration "a solemn scene" in which he imagined the beleaguered outgoing President George Washington rejoicing, "I am fairly out and you fairly in! See which of us will be happiest!" (LIBRARY OF CONGRESS)

A sly aristocrat-turned-revolutionary who lurked on the fringes of Jacobin leadership, Barras organized the coup that overthrew Robespierre and sent him to the guillotine. Barras then seized control of the Paris National Guard and key government ministries before partnering with a popular young Corsican colonel, Napoléon Bonaparte. Barras promoted Bonaparte to general and gave him command of the army. Thereafter Bonaparte ensured Barras the military support to sustain his political power, while Barras ensured Bonaparte the political support to sustain his military power.

To cement their partnership, Barras gave Bonaparte his mistress, Joséphine de Beauharnais, actually giving the bride away at the wedding. With Bonaparte's guns to back him, Barras dissolved the Convention, or national assembly, and replaced it with a new "republican government" led by a five-member executive committee of political allies called the *Directoire*, or Directory.

A British blockade of French ports, however, had crippled French foreign trade and drained the French treasury. Inflation and starvation had spread across France, provoking a wave of peasant insurrections. Bonaparte assuaged their anger and hunger with dazzling oratory that promised rich pastures in neighboring lands. "You have no shoes, uniforms or shirts and almost no bread," he called out to the people of France.

> Our stores are empty while those of our enemies are overflowing. I will lead you into the most fertile plains in the world. Rich provinces and great cities will be in your power. There you will find honor, glory, and wealth. It is up to you to conquer. You *want* to conquer. You *will* conquer. Let us march! *Marchons! Marchons!*[20]

By the thousands, starving peasants rallied to his side, and in lightning strikes that overwhelmed western Europe, Bonaparte's armies, inflated by hungry peasant mobs, overran and plundered Holland, the Rhineland, Switzerland, Italy, Venice, Dalmatia, and the Ionian Islands. They seized the Papal States and Vatican City, captured Pope Pius VI, and stripped him of his temporal powers. When Bonaparte's armies had advanced to about sixty miles from Vienna in the spring of 1797, Russia, Austria, and Spain sued for peace.

In Philadelphia John Adams had just taken the reins of America's government from George Washington.

Napoléon Bonaparte's conquests restored the French national economy. Hundreds of millions of francs in reparations poured into France from conquered lands—60 million francs of currency from northern Italy alone, along with 10 million more in looted gold, silver, and jewels. Backed by Bonaparte's bayonets, Barras eliminated political dissent, anointing himself "King of the Republic." He appointed Bonaparte Chief of the French Armies and named the wily Charles Maurice de Talleyrand-Périgord minister of foreign affairs.

A friend of Barras from the Jacobin revolution, Talleyrand was part of a small, steady stream of aristocrat émigrés who returned from exile to reclaim ancestral lands and their roles in national leadership. During the butchery of Robespierre's Terror, Talleyrand had spent two years in exile in the United States. Apart from fluency in English, he laid claim to considerable knowledge of North American affairs, but little else. After falling prey to several investment swindles while in the United States, he grew to hate America and everything American.

"If I have to stay here another year," he despaired in a letter to his friend, French novelist Madame de Staël, "I shall die."[21]

An injury to his foot when Talleyrand was an infant left him with an ugly limp to complement his grotesque face. Although unfit for military duty, his aristocratic origins opened doors to the church, and his seductive voice, brilliant wit, and persuasive political skills won him, at thirty-four, a prestigious bishopric that made him chief spokesman for the French clergy. The post fed his greed for wealth, pleasure, and power with a fortune in gifts, commissions, bribes, and flocks of mistresses and sycophants. When the French Revolution began, he displayed chameleonic instincts by discarding his clerical robes, renouncing the church, and swearing allegiance to secularism, state, and revolution.

When Barras and Bonaparte came to power, Talleyrand revived the concept of France's mystical "natural right" to give law to the world and echoed Bonaparte's call to recover the nation's colonial empire of the 1750s. With western Europe in thrall, only the British blocked French return to glory, and by ensuring British access to American raw materials, the Jay Treaty would bolster British military strength. Calling the Jay Treaty an act of war, Bonaparte ordered the French navy to disrupt Anglo-American trade on the Atlantic and in the Caribbean by seizing American ships bound for Britain.

By the time John Adams took his oath as second American President, the French had seized more than 340 American ships with cargoes valued at more than $55 million. Hundreds of American seamen were languishing in prisons in Brest, Bordeaux, and the French West Indies. Insurance

Born an aristocrat, the wily French Foreign Minister Charles Maurice de Talleyrand-Périgord had been a bishop in the church and fled to the United States when the French Revolution erupted. (LIBRARY OF CONGRESS)

rates for Caribbean-bound ships increased five-fold in two years, from 6 percent to 35 percent of cargo values, and priced American exports out of world markets. The President called an urgent meeting of his cabinet and a special session of Congress to respond.

In what proved the first of many self-destructive political decisions, Adams retained Washington's cabinet to ensure government stability during the change of administrations. What he did not know was that Alexander Hamilton was manipulating the three most important cabinet officials like marionettes: Secretary of State Pickering, Secretary of War McHenry, and Secretary of the Treasury Wolcott. None took a breath, much less made a decision, without consulting Hamilton.

An outspoken Republican who had refused to sign the Constitution, Elbridge Gerry of Massachusetts was nonetheless a close friend of Federalist President John Adams and one of the President's appointees to the three-man commission to negotiate peace with France.
(LIBRARY OF CONGRESS)

Having served as American envoy in France, however, Adams knew far more about France than his cabinet and, ignoring cabinet suggestions, he appointed a bipartisan, three-man commission, with two Federalists and one Republican, to negotiate rapprochement with France. Each was a symbol of American policies and politics. Adams named a personal friend and fellow Harvard graduate, Elbridge Gerry of Massachusetts. An outspoken friend of France and a staunch Republican, Gerry had refused to sign the Constitution at the Constitutional Convention because it lacked a bill of rights.

"France has already gone to war with us," John Adams instructed Gerry. "She is at war with us but we are not at war with her."[22]

To demonstrate national pride, Adams rejected the French government's expulsion of Pinckney as American envoy by ordering his return to Paris as a member of the peace commission. And for the third member, Adams looked to Virginia, America's largest and most powerful state—the home of Washington and Jefferson, two French favorites. Although Adams had never met him, he appointed John Marshall, Virginia's unquestioned Federalist leader and a steadfast Washington loyalist.[23]

To Polly's shock and distress, her husband accepted. She was three months pregnant, frail and frightened after having miscarried once and losing two infants shortly after childbirth. She could not cope with the three boisterous children who had survived infancy—Thomas, now thirteen, Jacquelin, ten, and Mary, three. Her husband was the family's foundation. He had never left them, save for three quick trips to Philadelphia for Supreme Court hearings.

John tried reassuring her and reasoning with her. Their devoted head slave, Robin Spurlock, he said, was fully capable of running the household and had, in fact, been doing so for years. In addition, Polly's parents and all three of her sisters lived nearby and would visit regularly to help care for her and the children. In any case, he told Polly firmly, he had made up his mind and was leaving for Europe—with or without her blessing.

Having fought in battle for his nation's independence, Marshall believed it his duty to obey his President's call to defend his nation's honor at the international conference table. In addition, he stood to gain enormous political and financial benefits. Politically the mission promised him national and international prominence and a voice in the nation's highest councils. As for financial gains, the Philadelphia banker Robert Morris, who had promised to finance the Marshall family's acquisition of the Fairfax Manor Lands, was now bankrupt. The Marshalls would have to find another source for the £20,000 to consummate the purchase, but the Anglo-French war had made cash scarce in every western European country except Holland.

John's younger brother James Markham, who had married Robert Morris's daughter Hester, was already scouring Dutch banks and financial markets for funds, but for reasons that remain unclear, he needed his brother's help. With formal diplomatic relations between France and the United States suspended, John Marshall would have to sail to Holland first, then apply for French permission to proceed to Paris for the negotiations, and that would give him time in Holland to help his brother raise the funds they needed.

As Polly sank into a mire of despair and depression, Marshall left Richmond for Washington on June 21, 1797—without his wife's blessing and hating himself for having hurt the woman he loved so entirely.

On his first evening in the nation's capital he met John Adams for the first time. They formed an instant friendship; the President insisted that Marshall stay for dinner, after which Marshall wrote to Polly: "I dined on Saturday in private with the President, whom I found a sensible, plain, candid, good tempered man and was consequently much pleased with him."[24]

While President Adams and Secretary of State Pickering worked out instructions for Marshall, Pinckney, and Gerry, Vice President Jefferson sent the French government a secret warning that a new Franco-American treaty would open the way for unfettered American commerce with Britain and ensure British victory in the war with France. In what was tantamount to treason, Jefferson told Joseph Létombe, the French consul in Philadelphia, to urge his government to "listen to them and then drag out the negotiations" with the American peace commission to permit the French navy to intercept American ships bound for England.[25]

Still racked by guilt over his abrupt separation from Polly, Marshall sent Polly six long letters over the next ten days. "Had you been with me," he wrote of a visit to Mount Vernon to see George and Martha Washington, "I should have been as happy as I could be."

> Do tell me and tell me truly that the bitterness of parting is over and your mind is at rest—that you think of me only to contemplate the pleasure of our meeting and that you will permit nothing to distress you while I am gone. I cannot help feeling a pang when I reflect that every step I take carries me further and further from what is to me most valuable in this world. . . . I am thinking of you always.[26]

Two days later he wrote, "I have been extremely chagrinned at not having yet received a letter from you. . . . I have much reason to be satisfied and pleased with the manner in which I am received here but something is wanting to make me happy. Had I my dearest wife with me I should be delighted indeed. Not having that pleasure, why do you not give me what is nearest to it?"[27]

Almost three weeks after he had left he at last heard from Polly: "I thank heaven that your health is better," he replied, but asked for "assurances that your mind has become tranquil and as sprightly as usual. . . . Remember that . . . melancholy may inflict punishment on an innocent for whose sake you ought to preserve a serene and composed mind. . . . Tell the boys I please myself with the hopes of their improvement during my absence and kiss little Mary for your ever affectionate J. Marshall."[28]

Before sailing, he pleaded that she "let me hear often that you are well, and I shall be happy. Farewell my dearest Polly. My heart is incessantly offering prayers for you. . . . Farewell my much loved wife."[29]

After Marshall's ship reached Amsterdam on August 29, he found his brother James Markham, and together they obtained the funds to consummate the Fairfax Manor Lands deal before John left for Paris.

On October 8, 1797, Talleyrand agreed to see the three American peace commissioners at his palatial Paris mansion off the Place de la Révolution, now the Place de la Concorde. When they arrived, however, an aide told them he was in conference and to return two hours later. When he finally saw them, Talleyrand announced he would not receive them officially or open negotiations until he received instructions from Barras and Bonaparte. Evidently unimpressed by the ornate surroundings, Marshall noted only, "The conversation which continued about fifteen minutes was perfectly unimportant. The minister in his manners was polite and easy."[30]

Ten days later a Swiss financier, Jean Conrad Hottinguer, showed up after dark at the Left Bank quarters of the Americans and told them President Adams had insulted Barras in a speech assailing French attacks on American ships. To begin negotiations, said Hottinguer, Barras would require an official apology, along with *douceurs*, or "sweeteners" for the

The entrance to Talleyrand's lavish mansion off the Place de la Révolution (later, Place de la Concorde) was a European Portal of Power, through which the naïve American negotiators—John Marshall, Charles Cotesworth Pinckney, and Elbridge Gerry—thought they could enter and obtain an immediate peace settlement with France. (UNITED STATES DEPARTMENT OF STATE)

directors—Talleyrand, Bonaparte, and the others. When Marshall and Pinckney questioned Hottinguer about the *douceurs*, the bankers asserted they were "gratifications" that were "customary distributions in European diplomatic affairs."[31]

Marshall asked whether such a payment would buy the release of captured American ships and cargoes still in French government hands. Hottinguer shook his head "no."

Would the payment at least earn suspension of French attacks on the high seas? Again, a firm "no."

Believing Hottinguer might be an adventurer, Marshall and Pinckney demanded that he return with a written request from the Foreign Ministry.

Two days later—again, at night—Hottinguer showed up with a second Swiss banker, Pierre Bellamy, a close friend of Talleyrand. He told Marshall that Talleyrand considered himself a friend of the United States, but the directors felt John Adams had insulted France and demanded "a spontaneous gesture of friendship or gift" to placate them enough to receive American envoys. The *douceurs*, he explained, were similar to "the fealty and remuneration demanded by the ancient kings of France." Bellamy said he believed a gift of 120 million francs—about $250,000— would suffice, along with a loan of $12.8 million as a show of good faith.

"You must understand," Bellamy told the Americans, "without money, you will not be received."[32]

Marshall rejected the demand outright, warning that if France preferred war, "we regret the unavoidable necessity of defending ourselves," and he and Pinckney showed the two men to the door.[33]

Hottinguer returned a week later, warning the Americans, "Think of the power and violence of France. Give them the gifts and loans and buy some time. I fear the Directory will declare war on America."

Pinckney exploded: "We are unable to defend our commerce on the seas, but we will defend our shores!"

"It is not a question of war, but money," Hottinguer insisted. "The Directors are waiting for money!"

"We have already answered that demand," Pinckney and Marshall answered in unison.

"No, you have not," snapped the banker. "What is your answer?"

"It is no!" both Americans shouted. Then Pinckney barked, "Not even a six pence!"

Hottinguer sighed but kept his calm, spending two more hours pleading, cajoling, threatening: a bribe would be of great advantage to the Americans, old allies should not bicker over money; the commissioners were risking war and endangering their nation by refusing to pay so small a sum.

"He stated that Hamburg and other states of Europe were obliged to buy peace," Marshall related, "and that it would be in our interest to do so."

An Oxford-educated lawyer who signed both the Declaration of Independence and Constitution, Charles Cotesworth Pinckney rejected efforts by the French government to extort bribes in exchange for a peaceful settlement of the "quasi-war" with America. His response to the French—"Millions for defense, but not a cent for tribute"—became a national battle cry in the United States. (LIBRARY OF CONGRESS)

Marshall replied, "Our case is different from that of one of the minor nations of Europe."

They were unable to maintain their independence. . . . America is a great and . . . powerful nation. . . . Our national independence . . . is dearer to us than the friendship of France. America had taken a neutral stance. She had a right to take it. No nation had a right to force us out of it. To lend a sum of money to a belligerent power . . . is to relinquish our neutrality and take part in the war. To lend this money under the lash and coercion of France is . . . to submit to a foreign government imposed on us by force.[34]

Talleyrand's efforts to extort bribes from the American commissioners knew no bounds, however. He sent a third banker, Lucien Hauteval, and when he failed to extort any money, Talleyrand sent Tom Paine, Connecticut artist John Trumbull, and other Americans with Jacobin sympathies—all to no avail.

As weeks elapsed, the commissioners grew anxious about the mounting costs of their stay. "Friends"—secretly enlisted by Talleyrand—steered them to a palatial mansion owned by Voltaire's niece, a delightful thirty-two-year-old widow whom the great philosopher had adopted as his daughter before adopting her as his mistress.

Madame Reine-Philiberte Marquise de Villette charmed the commissioners as much as she had her uncle, with magnificent suppers that they shared with leaders of Parisian society and with a private box at the theater, opera, and other entertainments. The commissioners luxuriated in their new quarters that, though inexpensive, were far more lavish than their previous lodgings and commanded a sweeping view of the magnificent gardens of Marie de Medici—today's Jardin du Luxembourg.

"Paris presents an incessant round of amusement and dissipation," Marshall exulted in an uncharacteristically thoughtless letter to Polly.

> Every day there is something new, magnificent and beautiful; every night you may see a spectacle which astonishes and enchants the imagination. The most lively fancy . . . cannot equal the reality of the opera. All that you can conceive and a great deal more . . . in the line of amusement is to be found in this gay metropolis but I suspect it would not be easy to find a friend. I would not live in Paris to be among the wealthiest of its citizens.[35]

When Polly received her husband's letter, she was staying with relatives in Winchester, Virginia, where she had gone after her father's death in early January. Three days later, on January 13, 1798, the Marshalls' third son, John, was born, but, in the absence of her husband and the wake of her father's death, Polly sank into a deep depression. The birth was not only difficult—as all births were for her—her husband had stayed away far longer than she had anticipated.

Already in despair over his absence when she lost her father, Polly Marshall collapsed in tears after reading the first part of his letter describing Paris as a "gay metropolis" with an "incessant round of amusement and dissipation." As she read further, she all but despaired of ever seeing her husband again—with good reason:

"I now have rooms," he foolishly confessed, "in the house of a very accomplished, a very sensible, and a very amiable lady whose temper . . . is domestic and who generally sits with us two to three hours in the afternoon. This renders my situation less unpleasant than it has been."[36]

Indeed, Madame de Villette overwhelmed Marshall and Gerry with favors, teaching them to speak French, showing them the sights of Paris—by day and by night. Pinckney had come to Europe with his wife and daughter and spent his free time with them, but, as Mrs. Pinckney noted, the thirty-two-year-old Marquise "always dines with the two *bachelors*," as she called Marshall and Gerry, "and renders their situation very agreeable."[37]

Although Marshall tried assuring his wife that "no consideration will induce me ever again to consent to place the Atlantic between us," the first part of his letter had done its damage. Convinced that her husband was in the clutches of a French courtesan, Polly sank into so deep a depression that her sister took her out to the country to care for her.

Polly's concerns were not without foundation.

"Why," Marshall heard the seductive French whisper one evening. "Why will you not lend us money," Madame de Villette had surprised Marshall in the quiet of her dimly lit salon. "If you would only give us the money, we could arrange everything satisfactorily. We gladly loaned you money during your revolution."[38]

Stunned by the lady's words at first, Marshall called in Pinckney. Both suddenly realized their hostess was also a Talleyrand agent. The French Foreign Ministry had duped them into renting lodgings subsidized by the French government to lure them into the arms of a seductress. Pinckney told his hostess he planned to return to America immediately. Madame de Villette hissed that if he ended his mission, France had a powerful political party in America ready to seize power from the Adams administration by force if necessary.

In April 1798 Marshall and Pinckney abandoned their quest. They sent Talleyrand a thirty-five-page "memorial . . . in which we review[ed] fully the reciprocal complaints of the two countries against each other" and summarized their intent in coming to France and their view of the reasons for their failure.[39] "There is not the least hope of an accommodation with this government," Pinckney concluded. "We sue in vain to be heard."[40]

Gerry, however, took issue with the two Federalists. He insisted that peace with France was within reach and that "to prevent war, I will stay."[41] He said he would apologize to the Directory for President Adams's anti-French statements and negotiate a peace treaty with the French as a private citizen.

Outraged by Gerry's disloyalty, Pinckney and Marshall showed Gerry to the door and never spoke to him again. Although Pinckney and Marshall intended to leave France together, Pinckney had brought his thirteen-year-old daughter along, and she was ill, forcing him to remain long after his mission ended.

On April 24, 1798, Marshall reached Bordeaux, "bid an eternal adieu to Europe and its crimes,"[42] and set sail for America aboard the *Alexander Hamilton*. He called the ship "excellent . . . but for the sin of the name, which makes my return in her almost . . . criminal."[43] Marshall believed that Hamilton's espousal of alliance with Britain threatened American independence as much as Gerry's espousal of alliance with France. He was convinced America would soon be at war with France or Britain or both.

Before he left he sent a letter to the American consul general in Paris asking that he tell the Marquise "in my name and in the handsomest manner everything which respectful friendship can dictate."[44] Although some historians suggest that the handsome forty-two-year-old Marshall had an affair with the Marquise, there is no evidence to support the suggestion—even in the notes of the all-knowing Talleyrand, whose omnipresent spies reported every word and every move—sexual as well as political—of every important figure in Paris, day and night.

By the time Marshall embarked, news of the failed mission had reached Philadelphia, where congressional Anglophiles and Francophiles turned on each other, shouting insults and even assaulting each other. Federalist Congressman Roger Griswold of Connecticut got into a shouting match with Vermont's Republican Congressman Matthew Lyon, with Griswold accusing Lyon of cowardice during the Revolutionary War.

Lyon sprang across the floor of the House and spat in Griswold's face—earning the Vermont congressman the epithet of "The Spitting Lyon." Griswold reacted by beating Lyon about the head with his cane. Lyon retreated to a fire pit for a pair of tongs to parry; Griswold tackled him, and other congressmen jumped into the fray to pull Griswold from the melee by the legs.

The Lyon-Griswold free-for-all was but the first of the congressional crises that threatened to bring down constitutional government in the United States—much to Talleyrand's delight. With Marshall and Pinckney out of the negotiations, Talleyrand planned extending negotiations with Gerry long enough to permit what he called the "French Party" in America—Jefferson's pro-French Republicans—to seize power.

Like many French foreign ministers before and after, Talleyrand completely misjudged the temper of Americans. Despite their calls for rapprochement with France, even Republican congressmen grew uneasy when dispatches from the commissioners arrived. The "unexampled arrogance" of Talleyrand outraged President Adams, who sent a message to Congress for funds to reinforce coastal defenses, build a navy, arm merchant ships, and call up an army of 15,000 men to repel a possible French invasion.

Vice President Jefferson called the President "insane," claiming Adams had concealed all but the negative aspects of the peace commission's dispatches from Paris. Republicans demanded to see all the commission's messages.

On April 3, 1798, the President obliged, with the secretary of state disguising the names of Hottinguer, Bellamy, and Hauteval as X, Y, and

A cartoon entitled "Congressional Pugilists" shows Roger Griswold of Connecticut (right) fighting with Vermont Republican Matthew Lyon on the floor of the House of Representatives. (LIBRARY OF CONGRESS)

Z to protect them from retaliation. Jefferson called them a "dish cooked up by Marshall where swindlers are made to appear as the French government,"[45] but the XYZ dispatches soon silenced the vice president and French partisans in Congress and across the nation. Indeed, they provoked a frenzy of war fever and violent anti-French demonstrations. More than a thousand young men in Philadelphia marched to the President's house to volunteer to fight against France. The President came out to address them, dressed incongruously for so short and stout a man, in military parade dress, complete with a sword in a gleaming scabbard that scraped the ground as he waddled to and fro.

When First Lady Abigail Adams greeted another group, she wore a flowerlike device she had sewn together herself, with radiating bows of black ribbon. Federalists converted it into a black cockade that became their symbol of opposition to the French tricolor cockade.

"Every [black] cockade will be another Declaration of Independence," wrote the editor of Boston's *Columbian Centinnel*.[46]

In Cambridge, Massachusetts, the President's alma mater, Harvard, canceled the French oration at graduation exercises. In Philadelphia wearers of Abigail Adams's black cockade ripped tricolor cockades off Republicans in the State House yard, setting off a riot that required a troop of cavalry to suppress.

Across the nation Federalist newspapers called for expulsion of French aliens for plotting with Jacobins and Republicans to overthrow the government. Frightened French émigrés—many of them royalists who had fled the guillotines of the French Revolution—crowded onto ships bound for Europe to escape the tar and feathers of American mobs.

In April Congress created a Department of the Navy, authorized acquisition of twelve ships—later thirty-six—with up to twenty guns each, and ordered them to seize French privateers and other raiders in or near American waters. It authorized merchant ships to arm and defend themselves against French attackers and to seize French ships and contribute them to the navy in exchange for 6 percent government bonds.

In May Congress imposed an embargo on trade with France, and the State Department rejected the credentials of the new French ambassador who, together with all French consuls, sailed back to France and left the United States without French diplomatic representation. As John Marshall sailed home from France, news reached the United States that Napoléon Bonaparte was massing an army to invade the United States.

CHAPTER 8

⟡

Our Washington Is No More

JOHN MARSHALL'S SHIP ARRIVED IN NEW YORK FROM FRANCE ON
June 17, bringing with it news of Bonaparte's latest military adventures.
Not satisfied with conquering half of Europe, he had set off in June 1797
for the Levant with the largest force to cross the Mediterranean since
the Crusades—400 transports carrying 35,000 elite troops, escorted by
thirteen ships of the line (battleships) and more than forty frigates and
corsairs. On June 12 he had reached Malta, confiscated the bullion and
treasures of the ancient Knights of St. John, then sailed for Alexandria to
conquer and plunder Egypt and the Middle East.

Bonaparte's outrageous plunder of Malta's national wealth provoked
demonstrations against French expansionism across Britain and in New
York, where it reached a peak of intensity when Marshall's ship tied up
in lower Manhattan. The city gave the man who stood up to the French
a hero's welcome—indeed, a welcome fit for a President and not seen
since Washington's presidential inauguration. The plaudits and cheers
only grew as his coach left New York for Philadelphia to report to President Adams.

Secretary of State Pickering met him six miles outside the capital with
a delegation of high-level government officials and three troops of cavalry
in dress uniform to escort him into the city. As artillery fired salvo after

salvo of welcoming blasts, Philadelphia's churches pealed their greetings to the returning envoy. Crowds filled the streets, jammed into every window and leaned over every rooftop to glimpse "the man who, at the hazard of his life, had displayed the most eminent talents and fortitude in the support of the interest and honor of his country."[1]

The Speaker of the House led a congressional delegation at a lavish banquet for him and 120 guests, including the entire cabinet and the justices of the Supreme Court. Vice President Jefferson did not attend. One of the traditional toasts for each of the sixteen states set the crowd aroar by echoing Pinckney's defiant cry: "Millions for defense, but not a cent for tribute."[2] Federalists across America adopted the words as their battle cry for war with France.

After Marshall conferred with the President, Adams sent Congress a message declaring, "I will never send another minister to France without assurances that he will be received, respected and honored as the representative of a great, free, powerful, and independent state."[3] Adams stopped short of advocating war, however, calling it "inexpedient," and Marshall assured the President that he too favored the longstanding Washington policy of neutrality.

Ultra-Federalists dominated Congress, however, and all but ignored the President's message of caution. They voted to expand the army to 50,000 men and call up 80,000 state militiamen to stand at the ready. Two weeks later the President named—and Congress confirmed— George Washington as commander-in-chief of the armed forces. The aging former President, however, had no intention of quitting his idyllic nest in Mount Vernon and immediately promoted Alexander Hamilton to second in command, with the rank of inspector general. In effect, he gave the ambitious New York lawyer direct control of America's military machine to complement his indirect control of the cabinet and the nation's political machine.

"That man," Abigail Adams warned of Hamilton in a letter, "would, in my mind, become a second Buonaparty [sic] if he was possessed of equal power."[4]

Anti-French frenzy reached a peak on June 18, 1798, when Federalists in Congress rammed through the first of four vicious Alien and Sedition Acts, effectively annulling the Bill of Rights, to limit criticism of government and rid the nation of French influence. The Naturalization Act prevented immigrant voting by stretching the residency period for naturalization from five to twelve years and forcing aliens to report regularly to immigration authorities. The Act Concerning Aliens gave the President powers to arrest and deport without trial any aliens he deemed "dangerous to the peace and safety of the United States." The Act Respecting Alien Enemies gave the President power to arrest, detain, and deport aliens in case of war—without presenting justification.

To retaliate for Talleyrand's treatment of Marshall and Pinckney, Congress waited until July 14, the French national holiday commemorating the storming of the Bastille, to pass the most oppressive of the four laws: the Act for the Punishment of Certain Crimes. In clear violation of the Constitution, the act annulled the First Amendment by restricting freedom of speech and of the press. It imposed fines of up to $2,000 and prison sentences of up to two years for anyone who opposed or interfered with law enforcement and made it a crime to publish "false or malicious writing directed against the President or Congress." Within a few weeks Federalist prosecutors charged Vermont Representative Matthew Lyon—the "Spitting Lyon"—with sedition.

The acts so outraged Vice President Thomas Jefferson that he called on state legislatures to restrict federal government powers. Declaring the Constitution a "compact" between states, he insisted that state legislatures could nullify federal laws that gave the national government powers not granted by the Constitution.[5] He then drew up formal resolves for state legislatures to declare the Alien and Sedition Acts "altogether void and of no force." He sent one to Kentucky, which he knew embraced his views, and a second to his protégé James Madison to present to the Virginia legislature. In effect, the Kentucky and Virginia Resolutions repudiated—or at least reinterpreted—the Constitution and threatened to rupture many of the ties that bound the states in union.

Aware of fervent pro-English sentiment among Hamilton's ultra-Federalists, English Prime Minister William Pitt sent President Adams a proposal for an Anglo-American alliance against France and Spain. Pitt offered to provide a British fleet if the United States provided troops to free the Americas from French and Spanish rule. Pitt also informed Hamilton, the effective commander of the American army, of his proposal, and Hamilton urged President Adams to accept. Ridding South America of Spanish rule, Hamilton told the President, would block "the channel through which the riches of Mexico and Peru are conveyed to France."[6]

Adams, however, steadfastly opposed America going to war—on either side—and he rejected Pitt's plan. While Hamilton fumed at the President's intransigence, John Marshall separated himself from Hamilton's ultra-Federalists, setting himself squarely behind the President by reiterating George Washington's beliefs:

"No man in existence," Marshall asserted, "is more decidedly opposed to such an alliance."

> The whole of my politics respecting foreign nations are reducible to this single position: We ought to have commercial intercourse with all, but political ties with none. Let us buy as cheap and sell as dear as possible. Let commerce go wherever individual and consequently national interest will carry it, but let us never connect ourselves politically. . . . Europe is eternally engaged in wars in which we have no interest. . . . We ought to avoid any compact which may endanger . . . the neutrality of the United States.[7]

Unwilling to involve himself further in the Anglo-French controversy, Marshall fled the national spotlight of the capital to rejoin Polly and the family.

His return sparked Polly's partial recovery, but not enough for her to go home to Richmond and reunite with her children, who were with her parents. Polly still smarted from fears and suspicions that her husband had succumbed to the wiles of Madame de Villette.

"Your mama and friends are in good health," Marshall reassured Polly after he arrived in Richmond. "Your sweet little [three-year-old] Mary is one of the most fascinating little creatures I ever beheld. . . . She comprehends everything that is said to her and is the most coquettish little prude and the most prudish little coquette I ever saw. . . . Poor little [eight-month-old] John is cutting teeth and of course is sick."[8]

> I hear nothing from you my dearest Polly but I will cherish the hope that you are getting better and will indulge myself with expecting the happiness of seeing you in October quite yourself. Remember, my love . . . to use a great deal of exercise, to sleep tranquilly, and to stay cheerful in company. Farewell my dearest Polly.

Virginia's governor joined other state officials and a contingent of Revolutionary War heroes in greeting John Marshall at the state capitol. As cheering crowds watched, a colorful procession of state militiamen and cavalry in dress uniforms celebrated his return. The brilliant attorney Bushrod Washington, George Washington's favorite nephew and a growing influence in state and national affairs, delivered a passionate welcoming address. Bushrod and Marshall had warmed to each other when they studied law together under George Whyte at College of William and Mary. They remained close and, indeed, worked together in support of ratification at Virginia's constitutional ratification convention.

The *Virginia Gazette and General Advertiser* of Richmond joined in hailing Marshall's return. "When future generations pursue the history of America," it declared, "they will find the name of Marshall on its sacred page as one of the brightest ornaments of the age in which he lived."[9]

Marshall, however, had tired of the fervor with which Americans greeted his return. Although elated that Richmond's enthusiasm would ensure revival of his law practice, he clearly opposed ultranationalist trampling of constitutional rights.

"I am not an advocate for the Alien and Sedition Laws," he declared. "Had I been in Congress when they passed, I should . . . certainly have opposed them . . . because they are calculated to create, unnecessarily, discontent and jealousies at a time when our very existence as a nation may depend on our union."[10]

Above all, Marshall believed in the sanctity of the Constitution, which he said the Alien and Sedition Acts had breached:

> In heart and sentiment, as well as by birth and interest, I am an American, attached to the genuine principles of the Constitution, as sanctioned by the will of the people. . . . I consider that Constitution the rock of our political salvation, which has preserved us from misery, division, and civil war—and which will yet preserve us if we value it rightly and support it firmly.[11]

Despite Marshall's opposition to the Alien and Sedition Acts, they exacted a steep toll. In New England, ultra-Federalist prosecuting attorneys used them to crush political opponents. In Vermont, Republican Representative Matthew Lyon, who owned and operated two newspapers, became the first American tried for violating the Sedition Act by criticizing President Adams's naval actions against France.

After forbidding Lyon from citing constitutional guarantees of free speech and free press, a Federalist judge found Lyon guilty and, on October 10, 1798, sentenced him to four months in jail and a fine of $1,000. Lyon nonetheless won reelection to Congress by a rousing two-to-one majority—from his Vermont jail cell. On his release Lyon sang out, "I am on my way to Philadelphia."[12]

Lyon was the first of twenty-five Republicans charged under the Sedition Act. Ten were convicted—all editors and printers.

Although the Alien and Sedition Acts had appalled John Marshall, Vice President Jefferson's Kentucky Resolution and Madison's Virginia Resolution outraged him even more. The Alien and Sedition Acts, he pointed out, "will expire of themselves . . . during the term of the ensuing Congress," but the Kentucky and Virginia Resolutions threatened to annul the Constitution and dissolve the Union.

The Kentucky and Virginia Resolutions angered George Washington as much as they had Marshall, and he encouraged popular Federalists to run against Republicans for Congress. He invited Marshall and Bushrod Washington to Mount Vernon and warned them that "the temper of the people of this state" had grown "violent and outrageous." He urged both men to run for Congress.

"Bushrod," he commanded, "it must be done!"

Bushrod shuddered and knew he had little choice but to obey. Washington had, after all, financed his college and law school studies and had supported the young man until he established himself in his profession. Marshall, however, insisted that his family obligations came first, and having given the former President a final answer, he rose before dawn on the third day of his visit to leave Mount Vernon before Washington awakened. To Marshall's astonishment, Washington awaited him, dressed in his uniform as commander-in-chief of the Continental Army.

"He said there were crises in national affairs which made it the duty of a citizen to forego his private affairs for the public interest," Marshall recalled. Washington told Marshall he had retired from the presidency "with the firmest determination never again to appear in public life. . . . Yet I saw him pledged to appear once more at the head of the American army. . . . I yielded to his representations and became a candidate."[13]

Before the campaign could get under way, however, Supreme Court Justice James Wilson died, and President Adams immediately offered the seat to Marshall. Much to the President's surprise and disappointment, Marshall declined because the Court would keep him far from home in the national capital several weeks a year and riding the circuit another twelve weeks.* Service on the two courts would make it difficult, if not impossible, for him to rebuild his law practice. In contrast, a seat in Congress would keep him in Philadelphia only a few weeks a year and leave him free to practice law the rest of the year.

---

*The Judiciary Act of 1789 extended the reach of federal laws and the federal judiciary across the nation by creating a federal district court with a single judge in each state and three circuit courts of appeal, with Supreme Court justices "riding the circuit" and two of the justices periodically joining each district court judge to hear cases in each state.

Adams then offered the seat to Bushrod Washington, who accepted and withdrew from the election campaign.

As it turned out, events in the Caribbean and Europe suddenly changed the complexion of the campaign. Construction and refitting of American warships progressed faster than anticipated. By midsummer the *U.S. Constellation* and two other frigates plowed through American coastal waters chasing French ships away, while the *Delaware*, a converted sloop with sixteen guns, captured the first French prize of the undeclared war with France. By midautumn the navy had launched a fourth frigate, the *U.S. Constitution*, and armed more than a thousand merchant ships. Together they cleared American coastal waters of French marauders and prepared to wage offensive warfare against the French.

President Adams ordered the navy to "sweep the West India [*sic*] seas" of French ships and seize French seamen as hostages for the thousands of American seamen languishing in French prisons. Although the French had captured more than 800 American vessels, by the end of 1798 the surprising American navy had retaliated by seizing 84 French vessels. Four American squadrons of five ships each had gained control of Caribbean waters, with the fearless Captain Thomas Truxton and his squadron taking so many French vessels that Washington called him the equal of "a regiment in the field."

On February 9, 1799, Truxton's *Constellation* engaged the big French frigate *L'Insurgeante* and, after a fierce battle off the island of Nevis, captured the vessel and added it to the American Navy. A year later, almost to the day, Truxton spotted the fifty-four-gun French frigate *La Vengeance* and ordered his crew to come about and pursue. The French vessel was carrying a huge cargo of money from Guadeloupe to France—the island's entire profits from a month's trade—along with eighty military passengers, thirty-six American prisoners, and a crew of thirty-two. The *Constellation* launched a barrage of cannon fire at the more powerful French warship, and after slightly more than an hour, the French struck their colors and surrendered.

French forces were suffering similar humiliations elsewhere in the world. On August 1, 1798, a week after Napoléon Bonaparte and his

Napoléon Bonaparte invades Egypt not knowing that Admiral Horatio Nelson's British fleet was about to sink the French fleet in Aboukir Bay, near Alexandria at the mouth of the Nile, and trap the French army on the African mainland. (PAINTING BY JEAN-ANTOINE GROS AT MUSÉE DE VERSAILLES, RÉUNION DES MUSÉES NATIONAUX)

troops had entered Cairo, Admiral Horatio Nelson's British fleet surprised and annihilated the French fleet of 55 warships and 280 transports in Aboukir Bay, at the mouth of the Nile near Alexandria. The British had trapped the French army in Egypt.

Hoping to establish an overland route back to France via the Levant and Constantinople, Bonaparte left half his army in Cairo and led 13,000 troops across the Sinai Peninsula to Palestine, where they captured Gaza and Jaffa and laid siege to the heavily fortified port of Acre. He ordered five assaults—all of them failures—before plague killed half of his men and forced the rest to limp back to Cairo.

Convinced that Barras and other directors had betrayed him to the English to prevent his accession to power, Napoléon Bonaparte made secret arrangements to sail back to France with a handful of trusted aides on two frigates that had survived Nelson's assault. He left in the middle of the night, leaving only a hastily scrawled note to announce his

clandestine departure to his second in command, General Jean Baptiste
Kléber.

The note shocked Kléber, who accused the Corsican of "desertion. . . .
There is no doubt: Bonaparte has sacrificed the country [Egypt]," Kléber
wrote, "and he has fled in order to escape the catastrophe of surrender."[14]
Within a year invading English troops would force the ill-fated French
expeditionary force to lay down its arms and surrender—but not before a
knife-wielding university student assassinated Kléber. (Infuriated French
troops burned off the assassin's right arm, then impaled him in a public
square in Cairo and left him to die.)

In Ireland the French suffered a similar humiliation when a British
fleet trapped and captured nine French warships and transport vessels
in Donegal Bay. Cut off from escape by sea, the French invaders cawed
like mad hens and surrendered, clearing England's North Atlantic trade
routes of the danger of French naval attacks.

As the aura of French invincibility disintegrated, conquered peoples
in Belgium, Luxembourg, Switzerland, and Italy rose in rebellion against
French occupation. Russia organized a new alliance with Britain, Naples,
Portugal, Sardinia, and the Turks to halt French expansion. An Anglo-
Russian army landed in Holland, while another Russian force joined the
Austrians to push the French out of the Bavarian and Italian Alps, Swit-
zerland, and the Rhineland.

In the French Antilles Santo Domingo's slave population rose up en
masse and butchered more than 10,000 French troops and 3,000 French
civilians, including Napoléon Bonaparte's brother-in-law, the army
commander-in-chief. The rebels seized control of the entire colony and
shut off the vital flow of sugar and coffee to mainland France.

In France proper, royalists staged a massive counterrevolution in the
central provinces, and when the Directory tried to draft 200,000 more
men to strengthen the army, one-third refused to report.

Besieged from all directions and stripped of revenue from foreign
plunder, France faced economic collapse unless Talleyrand could restore the flow of supplies and foodstuffs from her former ally, the United
States. The embargo on French goods had closed rich American markets

to important revenue-producing products such as wines, silks, linens, and china, while British ships prevented French transports from carrying essential goods from the French Antilles back to France.

Talleyrand responded by ordering immediate release of American seamen and other Americans from French prisons. He reopened French ports to American ships and ordered an end to French attacks on American shipping. In a contrite letter to Adams, Talleyrand issued a formal invitation to peace talks that purposely adopted the President's own language, pledging that "whatever plenipotentiary the Government of the United States might send to France . . . would be undoubtedly received with respect due to the representative of a free, independent, and powerful nation."[15]

President Adams issued a cry of triumph, but rather than risk another humiliation by sending high-level public figures, he named America's ambassador to Holland, William Vans Murray, as minister plenipotentiary to France to negotiate a peace agreement. Warned that Murray might not be a prestigious enough figure to extract concessions from the fox-like Talleyrand, the President sent Chief Justice Oliver Ellsworth of Connecticut and North Carolina Governor William R. Davie to join Murray.

News of the French peace overture raised Marshall to heroic heights in the esteem of Virginians, who equated the sudden French policy reversal to Marshall's tough stance earlier in the year—and he did nothing to dissuade them. Indeed, he plunged into the election campaign with great enthusiasm, spending more than $5,000 on barbecues for voters and happily joining their country dances around the bonfires. His investment was not unusual. As a young man, George Washington had drenched voters and their families with forty gallons of rum, twenty-six gallons of rum punch, thirty-four gallons of wine, and forty-three gallons of beer to win election to Virginia's colonial assembly, the House of Burgesses. Washington's final cost for victory was about one-half gallon of spirits per vote.

Despite Marshall's heavy investment in the electoral campaign, the outcome remained in doubt until the state's patriot-relic Patrick Henry declared for Marshall. Henry's endorsement proved decisive, and as Federalists whispered Marshall's name as a future presidential prospect, he went to Washington in early December to take his oath of office in the House of

Representatives. This time Polly went with him. She was six months pregnant and terrified by the prospects of having to suffer the loneliness and anguish she experienced during her husband's extended absence in Paris.

And she was unwilling to risk his encountering another Marquise de Villette.

Polly proved too shy and moody for the capital's social swirl, however, and stayed at home most of the time, paying few visits, receiving even fewer, and planting fears for her safety in her husband's mind.

As Washington had hoped, Marshall led a surge of popular support for Federalists in the South that gave them a twenty-seat majority in the House, and with a solid majority in the Senate and a Federalist President, they seemed to enjoy a firm grip on American government policies. The only Republican victory of note in the South was James Monroe's election as governor of Virginia.

Although Republicans had lost nominal control of Congress, Alexander Hamilton's political maneuvers divided the Federalist majority into what amounted to two new minority parties—moderate Federalists, who supported President Adams's policy of strict neutrality in Europe's military conflicts, and Hamilton's pro-British ultra-Federalists, who decried any negotiations with France.

Ultra-Federalist leader Robert Troup of New York said the President's decision to negotiate with the French had provoked "universal disgust." A heroic officer in the Revolutionary War, Troup had been Alexander Hamilton's roommate at King's College (now Columbia) in New York before entering the law and becoming a judge. "There certainly will be serious difficulty in supporting Mr. Adams at the next election, if he should be a candidate," Troup warned.

Two months later, as Davie and Ellsworth prepared to sail for Europe to join William Vans Murray, Hamilton—still inspector general of the army—appeared at the President's house. In an outburst that warranted a court martial, Hamilton berated the President that the peace mission to France would provoke war with Britain. Taking Hamilton's heroism in the Revolutionary War into account, the President simply dismissed Hamilton without demanding his resignation as army commander. Instead,

Adams sublimated his anger in a private letter that described the former Treasury secretary as an "overwrought little man" with a "total ignorance of . . . Europe, England and elsewhere."[16]

Infuriated by the President's curt rebuff, Hamilton scurried to the home of the Chief Justice to try to talk him into quitting the peace mission but met the same cold rejection from Ellsworth that he had from the President.

The Federalist Party divisions provoked a vicious floor fight between northerners and southerners over the choice of Speaker in the House of Representatives, with the crusty ultra-Federalist Theodore Sedgwick of Massachusetts winning the post. A devoted Anglophile, Sedgwick had faced President Adams a few weeks earlier in a near-violent shouting match over sending the peace commission to France.

Alarmed at the bitterness infecting the union, Marshall sidled in and out of various groups in the House, inserting warmth and joviality into enough arguments to earn friendships with a diverse number of House members—from Swiss-born Republican Albert Gallatin, on the one hand, to former South Carolina Governor John Rutledge, on the other. Rutledge was a moderate Federalist who had served on the Supreme Court for a while and remained one of the South's staunchest defenders of slavery. Marshall even drew close to the stern-faced Speaker Sedgwick, who always *looked* angry—even when he laughed.

Marshall got to know them all, made friends with all, steered clear of political ties to any, and won election as Federalist floor leader. "I hope," he responded, "a mutual spirit of tolerance and forbearance will succeed the violence which seemed in too great a degree to govern last year. I wish most devoutly that the prevalence of moderation here may diffuse the same spirit among our fellow citizens at large."[17]

As floor leader, Marshall wrote and delivered the customary congressional response to the President's annual State of the Union address. Given House Speaker Sedgwick's fierce encounter with the President and Marshall's friendship with Sedgwick, both Congress and the President expected Marshall to fire a barrage of criticism at Adams.

To the President's delight—and the distress of ultra-Federalist war hawks—Marshall declared Congress in total accord with the President's "pacific and humane policy." After praising the character of Adams's envoys to France, Marshall offered "our fervent prayers to the Supreme Ruler of the Universe for the success of their embassy and that it may be productive of peace and happiness."

> The uniform tenure of your conduct through a life useful to your fellow citizens and honorable to yourself gives a sure pledge of the sincerity with which the vowed objects of the negotiation will be pursued on your part, and we earnestly pray that similar dispositions may be displayed on the part of France. To produce this end . . . firmness, moderation, and union at home constitute, we are persuaded, the surest means.[18]

A week after Marshall's surprisingly conciliatory address to the President, a courier rushed onto the floor of the House to hand him a message. Marshall stood to interrupt the proceedings:

"Mr. Speaker!" his voice broke, and he paused before continuing.

> Information has just been received that our illustrious fellow citizen, the Commander in Chief of the American Army and the late President of the United States is no more. . . . After receiving information of this national calamity, so heavy and so afflicting, the House of Representatives can be but ill fitted for public business. I move you, therefore, to adjourn.[19]

Under the rules of order, Marshall still had the floor the following day when the House reconvened. Knowing this, Henry "Light-Horse Harry" Lee, the Revolutionary War hero and former Virginia governor who had been a close friend of Washington, had prepared a set of resolutions for Marshall to read.

"Mr. Speaker," Marshall began to read what was to be the most memorable eulogy in American history:

> Our Washington is no more! The hero, the sage, the patriot of America— the man on whom in times of danger every eye was turned and all hopes

were placed, lives now only in his own great actions and in the hearts of an affectionate and afflicted people.

Calling the public sorrow "deep" and "universal," Marshall went on to call Washington responsible "more than any other individual" for founding "our widespread empire." Marshall hailed Washington as having so often "quit the retirement he loved" to serve the nation—first, at the Constitutional Convention, then two terms as President, and again, as commander-in-chief of the army to confront the French in the quasi-war.

"Let us then, Mr. Speaker, pay the last tribute of respect and affection to our departed friend. Let the grand council of the nation display those sentiments which the nation feels." Marshall then presented three resolutions, the last of which called for a committee to join with a comparable Senate committee to consider "the most suitable manner of paying honor to the memory of the man, first in war, first in peace, and first in the hearts of his countrymen."[20]

Congress set aside December 26 as a day of national mourning. Although Washington's family had placed his casket in the family vault at Mount Vernon a week earlier, tens of thousands of mourners poured into the capital at Philadelphia for what would be the largest funeral procession in American history. Marshall headed the committees that made the funeral arrangements and later planned the great Washington monument Americans revere today on the Mall in Washington, DC.

Among the mourners, besides Marshall himself, were President and Mrs. Adams, Alexander Hamilton, and Henry Lee, who repeated the eulogy that he had written for Congress that Marshall had delivered.*

---

* Marshall never claimed the eulogy as his own composition and, indeed, always emphasized that "General Lee immediately called on me and showed me his resolutions. He said it had now become improper for him to offer them [because the House had risen on Marshall's motion] and wished me to take them." (JM to Charles W. Hanson, March 29, 1832, in JM *Papers*, 12:189–190). Marshall also credits Lee in his *Life of Washington*.

Conspicuously absent was Vice President Thomas Jefferson, who remained in his aerie at Monticello, near Charlottesville, Virginia, although he returned a few days later to preside over the Senate. His seat had been draped in black, but he failed to utter or write a word about George Washington or his passing—not even sending a note of condolence to Martha Washington.

Apart from freeing his slaves after Martha Washington's death, Washington's long and detailed will left his public and private papers to his favorite nephew, Associate Justice Bushrod Washington. Bushrod, in turn, convinced John Marshall to collaborate on writing the first definitive biography of Washington. A year after Washington's death, Tobias Lear, Washington's longtime private secretary, sent the first of five trunks of Washington's personal and public papers, which Marshall and Bushrod Washington began converting into a monumental five-volume *Life of George Washington*. It was published from 1804 to 1807 and, until the Civil War, remained the definitive history of eighteenth-century America, including the history of the American Revolution, the evolution of American government and the Constitution, and the life of Washington as a military and political leader.

"He was a real republican," Marshall wrote of Washington, "devoted to the constitution of his country, and to that system of equal political rights on which it is founded.

> Real liberty, he thought, was to be preserved, only by preserving the authority of the laws, and maintaining the energy of government. . . . No man has ever appeared upon the theatre of public action, whose integrity was more incorruptible, or whose principles were more perfectly free from the contamination of those selfish and unworthy passions, which find their nourishment in the conflicts of party. No truth can be uttered with more confidence than that his ends were always upright, and his means always pure.[21]

CHAPTER 9

Midnight Judges

On January 1, 1800, the passing of Washington combined with French peace overtures to provoke demands from House Republicans to disband the standing army. Still under the command of Inspector General Alexander Hamilton, the army had produced a federal deficit of $5 million and forced Congress to impose burdensome property taxes.

Like the Whiskey Tax in 1794, the property taxes provoked widespread protests and at least one small rebellion, when Pennsylvania auctioneer John Fries roused neighbors to resist federal tax assessors. Pennsylvania militiamen crushed the rebellion, capturing thirty and charging Fries and two others with treason. Associate Justice Samuel Chase, then serving in circuit court, sentenced all three to death, outraging Jefferson's Republicans. To a man, they called on the President to pardon Fries, disband the army, and end the hated tax.

President Adams favored disbanding the army—if only to strip Alexander Hamilton of military power—but he felt unsure about doing so before the French signed a peace agreement and ended their threat to the nation. Marshall agreed. As much as anyone, Marshall opposed the principle of a standing army in a free republic but knew "the cloven-footed devil Talleyrand"[1] well enough to fear that the Frenchman would interpret relaxation of America's military posture as a sign of indecision and weakness.

"The whole world is in arms," Marshall reasoned, "and no rights are respected but those that are maintained by force. In such a state of things we dare not be . . . totally neglectful of that military position to which . . . we may be driven for the preservation of our liberty and national independence."[2]

While Republicans besieged him with demands to release Fries, President Adams added to their outrage by signing an extradition order that sent a seaman to his death on the gallows in Jamaica for mutiny and murder.

Thomas Nash had been in the crew that mutinied and slayed the officers on the Royal navy frigate *HMS Hermione* in 1797. After sailing to a Spanish port and selling the ship, they scattered, with Nash turning up two years later in a bar in Charleston, South Carolina—drunk and boasting of his exploits. The British consul demanded his arrest and extradition. After rejecting Nash's claims that he was an American named Jonathan Robbins, a court issued—and President Adams signed—an extradition order.

All but wearing his presidential ambitions on his jacket, Vice President Jefferson led a chorus of Republicans accusing the President of conspiring with the British to murder an impressed American seaman. Concealing clear evidence to the contrary, Jefferson enlisted New York Congressman Edward Livingston in a cruel scheme to impeach President Adams and force a father of American independence into retirement and disgrace for high crimes and misdemeanors.

The "mutual toleration and forbearance" that Marshall had hoped to promote in Congress was fast slipping away. Knowing full well that Thomas Nash was a British citizen, the young New York Congressman Edward Livingston wisely withdrew from Jefferson's scheme to impeach John Adams and moved instead to censure the President for "dangerous interference . . . with judicial decisions . . . [and] the constitutional independence of the judiciary."[3]

Infuriated by the slanderous attack on the President and the vice president's behind-the-scene manipulations of Congress, Marshall sprang to Adams's defense like a wounded wolverine:

"The people of the United States," Marshall glared at Livingston, "have no jurisdiction over offenses committed on board a foreign ship against a foreign nation."

> The President is the sole organ of the nation in its external relations and its sole representative with foreign nations. Of consequence the demand of a foreign nation can only be made to him. He possesses the whole executive power. . . . He is charged to execute the laws. A treaty is declared to be a law. He must then execute a treaty.[4]

Marshall went on for three hours, crushing every one of Livingston's arguments with citations from tomes of law that many members of Congress had never heard of, let alone read or studied: from ancient Greece and Rome, from England—Coke, Grotius, Hawkins—and on and on.

Nash was *not* an American, Marshall all but shouted—and congressional Republicans had the proof in their hands. Not only did Nash lack the papers American seamen routinely carried as proof of their citizenship, but he also spoke with a thick Irish brogue and had bragged of his Irish birthright to at least two shipmates who testified under oath to his participation in the mutiny and murder of the ship's officers.

Marshall cited and read provisions of the Jay Treaty with England that required each country to extradite accused murderers to the other country. The Thomas Nash case was *not* a case of law and equity, Marshall went on, but a *political* issue. Nash had never stood trial in the United States; no American court had issued a ruling in his case.

Infuriated at Livingston's ignorance of the law, Marshall raged that the constitutional right to trial by jury did not apply to alien fugitives accused of crimes that occurred outside the United States on foreign territory. A crime on a British ship in waters outside the United States fell within the jurisdiction of British—not American—courts.

"The [American] Constitution," Marshall lectured Livingston, "is not designed to secure the rights of the people of Europe or Asia, or to direct and control proceedings against criminals throughout the universe." American courts have no jurisdiction in extradition matters. The President's action in signing extradition papers did not involve a legal matter. His decision dealt exclusively with relations between the United States and Britain as defined by treaty.[5]

In oratory that seemed more appropriate for the Supreme Court than the House of Representatives, Marshall destroyed every argument for censure, humiliated Livingston, and sent the New York congressman's motion crashing to defeat.

Marshall's reasoning became and remains a centerpiece of American constitutional law, drawing a clear line between legal and political issues. In simplest terms, if it goes to court, it is legal; if not, it is political. The Nash case involved the exercise of treaty rights and obligations and was, therefore, strictly political.[6]

Although he had not sought the role, Marshall emerged from the Nash case as the most respected mediator and jurist in Congress as well as a staunch defender of the President, the presidency, and presidential authority as defined by the Constitution. Despite the accolades, Marshall was, at heart, quite an ordinary man, but a straight-thinking one, governed solely by logic and a love of justice—undeterred by flattery or verbal ornamentation unrelated to the matter at hand. Indeed, Treasury Secretary Oliver Wolcott inadvertently complimented Marshall in a criticism that characterized him as "too much disposed to govern the world according to the rules of logic."[7]

Speaker Sedgwick—as fervent a Hamiltonian ultra-Federalist as Wolcott—was more generous, calling Marshall a "great and commanding genius," a beacon to "enlighten and direct national councils."

He is a man of a very affectionate disposition, of great simplicity of manners and honest and honorable in all his conduct. He has a strong attachment to popularity but is indisposed to sacrifice it to his integrity. . . . This gentleman, when aroused, has strong reasoning powers; they are almost unequalled.[8]

Most members on both sides of the aisle agreed, commending Marshall's logic, his all but unearthly analytical skills, and his thorough grasp of every point of law and point of view in a complex dispute.

No one was more delighted with Marshall's performance than the President himself. Politically isolated, Adams's chances for reelection had all but vanished until Marshall ignited a spark of hope not only with his steadfast support but in rallying others to the President's side by exposing the unfairness and lies that underlay criticisms of the President by both Hamiltonians and Jeffersonians.

As reports from France began to show progress toward peace, American political antagonisms softened somewhat. Sensing an opportunity to gain a foothold in national political affairs, New York's popular former Senator Aaron Burr Jr. organized a slate of aging popular heroes—former governors, retired generals, and so on—to stand as the state's candidates for the Electoral College that would elect the President later in the year. With the rest of the nation evenly divided between Federalists and Republicans, Jefferson knew that New York's Electoral College votes would determine the next President of the United States, and Jefferson asked Burr to run, assuring the New Yorker that he would win the vice presidency. Electors in the Electoral College cast all their votes for a President, and the candidate receiving the second-most votes automatically became vice president. If, as expected, Burr delivered New York to the Republicans, Jefferson would probably win the necessary majority in the Electoral College to ensure his election as President, while Burr, with his New York votes, would probably win enough votes from other states to finish second in the overall voting and accede to the vice presidency.

Organizing the Federalist campaign was Inspector General Alexander Hamilton, the acting commander-in-chief of the American army after the death of Washington. Ironically, Burr and Hamilton had just teamed up successfully in winning acquittal of a man charged in the grisly slaying of a young lady, whose battered body had been fished out of a well.

When Burr and Hamilton left the courthouse, however, they inexplicably left behind the last traces of their long personal and professional friendship. Comrades with John Marshall and James Monroe at the Battle of Monmouth Courthouse, the two heroic Men of Monmouth had remained friends until the 1800 presidential election campaign suddenly sent them veering onto paths of mutual destruction that would lead one to his death, the other to exile in a foreign land.

It was Burr who inadvertently fired the first shot at his friend by organizing a radically new type of election campaign that would defeat Hamilton's party. In a campaign that would set standards for election campaigns decades thereafter, Burr recruited a small army of street-corner campaigners, sending members of various ethnic groups to German, Irish, and other neighborhoods in New York City to rally voters in their own native languages. Other campaigners went door-to-door collecting funds in wealthier neighborhoods, while Burr, the immaculately dressed former US senator, walked the streets shaking hands and flattering individual voters with his presence.

Burr also opened his palatial home to feed campaigners, coordinate their activities, and let them rest when they needed. A Federalist newspaper chastised him, calling street-corner electioneering beneath the dignity of a presidential candidate. Undeterred by critics, Burr organized an armada of wagons, carriages, and chairs to haul voters to the polls on Election Day.

On May 1 voting results showed that Aaron Burr had changed the course of American political history. He had not only invented a new type of election campaign; he had also scored a stunning victory that ensured the first political change in government in the young republic, giving Thomas Jefferson's Republican Party New York State's Electoral College votes and all but certain victory in the presidential election.

Stunned by Burr's victory, Hamilton and his Federalist supporters asked New York's Federalist Governor John Jay to overturn the results. When warned such action might provoke civil war, one Federalist grumbled, "A civil war would be preferable to having Jefferson."[9]

But Hamilton was apoplectic. His own ambitions for retaining power in the federal government all but shattered, he warned Governor Jay that

*Vice President Aaron Burr Jr. faced a powerful array
of forces led by Thomas Jefferson, who was intent on
destroying Burr's growing political power.* (LIBRARY OF
CONGRESS)

Jefferson was "an atheist in religion and a fanatic in politics" who would
"overthrow the government" and stage "a revolution in the manner of
Buonaparte [*sic*]."[10]

In the eyes of some, Hamilton seemed to have crossed the line into insanity. A coauthor of the Constitution and its early champion, Hamilton
now asked a governor and former US Chief Justice to ignore that document and reverse the results of a popular election. In doing so, Hamilton all but disgraced himself in the eyes of Jay, President Adams, John
Marshall, and other Federalist leaders. Adams responded by purging his
government of Hamiltonians. Navy Secretary Stoddard had called them

"artful designing men," and Adams now believed them to be dangerous as well.

Not wanting to give them time to stage a European-style coup, the President sent Secretary of War McHenry what seemed an innocuous note on May 5, 1800: "The P. requests Mr. McHenry's company for one minute."[11]

The mild-mannered McHenry responded by leaving a dinner party to go to Adams's office, where he settled into a comfortable chair. The President stood silently at first, then began pacing the room, and finally exploded into uncontrollable rage "in such a manner . . . as to persuade one that he was actually insane."[12] Unleashing a stream of invectives that he had obviously bottled up for years, he blasted Hamilton, Hamilton's puppets in the cabinet, ultra-Federalists in Congress, and others who opposed his policies and initiatives.

"Hamilton is an intriguant," the President shouted unpresidentially, "a man devoid of any moral principle—a bastard, and . . . a foreigner." He charged Hamilton with plotting to undermine his presidency and deny his reelection. The President turned and pointed a finger at McHenry, accused him of plotting with Hamilton to destroy the peace initiative with France.

"You are subservient to Hamilton, but I shall take care of that. You cannot, sir, remain longer in the office!"[13]

As crowds gathered outside the President's house, rumors circulated in Congress that Hamilton was planning a march on the capital to overthrow the President. Others predicted Adams would declare martial law, charge Hamilton with treason, and condemn him to death. Any of these eventualities would leave the Constitution in shreds, America's experiment in self-government at an end, and the nation in civil war.

John Adams acted quickly to tighten his reins on executive power, firing everyone he suspected of working with Hamilton. Four days after firing McHenry he asked for Secretary of State Pickering's resignation, only to have Pickering refuse. He told the President that the certainty of Jefferson's election in the fall left the Adams administration with only a few months in office and that he intended to serve his full term.

Fired as Secretary of State by President John Adams, Timothy Pickering returned home to Massachusetts and called for the New England states and New York to secede from the United States and combine with Canada to form a new nation. (LIBRARY OF CONGRESS)

Already incensed by Federalist newspaper editorials that called him "old, querulous, bald, blind, toothless Adams,"[14] the President exploded in rage. As surviving cabinet members looked on in disbelief, he accused Hamilton of instigating the editorials and fired Pickering. To counter any plots that may have been afoot, the President exercised his powers as commander-in-chief to order demobilization of the army, and in July 1800 he forced Hamilton to resign as inspector general. Although Adams infuriated Hamiltonian Federalists, most Americans cheered the President and the break-up of the military, which the Treasury Department had used as a police force to collect unpopular property taxes.

After demanding and accepting resignations from other members of his government who disagreed with his policies, the President announced he was pardoning John Fries and his two coconspirators, along with all other participants in the Fries rebellion. Citing his experience as a lawyer, the President insisted that Fries was guilty of leading only a riot, not a rebellion; there was no evidence that he or the other farmers had committed treason or intended overthrowing the government.

Jefferson tried to take advantage of Adams's administration turmoil by promising his editor friend James T. Callender $100 to publish a book of scurrilous essays called *The Prospect Before Us*. It claimed, among other things, "The reign of Mr. Adams has been one continued tempest of malignant passions. As President, he has never opened his lips or lifted his pen without threatening and scolding."[15]

Adams retaliated by ordering prosecutors to charge Callender with violating the Sedition Act. Supreme Court Justice Samuel Chase presided over the trial and, after pronouncing Callender guilty, fined him $200 and sentenced him to nine months in jail—the harshest penalty meted out under the Alien and Sedition Acts. Although Jefferson denied any involvement, Callender emerged from prison furious at his patron—not just for abandoning him to a trial by political wolves but also for failing to pay his fine and give him the $100 he had promised for publishing *Prospect*. Callender retaliated by publishing letters from Jefferson proving his instigation and complicity in writing the essays.

Survivors of the cabinet cleansing sat in silence at their next meeting, scarcely daring to breathe in the face of President Adams's fury. His face still twisted by anger, the President announced his intention to name John Marshall to replace McHenry as Secretary of War. Marshall, however, declined, asserting that "my private affairs claim an immediate attention incompatible with public office."[16]

By then Richmond had metamorphosed into a thriving, modern city, where Marshall reigned happily as the most beloved public figure. Unlike the tumbledown frontier town of twenty years earlier, the city boasted a magnificent statehouse that Thomas Jefferson had "designed" by copying the Maison Carré, the beautifully preserved Roman temple in Nîmes, France.

In planning Virginia's Capitol in Richmond (bottom), Thomas Jefferson copied the design of La Maison Carré (top), a Roman temple built in Nîmes, France, in 16 B.C.

With Marshall the only man in government he trusted, President Adams increased the ante, responding to Marshall's refusal to leave Richmond by offering him a higher post. Indeed, the President offered John Marshall the highest office in the American government other than the presidency itself, with more authority than any cabinet member had ever commanded in the nation's short history.

Marshall was to be secretary of state, with a new, additional designation: head of cabinet. Until further notice, Adams told the rest of the cabinet, they were to obey Marshall's directives as if they came from the President's own lips. He then left the executive mansion for a trip to inspect what would soon be the new capital in Washington City, where Marshall met him a few days later.

Marshall had returned to Richmond to bolster his law practice and was as surprised as everyone in Washington when he received the President's letter of appointment. Even more surprising were the powers the President had added to the secretary of state's normal responsibilities—a clearly unconstitutional authority to act as presidential surrogate in Adam's absence.

Most congressmen, however, were pleased by the Marshall appointment—Republicans as well as Federalists—and Marshall himself was ecstatic. Despite his enormous power and prestige in Richmond, he called the job as secretary of state "precisely that which I wished and for which I had vanity enough to think myself fitted. . . . I determined to accept the office."[17] Although he never said as much, others in government believed his new office would eventually catapult him to the presidency.

When the President and secretary of state–designate arrived in Washington, both stayed at Washington City Hotel, a three-story brick building that had just opened opposite the Capitol on the site of today's Supreme Court. Together they roamed the muddy roads and, with Marshall displaying skills he had learned from his surveyor-father, they staked out squares in what they believed would one day evolve into a great city. At the time, though, it was little more than a developing outpost of civilization.

In fact, the city was a gigantic marsh fringed by forests and perforated by islands of reclaimed land with clusters of shabby wooden boarding houses, inns, taverns, and stables near Capitol Hill.

The two principle government buildings—the Capitol and the Executive Mansion—were still under construction on relatively high ground above the marsh. Although the north wing of the Capitol building was nearly complete, the south wing was a skeleton of its future self, and only a long, unpainted wooden shed stood where the majestic central dome would one day soar and tie the two wings together.

There was no church, hospital, or park in Washington. Clusters of squalid slave shacks added to the horror. Snakes slithered in and out of low-lying houses; a heavy rain turned mud into torrents of ooze, the air into suffocating stench; mammoth rats competed with pigs, cattle, and other livestock for footing and food on the few slime-coated islets of high ground. Clouds of insects swarmed through the air, disease was rampant, influenza reached epidemic proportions in winter, and small pox decimated the remnants of humanity without the means of escape in summer.

"We want nothing here," the witty New York Senator Gouverneur Morris liked to tell visitors, "nothing but houses, cellars, kitchens, well-informed men, amiable women, and other little trifles of the kind, to make our city perfect."[18]

British Minister Anthony Merry lacked Morris's sense of humor:

I cannot describe . . . the difficulty and expense which I have to encounter in fixing myself in a habitation. By dint of money I have just secured two small houses on the common which is meant to become in time the city of Washington. They are mere shells of homes, with bare walls, and without fixtures of any kind, even without pump or well. . . . Provisions of any kind, especially vegetables, are frequently hardly to be obtained at any price. So miserable is our situation.[19]

A French diplomat was no kinder in his appraisal: "My God!" he lamented. "What have I done to be condemned to reside in such a city?"[20]

Members of Congress received only $6 a day for their services in the House and $7 in the Senate, and all but the wealthiest members had to leave their wives and families at home when they attended Congress. Forced to live as bachelors, they had settled into relatively attractive brick boarding houses when Philadelphia was the capital. Now they would have to live in cheap, squalid, wooden shanties. Affluent government officials would avoid the city as much as possible by living in nearby Georgetown.

President Adams stayed in Washington only long enough to officiate over the formal transfer of the federal government from Philadelphia. The Residency Act of 1790 that had designated Washington the new capital had required transfer to be completed within ten years, and the President ordered government operations to begin on June 15, 1800.

With no executive offices ready for occupancy, it was fortunate that executive-branch papers fit into only seven packing cases. Marshall found a corner for them in a small, unfinished Capitol anteroom that he converted into an office. When the President left for his Massachusetts home for the summer, he put the entire government in Marshall's hands and charged him with prodding construction crews to finish in time for the President and Congress to take up the nation's business in the fall.

Though honored by the President's trust, Marshall had to cancel plans to spend the summer with his family in the cool mountains near the Virginia Mineral Springs, about 120 miles west of Richmond. Alone and all but suffocating in the stifling heat of his makeshift office, he missed Polly and the children desperately. She had given birth the previous February to their fourth son, James Keith, and although he hoped she might join him at first, he realized that Washington's merciless heat and rampant summer diseases made it too dangerous.

"My dearest Polly," he wrote on August 8. "I have this moment received yours of the 5th and cannot help regretting that it affords me no hope of seeing you soon."

> I am delighted with the account you give me of Mary's dinner with you and of John's good breeding. Tell him I say he is a fine boy for his attention to his sister and his love for his Mama. I approve of you sending the boys up country.
>
> I am my dearest Polly
> Your
> J Marshall[21]

Though lonely, Marshall had more than enough government business to occupy his time—attacks on American ships by Barbary pirates and by both the British and Spanish navies, the killing of two Indian men and wounding of two children in western Connecticut, construction delays in Washington, and official letters to write, including one expressing empathy "to the King of Great Britain . . . on the fortunate escape of his majesty from the blow of an assassin."[22]

Marshall also assumed an obligation undertaken by First Lady Abigail Adams to make regular calls on Martha Washington, who still grieved for her husband.

"I have just returned from a visit to Mount Vernon, where I passed an evening," he reported to Polly.

> Mrs. Washington asked me to bring you to see her when you should visit this city. She appears tolerably cheerful but not to possess the same sort of cheerfulness as formerly. You as a widow would I hope show more firmness.
>
> Farewell my dearest Polly
> I am your ever affectionate
> J Marshall[23]

Although President Adams considered it beneath the dignity of a sitting President to campaign actively, he nonetheless took a longer-than-necessary route home to Quincy, Massachusetts, for the summer. Traveling westward to York and Lancaster, Pennsylvania, he reminded voters of his generous decision in favor of their neighbor John Fries. Despite the furor over cabinet firings and his angry accusations of Hamilton, Adams remained a popular President—admired as Washington's handpicked heir to the chief magistracy and, after dismissing Pickering and Hamilton, a staunch proponent of peace and opponent of property taxes.

Before the President returned to Washington in the fall, Hamilton retaliated for the President's dismissal of Pickering by publishing a vicious fifty-four-page *Letter from Alexander Hamilton, Concerning the Public*

Conduct and Character of John Adams, Esq., President of the United States.
With it Hamilton sabotaged his own as well as the President's political
career.

In language that bordered on hysteria, Hamilton accused the President of "vanity without bounds . . . ungovernable temper . . . [and] par-
oxysms of anger which deprive him of self-command. . . . Mr. Adams has
repeatedly indulged himself in virulent and indecent abuse of me. . . .
Great and intrinsic defects in his character . . . unfit him for the office of
Chief Magistrate."[24]

Hamilton's cruel attack stunned the President's wife, Abigail, who
all but cried at "the shafts and arrows of disappointed ambition" that
Hamilton—she called him "the little Gen'll,"—had hurled at her husband.[25] Adams, in turn, called Hamilton "the most treacherous, mali-
cious, insolent, and revengeful enemy of the First Magistrate."[26]

Hamilton's pamphlet even shocked Adams's enemies in the Republican Party. Lawyer St. George Tucker, who had studied with Marshall
under George Wythe at College of William and Mary and had replaced
Wythe as law professor there, expressed indignation: "If there is anything . . . more virulent, more bitter, more injurious to Mr. Adams's
feelings as a man or more derogatory to his character as chief magistrate
of the Union . . . I have not been able to find the passages."[27]

Confident he had cleansed his administration of Hamiltonian influ-
ences and assuaged by a flood of supporting letters, the President dismissed Hamilton's pamphlet and prepared to return to his presidential
duties.

During the President's absence John Marshall had indeed administered the entire government. Under normal circumstances the secretary of state's responsibilities reached far beyond foreign affairs to cover
functions that would be handled two centuries later by the secretaries of
commerce, interior, agriculture, energy, transportation, and homeland
security as well as the director of intelligence and other agency heads. But
the President had also charged Marshall with supervising construction
work in the new capital city, even attending to furnishing the future presidential residence.

With $15,000 allocated for the purpose, Marshall commissioned Thomas Claxton, a well-known purchasing agent for furniture, to find appropriate pieces for the new mansion. "Two rooms, that is, the oval room on the second floor intended for the drawing room for Mrs. Adams and the northwest room on the first floor intended as the drawing room of the President, may be richly furnished. We wish the other rooms to be furnished in a plain and elegant manner."[28]

With only five assistants, however, Marshall was unable to work miracles.

Events overseas were simply beyond his control. With the Anglo-French war raging, the British continued seizing American ships and cargoes bound for France and impressing captured American seamen into the British navy. The French did much the same, although they imprisoned most captured seamen because of language barriers that made it too difficult to integrate Americans into French crews. Marshall warned both the British and French that their aggressive acts had forced the United States to gear for war.

"We have repelled and we will continue to repel injuries . . . and hostility," Marshall told the English and French, "but this is a situation of necessity not of choice."[29]

> It has been the object of the American government from the commencement of the present war to preserve between the belligerent powers an exact neutrality. Separated far from Europe, we mean not to mingle in their quarrels. This determination was early declared, and has never been changed. In pursuance of it, we have avoided and we shall continue to avoid any political connections which might engage us further than is compatible with the neutrality we profess.[30]

When John Adams returned to Washington in November, he found the exterior of the executive mansion transformed into a palatial structure, but the interior a vast unfinished space, sustained by stark bearing walls devoid of plaster. Workers had yet to finish a single room in the President's private quarters, and the President's household staff had to appropriate the East Room for hanging laundry. But Adams was too moved by what he sensed as an important moment in American history:

"I pray heaven to bestow the best of blessings on this House and all that shall hereafter inhabit it," he wrote to his wife Abigail. "May none but wise and honest men ever rule under this roof." He assured her that "the building is in a state to be habitable" and told her he intended spending the remaining days and nights of his presidential term as the first resident President in what Americans would later call the White House.

"I shall say nothing of public affairs," he told Abigail. "I have seen only Mr. Marshall. . . . And now I wish for your company. It is fit and proper that you and I should retire together." She joined him a few days later.[31]

As one of the few people whom the beleaguered President trusted completely, Marshall took Adams on a whirlwind tour of the capital to display the summer's meager improvements—along with a stack of ledger sheets accounting for every penny of government funds he had spent. Workers had completed the North Wing (now the Senate) of the Capitol, and more than a half-dozen boarding houses had sprouted on Capitol Hill to receive the new Congress. A few new shops housed a tailor, shoemaker, printer, laundry, grocery, stationery, and restaurant. In an expansive mood after his jaunt, Adams asked the secretary of state to prepare the annual presidential address to Congress.

Marshall prepared an optimistic address that described substantial growth in government revenues and domestic commerce. Abroad, America seemed at peace with almost all the world's nations but France and Britain, but peace with France seemed imminent, and talks aimed at reconciliation with Britain were well under way in London. The President's diplomat-son John Quincy Adams had negotiated a new treaty of friendship and commerce with Prussia, foreign trade was booming, and the Alien Act had expired quietly, eliminating a continuing source of voter bitterness toward Adams and the Federalists.

"The secret of Mr. Adams's satisfaction [with Marshall]," former Treasury Secretary Oliver Wolcott chortled sarcastically, "was that he obeyed his Secretary of State without suspecting it."[32]

All the good news, however, came too late to affect the election. A week after delivering his annual address to Congress, John Adams learned he had probably lost the presidency—that Vice President Thomas Jefferson was likely to be the new President. Adding to President Adams's woes, his youngest son, thirty-year-old Charles, died from the effects of alcoholism.

With Republicans all but certain to take control of both houses of Congress, Marshall warned the President that Jefferson planned establishing a "popular" dictatorship similar to the one Robespierre's Jacobins had established in France before his assassination. The Jacobins had replaced the National Assembly with the *Convention Nationale*, and assigned legislative, executive, and judicial powers to the majority. Vested with absolute powers over all phases of government, majority leaders routinely ignored or ran roughshod over minority rights and objections.

"Mr. Jefferson," Marshall charged, "appears to me to be a man who will . . . sap the fundamental principles of government."[33]

Marshall urged Adams to reinforce and expand the judiciary, which remained the weakest of the three federal branches. With power concentrated in only two branches of government, he reasoned, collusion between them—as between Parliament and the British king—was inevitable, and tyranny the likely result. "We the people" had no protection against oppressive laws that Congress deemed "necessary and proper," as stated in the Constitution.

"It is believed and feared," Marshall warned, "that the tendency of the [Jefferson] administration will be to strengthen state governments at the expense of that of the Union and to transfer as much as possible the powers remaining to the floor of the House of Representatives."[34]

With each of three branches commanding equal power, he argued, collusion would be more difficult, if not impossible—especially if a powerful judiciary voided laws and presidential proclamations it deemed unconstitutional.

The framers of the Constitution, however, had failed to enumerate powers of the federal judiciary and left it all but impotent. The nation's geography weakened it still more. Established as an appeals court with almost no original jurisdiction, the Supreme Court meant nothing to most Americans. More than 90 percent lived and worked on farms scattered across the vast American wilderness. Few had time, means, or money to appeal local court decisions to a Supreme Court in a far-off national capital. Indeed, the original plans for the new city of Washington had not even designated a location for the Supreme Court.

Three Supreme Court Chief Justices had come and gone during the first decade of constitutional rule without leaving a trace of their presence. Although George Washington called the Court a "keystone of our political fabric [sic],"[35] Congress had passed so few federal laws that his first appointee, John Jay, heard only five cases during the nearly six years he served as Chief Justice. With so little to do, he grew bored and decided to become governor of New York state. Jay's successor, John Rutledge of South Carolina, heard only two cases during his single year on the bench, and his successor, Oliver Ellsworth of Connecticut, heard only four cases in four years as Chief Justice. In all, the High Court had heard a total of eleven cases in the eleven years of its existence—one a year.

In its waning days of power the Federalist majority in Congress responded to Marshall's and Adams's calls for an expanded federal judiciary by passing the Judiciary Act of 1801. The Act expanded the number of circuit courts to sixteen, added twenty-three district judgeships, reduced the number of Supreme Court justices from six to five, and eliminated the need for Supreme Court justices to "ride the circuit."

At the time federal court cases originated in district courts, with decisions appealed in the nearest circuit court, where one or, if possible, two Supreme Court justices would "ride" into town to join a district court judge in hearing the appeal. Apart from the small number of appeals such courts could hear, the courts were so far from each other that travel was an enormous hardship for appellants and judges alike.

The Judiciary Act of 1801 not only expanded opportunities for appeals, it relieved justices of arduous travel and freed them to focus solely on Supreme Court cases. It also eliminated conflicts of interest that arose when they heard appeals of decisions to the Supreme Court that they themselves had rendered while serving in circuit courts. Freed from circuit

America's first Chief Justice, John Jay, heard only five cases during nearly six years of his tenure and grew so bored with the post that he quit. Jay wears the traditionally ornate robes of British jurists that Marshall discarded in favor of politically neutral black robes. (LIBRARY OF CONGRESS)

court duty, Supreme Court justices would meet twice a year for two-week sessions in December and June and would hear all cases for the first time.

With no Republicans in the federal judiciary, Adams counted on the army of Federalist judges serving lifetime appointments to turn the judiciary into a Federalist bulwark against absolute Republican rule.

"I dread this above all the measures meditated," Jefferson complained of the Judiciary Act of 1801, "because appointments . . . render it difficult to undo what is done." For Jefferson and the Republicans, the expansion and reach of the Federal judiciary threatened the jurisdiction of state courts, whose judges were elected by local freeholders and responsible to the people. But Federalists argued that the expanded network of federal courts would expand individual rights, giving farmers, artisans, and ordinary citizens in distant parts of the country easier access to the federal court system and broader protection against tyranny by local and state officials and courts.

President Adams spent his remaining weeks in office packing the expanded judiciary with Federalist judges committed to strong central government and protection of property rights—the very opposite of Jefferson's stated political goals. As Jefferson howled in protest, Adams kept appointing new judges, the Federalist Senate continued confirming them, and Secretary of State John Marshall kept signing their commissions—until 11:59 p.m. on the eve of Jefferson's inauguration.

Adams left office at midnight, having filled every seat in the federal judiciary with Federalists, earning them the collective epithet of "Midnight Judges." Not a single Republican sat on the federal bench anywhere in the nation the next day, when Jefferson assumed the presidency.

"The Federalists have retired into the judiciary as a stronghold," Jefferson wailed, "and from that battery all the works of republicanism are to be beaten down and erased."[36] Intensifying Jefferson's anger at the Midnight Judges was their identity: one was President Adams's brother-in-law, another was John Marshall's brother, James Markham, and two were John Marshall's brothers-in-law.

"Mr. John Marshall has taken particular care of his family," editor James Callender remarked in the *Richmond Examiner* of March 13, 1801.

Just before Adams's term ended, Oliver Ellsworth resigned as Chief Justice, and the President asked his old friend, New York's Federalist Governor John Jay, to return to the court. Jay had planned to retire, however, and declined. With his term near its end, Adams was left with but one choice for Chief Justice. "When I waited on the President with Mr. Jay's letter declining the appointment," Marshall recalled, "the President asked thoughtfully, 'Whom shall I nominate now?'"

I replied that I could not tell.

After a moment's hesitation he said, "I believe I must nominate you."

I had never before heard myself named for the office and had not even thought of it. I was pleased as well as surprised and bowed in silence. Next day I was nominated.[37]

> Gentlemen of the Senate.
>
> I nominate John Marshall Secretary of State to be a Chief Justice of the United States in the place of John Jay who has declined his appointment. *John Adams*
>
> United States
> Jan 20th 1801.

President John Adams's simple letter to the Senate nominating John Marshall as the nation's fourth chief justice of the Supreme Court. Twenty-five years later, Adams would call his "gift of John Marshall to the people of the United States . . . the proudest act of my life."
(NATIONAL ARCHIVES AND RECORDS ADMINISTRATION)

On February 4, 1801, as the nation waited for the official count of Electoral College votes in the presidential election, forty-five-year-old John Marshall took the oath of office as Chief Justice of the US Supreme Court in an anteroom of the Capitol north wing and began what would be a historic—and turbulent—thirty-five-year tenure in the US Supreme Court.

The official portrait of Chief Justice John Marshall after his appointment by President John Adams. (FROM *THE LIFE OF JOHN MARSHALL*, BY ALBERT J. BEVERIDGE, VOL. II: FRONTISPIECE)

"I pray you," he wrote to President Adams, "to accept my grateful acknowledgment for the honor conferred on me in appointing me Chief Justice of the United States."

> This additional and flattering mark of your good opinion has made an impression on my mind which time will not efface. I shall enter immediately on the duties of the office and hope never to give you occasion to regret having made this appointment.[38]

With the initial rap of his gavel, Marshall sounded the opening volley in a brutal political war with Thomas Jefferson over the meaning and interpretation of the Constitution—a war that would shape American government, provoke civil war, and determine the nation's course for centuries to follow.

CHAPTER 10

Mr. Chief Justice

"HE HIT THE CONSTITUTION MUCH AS THE LORD HIT THE CHAOS, AT A TIME when everything needed creating," declared constitutional scholar John Paul Frank, describing John Marshall's accession to the Chief Justiceship. "Only a first-class creative genius could have risen so magnificently . . . to uphold the power of the federal government . . . and to restrict the power of the states."[1]

Britain's legal authority Lord Bryce agreed that Marshall's "legal judgments . . . have never been surpassed and rarely equaled by the most famous jurists of modern Europe or ancient Rome."[2]

With only the Senate wing of the Capitol completed when Marshall took his oath of office, the House and Senate took turns using the Senate chamber, stuffing congressional offices and the Library of Congress into any remaining spaces while awaiting completion of the other wing and the connecting midsection of the Capitol. Congress relegated the Supreme Court to "a half-finished committee room meanly furnished and very inconvenient" on the Capitol ground floor. The Court had no space for its own library or offices, no clerks or secretaries—not even a bench. Justices sat at individual desks, along with the Reporter of Decisions*—and they had to share their meager space with district and circuit courts.

---

*The appointee of the court charged with editing and publishing the court's decisions in bound volumes.

Marshall surprised his colleagues when he arrived to take his oath in an austere black robe—in stark contrast to the ermine-fringed robes of scarlet silks and rich purple velvets that other justices wore, in the traditional dress of London's King's Bench.

Their dress was understandable, of course: the oldest members had been raised as British subjects. Sixty-eight-year-old Associate Justice William Cushing of Massachusetts—President Washington's first appointee to the Supreme Court—had won admission to the bar in 1755, the year John Marshall was born and George II ruled North America and the British empire. Maryland's Samuel Chase, fourteen years older than Marshall, was a gruff, outspoken giant of a man, well over six feet, fiercely conservative, steeped in English law, and thoroughly intimidating. New Jersey's William Patterson was ten years older than Marshall and had been a delegate to the Constitutional Convention, a US senator, and governor of his state.

In contrast to Marshall and Chase, forty-five-year-old Alfred Moore of North Carolina stood only four feet, five inches tall and weighed eighty-five pounds. A founder of the University of North Carolina, Moore made up for his diminutive stature with lightning-fast wit and caustic sarcasm. Thirty-eight-year-old Bushrod Washington was the youngest member of the court—seven years younger than Marshall—but already a close friend when Marshall became Chief Justice. Bushrod and Marshall had studied law together with George Wythe at College of William and Mary and later served together both at the Virginia ratification convention and in the Virginia House of Delegates. He and Marshall were still collaborating on their massive biography of Bushrod's uncle, George Washington.

Eager to establish warm relationships with his new colleagues, Marshall invited them to dine, and before they had finished their first meal together, his winning ways had conquered them all. As they sipped their last glasses of Madeira before adjourning, he reminded his colleagues of the resentment many Americans harbored against England. He convinced them to do away with opulent English-style judicial wear in favor of black robes like his, as symbols that they carried no colors in making judicial decisions.

Marshall's warmth, humor, and intelligent conversation produced instant collegiality and bonhomie among the justices that none had ever experienced in the bleak capital city. The absence of their wives and families and the reticence of congressmen to draw too close to men who might one day judge them had made the capital a dull, lonely place for the justices. They eagerly embraced Marshall's invitation to lodge in the same boarding house and share meals together.

"Our intercourse is perfectly familiar and unrestrained," Associate Justice Joseph Story effused to his wife after he joined the Court, "and our social hours when undisturbed with labors of law, are passed in gay and frank conversation, which at once enlivens and instructs. . . . We live with perfect harmony."[3]

The harmony of the justices contrasted sharply with the angry dissonance in the Senate when Vice President Jefferson announced the Electoral College votes of the 1,800 presidential election: John Jay, 1; Charles Cotesworth Pinckney, 64; President John Adams, 65; Aaron Burr Jr., 73; Thomas Jefferson, 73.

Ironically, Jefferson had not *won* the election as much as Alexander Hamilton had *lost* it. By dividing Federalist votes in the Electoral College, Hamilton had cost John Adams the presidency. In fact, Federalist unity would easily have given Adams both a popular and Electoral College majority. Hamilton's machinations had not only toppled a popular President; they had produced a tie that sent the nation into a constitutional crisis that had some congressmen threatening secession—even civil war.

Although the Twelfth Amendment would later require separate votes for President and vice president, all votes in the Electoral College in 1800 were cast for individual candidates. The candidate with the most votes became President and the one with the second-most votes vice president. Each elector had two votes to cast. If a tie resulted, the Constitution required the House of Representatives to break the deadlock. Burr seemed to have precluded that eventuality months earlier, however, by stating, "It is highly improbable that I shall have an equal number of votes with Mr. Jefferson, but if such be the result, every man who knows me ought to know that I would utterly disclaim all competition."[4]

Shortly thereafter, however, Burr's close friend, New York's politically powerful Republican Governor George Clinton, apparently roused Burr's dormant ambitions: "If you, Mr. Burr, was the candidate for the presidential chair," the governor announced, "I would act with pleasure and with vigor."[5]

With Clinton's words ringing in his ears, Burr listened carefully as Jefferson announced the Electoral College tally. He then shocked Jefferson, the Republican Party, Congress, and the nation by renouncing his earlier intention to serve as Jefferson's vice president and challenged the Virginian for the presidency.

"I never thought him an honest, frank-dealing man," Vice President Jefferson growled at Burr, "but considered him a crooked gun, or other perverted machine, whose aim or stroke you could never be sure of."[6]

Jefferson's angry attack on Burr, however, spurred many Federalists to support the New Yorker. Burr's religious roots as grandson of Jonathan Edwards and his gallant service to the nation as a colonel in the Revolutionary War contrasted sharply with Jefferson's evident cowardice during the Revolution, his open scorn for organized religion, and his letter to Mazzei insulting the "father of our country." By supporting Burr, some Federalists hoped he might react to Jefferson's assaults on his character by switching to the Federalist party.

Of the many ironies of the 1800 election, the most puzzling was the constitutional obligation of House Federalists to choose their nation's next President from the two Republicans their nominal leader Alexander Hamilton most detested. If they failed, they would leave the nation without a chief executive to head the government when the incumbent President, vice president, and Congress left office on March 4.

Adding still more drama to the Burr-Jefferson impasse, an article signed *Horatius* in the *Washington Federalist* asserted falsely that in the event of a deadlock on March 4, Congress could appoint a President until another election was held. Alarmed by the article and convinced the author was John Marshall (it was not), James Monroe wrote to warn Jefferson of "intrigues" by Jefferson's political enemies.

"There has been much alarm at the intimation of such a projected usurpation," Monroe told Jefferson, "and a spirit fully manifested not to submit to it."[7]

Monroe's son-in-law, the prominent attorney George Hay, assailed Horatius, demanding that he "come forward," identify himself, and defend his opinion. Writing under the pseudonym *Hortensius*, Hay asserted that Horatius had created "anxiety and alarm . . . throughout America." Hay warned that if Congress elected "a stranger to rule over us . . . the usurpation will be instantly and firmly repelled. The government will be at an end."[8]

Jefferson seconded Hay: "We thought best to declare openly and firmly," Jefferson proclaimed, "that the day such an act passed, the Middle States would arm and that no such usurpation, even for a single day, should be admitted to."[9] Jefferson pledged resistance "by arms" and said he would act to set aside the Constitution and call "a convention to reorganize and amend the government."[10]

To prevent Jefferson from acting, House members resolved to remain in session until they elected a new President.

They began voting at one o'clock that afternoon. Sixteen states made up the Union, with Vermont, Kentucky, and Tennessee having joined the original thirteen. Eight state delegations in the House had Republican majorities, and six had Federalist majorities, with two delegations evenly divided. Each state had one vote, and the next President would need to win nine states.

Tensions grew as each state called out its preference:

"Connecticut! . . . Delaware! . . . Massachusetts! . . . New Hampshire! . . . Rhode Island! . . . South Carolina!"

"Burr!" each shouted in reply as the clerk called the roll of the states.

"Georgia . . . Kentucky . . . New Jersey . . . New York . . . North Carolina . . . Pennsylvania . . . Tennessee . . . Virginia . . .

"Jefferson!"

" . . . Vermont . . . "

"Vermont!" the clerk's voice rang out a second time.

Still, only silence. Vermont delegates had clustered together, whispering to each other, caucusing. Angry shouts rang out in the hall, demanding their reply.

"Vermont!"

In the end Vermonters were evenly divided and agreed to abstain from voting. Maryland abstained for the same reason.

Delegates stood, stretched, then clustered—grumbling, arguing, and gesturing until the Speaker called for order and a second ballot. The results were the same: six states for Burr, eight for Jefferson—and a collective moan from all.

A third ballot followed, with no change . . . three more with similar results. With the completion of each ballot, the chorus of moans turned into a crescendo of frustrated shouts and outrage. When calm returned, members agreed to adjourn for an hour before resuming their balloting.

The House reconvened and voted eight more times that afternoon and evening—past nine. Members sent away for food, pillows, and blankets, preparing to spend the night if they had to. All knew that unless they succeeded in electing a President, the nation would be without a chief executive or vice president three weeks later and be unable to function. Clerks awakened members for another vote at 1 a.m., but the count stayed the same . . . again, at 2 a.m. . . . at 2:30 . . .

The twenty-seventh ballot came at dawn, just as someone revived rumors of Hamilton leading the army to Washington. The rumors spawned more rumors: Virginia Governor Monroe, according to one report, had responded to Hamilton's insurgency by sending militiamen to secure the federal arsenal in New London, Virginia. Another rumor insisted that a citizen mob in Philadelphia had seized a federal arsenal and was marching to defend the capital against Hamilton.

None of the rumors had any basis in fact.

On Friday, February 13, the House reconvened for two more useless ballots before adjourning until the following morning.

A new rumor emerged that House Federalists would name Chief Justice Marshall acting President. After Jefferson repeated his pledge of civil war if Congress attempted to seat a Federalist as President, rumors reached the Capitol that 500 armed Marylanders were on their way to back Jefferson's threat.

"Nothing new today," wrote Pennsylvania's Republican Senator Albert Gallatin after the House reconvened on Saturday, February 14. "Three more ballots, making in all 33; result the same."[11]

When the House reconvened on Monday morning, February 16, a thirty-fifth ballot failed to break the impasse, and Delaware's lone delegate, the exhausted Federalist James Bayard, stunned his colleagues by grumbling he might shift his vote from Burr to Jefferson on the next ballot.

Like other Federalists, he had received one of the dozens of letters Alexander Hamilton had rained on the House to influence votes. In one letter Hamilton admitted he had often vilified Jefferson as "a contemptible hypocrite, tinctured with fanaticism . . . crafty and persevering in his objects . . . not scrupulous about his means of success nor even mindful of the truth."[12] But, Hamilton added, Burr was worse—"a man without principles"—and Hamilton said he preferred "a man with misguided principles [Jefferson] as President to one with no principles at all [Burr]."[13]

Marshall, who had served with Hamilton and Burr at Monmouth, responded curtly: "To Mr. Jefferson, I have felt almost insuperable objections."

> His foreign prejudices seem totally to unfit him for the chief magistracy of a nation which cannot indulge those prejudices without sustaining deep and permanent injury. . . . The morals of the author of the letter to Mazzei cannot be pure. . . . I cannot bring myself to aid Mr. Jefferson.

In the end Marshall decided to remain neutral, saying, "I can take no part in this business."[14]

On Tuesday, at noon, February 17, the House voted a thirty-fifth time, and Bayard succumbed to "the current of public sentiment, which I thought it neither safe nor politic to counteract." He announced he would switch his vote from Burr and deliver Delaware to Jefferson.[15]

"Deserter!" shouted a Federalist House member.

"Coward!" others echoed, waving their fists.

Some charged Jefferson had bought Bayard's vote with promises of patronage; others turned and stomped out the door, shouting they would "go without a constitution and take the risk of civil war" before accepting "such a wretch as Jefferson."

"The clamor was prodigious," Bayard recalled, "the reproaches vehement," but he said he feared further prolongation of the House stalemate would come "at the expense of the Constitution."[16]

As the shouting abated and a handful of more thoughtful House leaders gathered about Bayard, they admitted they had but two choices: "Risk the Constitution and a civil war or take Mr. Jefferson."[17] Before casting their votes, however, they huddled for long minutes in a corner of the chamber, whispering, gesturing curiously, and finally disbanding—some even wearing grim smiles. They had found a way to clear Jefferson's way to the presidency without voting for him—even sparing Bayard the epithet of turncoat.

Bayard withdrew his vote, along with Federalist delegates from Maryland, Vermont, and South Carolina, all of whom abstained from voting, thus leaving only Jeffersonian Republicans to vote in those states. In the final ballot Republicans carried ten states, allowing Thomas Jefferson to claim victory as third President of the United States.

A collective explosion of joy shook the nation's cities, towns, and villages—not because Jefferson had won but because the nation had avoided civil war. Sixteen cannon blasts (one for each of the states) resounded in Baltimore and other large cities, and church bells pealed in Richmond, Philadelphia, New York. "Three hundred Philadelphia Republicans are now drunk beyond the hope of recovery," proclaimed the *Gazette of the United States.* "Gin and whisky prices are said to have risen in price 50 per cent."[18]

"The voice of the people has prevailed," the *National Intelligencer* reported more calmly, "and Thomas Jefferson is declared by the Representatives of the People to be duly elected President of the United States."[19]

Jefferson rejoiced in a letter to Lafayette: "The storm we have passed through proves our vessel indestructible."[20]

Jefferson's victory astonished the British and Europeans as much as it did Americans. For the first time in modern history an incumbent political party had ceded control of government to an opposition party without violence. The bitter House balloting had tarnished the transition somewhat, but no shots had been fired, there had been no assassinations, no coup d'état, no military intervention. At the very least the results suggested that a self-governing republic might well survive in a world ruled largely by absolute monarchs.

"This whole chapter in the history of man is new," Jefferson crowed to a friend two weeks after his inauguration.[21]

In a disingenuous show of attempted reconciliation, Jefferson invited his cousin Chief Justice John Marshall to administer the oath of office at his inauguration. On March 4, 1801, some 300 officials and guests crowded into the Senate chamber for the first presidential inauguration in the nation's new capital.

Without ceremony the new vice president, forty-five-year-old Aaron Burr Jr. of New York, took his chair as President of the Senate. Seated beside him was Jefferson's fellow Virginian John Marshall. When Jefferson entered, Burr ceded his chair and sat in an adjacent seat, thus sandwiching Jefferson between two of the men he disliked most in the political world—Marshall and Burr. According to custom at the time, Jefferson rose to make his inaugural speech before taking his oath of office. He seemed to reach out to political opponents as well as allies:

"Every difference of opinion is not a difference of principle," he proclaimed. "We are all Republicans, we are all Federalists."[22]

John Adams was having none of it. The former President left the capital before dawn on Inauguration Day, refusing to congratulate the new President or attend any of the ceremonies associated with his assumption of office. He slipped out of the capital like a thief in the night. He would never again exchange a word with Hamilton, and it would take more than a decade—and his wife's cajoling—before he would begin a civil correspondence with Jefferson.

"I believe he left the city at 4 o'clock in the morning," John Marshall wrote of Adams to Charles Cotesworth Pinckney, his old friend from XYZ days. Pinckney had retired from Congress to his South Carolina planta-tion. "I have administered the oath to the [new] President. You will before this reaches you see his inauguration speech. . . . It is in direct terms giving the lie to the violent party declamation which elected him."

> The Democrats* are divided into speculative theorists and absolute ter-rorists. With the latter I am not disposed to classify Mr. Jefferson. If he arranges himself with them it is not difficult to foresee that much calam-ity is in store for our country—if he does not, they will soon become his enemies and calumniators.[23]

Despite President Jefferson's plea for reconciliation, his shaky victory exacerbated the nation's political chaos. Burr now seethed with hatred for Hamilton and Jefferson; Jefferson seethed with hatred for Burr and Ham-ilton; and the American people seethed with hatred for Congress, whose Alien and Sedition Acts had temporarily stripped them of constitutional rights to free speech and a free press.

Americans also harbored deep disgust with the political system for having forced from office a President they respected as the logical succes-sor to George Washington and who had actually more supporters than the new incumbent. By splitting the Federalist party, Hamilton destroyed it as a viable political force and created dangerous tears in the fragile na-tional political fabric. The Federalists lost not only the presidency and vice presidency, they lost control of both houses of Congress, with Jeffer-son's Republicans winning 18 of 32 Senate seats, or 56.3 percent of the votes, and 64 of 105 seats in the House of Representatives, or a 61 per-cent share of the votes. In effect President Jefferson and the Republicans had won a mandate to govern as they saw fit.

---

*Under Jefferson's leadership the Republicans also became known as Democrat-Republicans and, more simply, Democrats. The three terms were used interchange-ably, but only the term "Republicans" will appear in these pages except in quotations such as this one that use alternatives.

Annoyed at public mutterings that he had not won a majority of the popular vote and was, therefore, a minority President, Jefferson did not wait long to abandon his pledge of political reconciliation. At the end of the summer after the presidential inauguration Chief Justice Marshall issued the first decision of his tenure, and Jefferson reacted with fury, pledging to dilute the Court's powers.

Complaining that the finality of the Court's decisions left no opportunity for appeal, Jefferson charged that decisions by an unelected body like the Supreme Court contained "the germ of dissolution of our federal government." He called the Court "irresponsible . . . advancing its noiseless step like a thief over the field of jurisdiction, until all shall be usurped from the states."[24]

What stirred Jefferson's ire was Marshall's ruling in the case of Silas Talbot, captain of the legendary American frigate *Constitution* ("Old Ironsides"). Talbot had ordered his men to fire across the bow of a French corvette towing a merchant ship it had captured. Owned by businessman Hans Seeman from the neutral city-state of Hamburg, the captured merchant ship *Amelia* carried nine cannons to repel pirates, and its French captors had hoisted a French flag on its mast, giving it the appearance of an armed French ship. US and French ships were still fighting their undeclared "quasi-war" in the Caribbean, and under orders from then-President Adams to seize French ships threatening American trade, Talbot seized the *Amelia* and took it to an American port.

Talbot claimed half the value of ship and cargo from Seeman for rescuing the *Amelia* from the French. Seeman refused to pay, arguing that France and the United States were not legally at war, that the ship was a neutral vessel, and that international rules of the sea would eventually have required the French to release it to its owner.

Like many cases before the Supreme Court, both sides had valid arguments, with no absolute right or wrong and an almost infinite number of arguments and possible settlements. Before the justices reviewed the testimony, Marshall convinced them to adopt two new principles to augment the Court's standing as an independent third branch of government.

First, he asked the justices to work out their differences in private and agree to a single compromise decision for each case; second, he suggested that he, the Chief Justice, announce the decision as being the sole opinion of the court, with no mention of dissent. By speaking with one voice, he argued, the court would render its decision *absolute*, with no room for subsequent questioning or argument by appellants citing dissenting justices and undermining the impact of the decision.

Sensing the grandeur and power that Marshall's reforms would give the court, the justices agreed—and in the four years that followed, the Supreme Court rendered forty-six decisions, all of them pronounced by Chief Justice Marshall's lone voice, like Moses from on high, thundering, "It is the opinion of the Court . . . "

In the Talbot case Marshall and the justices examined every element as a separate legal question. On the question of whether Talbot's seizure was lawful, "the opinion of the court" found legitimate arguments for both sides. On the one hand, Marshall declared, "the powers of war being, by the Constitution of the United States, vested in Congress, the Acts of that body can alone be resorted to as our guides in this enquiry." Clearly Congress had *not* declared war, and the Court ruled, on the one hand, that Talbot had acted beyond his authority by attacking the French corvette and seizing the Seeman ship.

On the other hand, Marshall went on, the President, as commander-in-chief, had ordered Captain Talbot (and other naval commanders) to intercept French ships that might threaten American commerce. "The *Amelia*," Marshall pointed out, "was an armed vessel commanded and manned by Frenchmen [and flying a French flag]. . . . It is not then to be questioned, but that there was probable cause to bring her in for adjudication"[25] in accordance with the President's order.

Having now declared the seizure legal, the Court tried fixing the amount Seeman should pay Captain Talbot to recover his ship and cargo. "According to the law of nations," Marshall explained, "a neutral is generally to be restored without salvage." The Court, therefore, disallowed Captain Talbot's claim for 50 percent of the value of the ship and its cargo, but it recognized that because it had a French flag on its mast and cannons on its deck, Talbot had no way of knowing the ship was not an enemy ship and was, in fact, neutral.

"Considering the circumstances," Marshall ruled, "one-sixth appears to be a reasonable allowance." From that amount, however, the Court allowed Seeman to deduct port fees and litigation costs to recover his property. In the end each side won some and lost some: Seeman got his ship and cargo back, and Talbot and his crew obtained token compensation for capturing it and restoring it to its proper owner.[26]

The biggest winner, however, was the US Supreme Court, which shored up its standing as a federal institution by *mediating* a complex case instead of arbitrarily judging one side or the other absolutely right or wrong. Its unanimous decision not only dispensed justice to all but left no room for challenge.

President Jefferson was irate, however: "Nobody knows what opinion any individual member gave," he railed after reading the Talbot case. The public, he insisted, had a right "to know whether those decisions were really unanimous."

> The opinions were prepared in private. Some of these cases have been of such importance, of such difficulty, and the decisions so grating to a portion of the public as to have merited the fullest explanation from every judge *seriatim* [individually, in a series] of the reasons which had produced such convictions on his mind.[27]

Jefferson grew even more irate after Marshall simply ignored the President's provocative charges. Chafing from irrational bitterness toward Marshall, Jefferson challenged the Chief Justice and the Supreme Court to legal combat that would threaten to undermine the still-fragile structure of American government. Indeed, his first salvo set off one of the most critical constitutional conflicts in American history when he effectively nullified appointments of four justices of the peace—so-called Midnight Judges whom President Adams had appointed just before leaving office.

Still secretary of state at the time, John Marshall had not had time to deliver the commissions before he left office. When President Jefferson's new Secretary of State James Madison found them on his desk, Jefferson told Madison to withhold them, that he would replace the appointees with Republicans. When William Marbury and the three other Adams appointees subsequently demanded their commissions, Madison refused.

"If there is any principle of law never yet contradicted," President Jefferson asserted in supporting Madison, "it is that delivery is one of the essentials to the validity of the deed. Although signed and sealed, as long as it remains in the hands of the [original] party, it is not a deed and can be made so only by its delivery."[28]

A Georgetown business man, Marbury appealed to Congress, which had approved the appointments, but the Federalists were gone, and Jefferson's Republicans who formed the new majority rejected his appeal. Marbury turned directly to the Supreme Court for help, but before his attorney could plead the case of *Marbury v. Madison*, Jefferson's Republican Congress slammed shut the doors of the Supreme Court—actually shut it down by law and scattered its justices into legal obscurity. Marbury would have to wait more than two years for justice.

The sudden court shutdown came in response to Jefferson's warning that Federalists "have retreated into the judiciary as a stronghold, the tenure of which makes it difficult to dislodge them."[29] The President's puppet Congressman William Branch Giles of Virginia moved immediately for "an absolute repeal of the whole judiciary system, terminating the present officers and creating an entirely new system . . . restraining the jurisdiction of the courts."[30]

Congress agreed. It repealed the Judiciary Act of 1801 and replaced it with a new Judiciary Act of 1802, which effectively dismantled the federal judiciary and closed the Supreme Court for two years. The new law reset the number of circuit courts at six, eliminated more than a dozen judgeships, restored the number of Supreme Court justices to six, and forced the justices to resume "riding the circuit" to distant district courts.* The

---

*Although they continued complaining about the discomforts of "riding the circuit," Supreme Court justices would do so until 1891, when it became evident that a justice who decided a case in circuit court often found it difficult to be impartial if

act eliminated the summer session of the Supreme Court. It would now meet for only two weeks, once a year instead of twice a year. By scattering the justices around the country the rest of the year, the new law would prevent Chief Justice Marshall from organizing his colleagues into a powerful, cohesive third branch of government.

In the absence of presidential and congressional term limits, the new restraints on the judiciary represented a coup d'état that gave the President and Congress complete control of the federal government. With both branches dominated by southern Republicans, a handful of powerful plantation owners would rule the nation by casting the votes of the 1.7 million slaves they owned.*

The few Federalists left in Congress howled in protest, calling the new law unconstitutional and citing Article III, Section 1, that "judges . . . shall hold their offices during good behavior" and remain immune from removal except by impeachment and conviction for high crimes and misdemeanors." But Republicans countered that Article II, Section 1 gave Congress sole power to "ordain and establish" inferior courts "from time to time."

New York's Federalist Senator Gouverneur Morris charged into the fray before the final vote with a stirring plea that asked, "What will be the effect of the desired repeal?"

> Will it not be a declaration to the remaining judges that they hold their offices subject to your will and pleasure? And what will be the result of this? It will be that the check established by the Constitution is

---

he had to help decide the same case later in an appeal to the Supreme Court. Each justice still maintains a tie to—and, indeed, can sit in—a circuit court, now called a Court of Appeals, but the justices limit their involvement to issuing stays and other procedural matters.

*The Constitution, however, counted each slave vote as only three-fifths of a vote, thus reducing the votes of 1.7 million slaves to the equivalent of about 1 million white votes—still enough to give wealthy southern plantation owners full control of state legislatures in the six slave states and a disproportionate influence in the US Congress and national government. At the time state legislatures selected the two US senators from each state.

destroyed. . . . Cast not away this only anchor of our safety. . . . I know the difficulties through which it was obtained. I stand in the presence of almighty God and of the world, and I declare to you that if you lose this charter, never, no, never will you get another! . . . We stand on the brink of fate. Pause! Pause! For heaven's sake, pause![31]

Morris's eloquence produced a tie vote on the measure and so moved Republican Vice President Aaron Burr Jr. that he abandoned Jefferson's Republican camp and, to the cheers of Federalists, cast a tie-breaking vote to send the repeal proposal to committee for further study.

"That vote," Morris conjectured, "might, I believe, have made Burr President at the next election."[32]

Five days later, however, another Republican arrived to add to their majority, while a Federalist absented himself, giving the Republicans enough votes to enact the Judiciary Act of 1802 and repeal the Judiciary Act of 1801.

With repeal of the old act, Jefferson immediately stripped Federalists of power in the judiciary by replacing Federalist attorneys and marshals with Republicans—"as a protection to Republican suitors in courts."[33]

For Jefferson the new act was a total victory over John Marshall, over the Supreme Court, over Burr, over federalism. In effect he succeeded in voiding Article III of the Constitution and emasculating the Supreme Court by exiling its justices from the national capital for all but two weeks a year.* By scrapping the court sessions of 1802, the bill effectively shut

---

*The Constitution gave Congress the power to fix the number of justices on the US Supreme Court. The Judiciary Act of 1789, which created the federal judiciary, fixed the number at six. The Judiciary Act of 1801 reduced it to five, the Judiciary Act of 1802 restored the number to six, and it climbed to seven in 1807, nine in 1837, and ten in 1865, with each increase often reflecting the effort of the majority party in Congress to influence the politics of the Court. In 1869 Congress acted to reflect the increase in the number of states and reduce the incidence of tie votes by fixing the number of justices at nine, where it has remained ever since.

the Supreme Court for nearly two years, until February 1803, and with no Supreme Court to stand in his way, Jefferson had free rein to rule unchallenged in Washington. Led by Jefferson's powerful Virginia Republicans, Congress had staged a revolution without firing a shot and ceded all undesignated powers to the states in accordance with the Virginia and Kentucky Resolutions.

"Who is so blind as not to see that the right of the legislature to abolish the judges at pleasure destroys the independence of the judicial department?" Alexander Hamilton raged in far-off New York City. Marginalized from national politics after Jefferson's presidential victory, Hamilton had retreated to private law practice but tried to keep his political views before the public in his Federalist newspaper, the *New-York Evening Post*. Warning of possible civil war, Hamilton feared that without an independent judiciary, "the Constitution will be no more."[34]

As it turned out, they were Hamilton's last words on the Constitution. The man who wrote most of the *Federalist* essays extolling the Constitution fell into unrelenting despair a month later when his oldest son, Philip, died of a pistol-shot wound in a duel with a Republican who accused his father of plotting to overthrow President Jefferson. For Alexander Hamilton, nineteen-year-old Philip—a graduate of King's College (now Columbia) like his father—had been the family's "eldest and brightest hope."[35]

In Washington, however, Delaware Federalist James Bayard continued the Hamiltonian rhetoric and demanded to know, "Are the gentlemen afraid of the judges? Are they afraid that they will pronounce the repealing law void?"[36] Even Jefferson's loyal Republican protégé, Virginia Governor James Monroe, opposed the 1802 legislation, telling Jefferson that "a postponement by law of the meeting of the [Supreme] Court is . . . an unconstitutional oppression of the judiciary by the legislature to carry a preceding measure [removal of circuit court judges] which was also unconstitutional. Suppose the judges were to meet . . . denouncing the whole proceeding as unconstitutional and the motive impure?"[37]

Jefferson, however, refused to budge. Despite his absence from the Constitutional Convention, he insisted that the Constitution gave each branch of government "a right in cases which arise within the line of its proper functions . . . to decide without appeal on the validity of an act according to its own judgment and uncontrolled by the opinions of any other department." In effect he said "We the People" wrote the Constitution, and only "We the People"—that is, the legislature—had the right to interpret it.[38]

Expanding on Jefferson's specious argument, Kentucky Republican John Breckenridge told the Senate that the Constitution had "intended a separation of the power vested in the three great departments, giving to each exclusive authority on the subjects committed to each."

> The legislature have the exclusive right to interpret the Constitution in what regards the law-making process and the judges are bound to execute the laws they make. Let gentlemen consider well before they insist on a power in the judiciary which places the legislature at their feet.[39]

Gouverneur Morris returned fire, asserting that "the moment the legislature declare themselves supreme, they become so. The sovereignty of America will no longer reside in the people, but in the Congress, and the Constitution is whatever they choose to make it."[40]

New Englanders were irate over Republican emasculation of the judiciary. Former Secretary of State Timothy Pickering, now a senator from Massachusetts, renewed his perennial call for New England's secession.

"I . . . anticipate a new confederacy exempt from the corrupt and corrupting influence and oppression of the aristocratic democrats of the South," he wrote to his friend, former Senator George Cabot of Boston. "There will be (and our children, at farthest, will see it) a separation." Pickering predicted that Canada would join New England to form a northern confederacy "with the assent of England. . . . A continued tyranny of the present ruling sect will precipitate that event."[41]

To President Jefferson's delight, what Pickering called the "tyranny of the present ruling sect" had crased the face of Chief Justice John

Marshall—and indeed the entire US Supreme Court—from the govern-mental picture in Washington. Like his colleagues, Marshall now spent his days riding the circuit over dusty, muddy, rutted dirt roads and trails through the savage southern wilderness.

Just as Marshall's face had faded from his mind, however, another more dangerous one loomed in the presidential doorway: James T. Cal-lender, the editor to whom Jefferson had sent the confidential papers documenting Alexander Hamilton's affair with Mrs. Reynolds.

After Callender had gone to prison for articles assailing President John Adams, then-Vice President Jefferson had refused to help, offering Cal-lender a mere $50 after the editor's release from prison and reneging on his promise to pay Callender $100 for publishing a political attack on former President Adams. Callender retaliated in the summer of 1802 by publishing a story that would forever tar Jefferson's reputation:

"It is well known," Callender wrote, "that the man whom it delights the people to honor, keeps and for many years has kept, as his concubine, one of his slaves. Her name is Sally. . . . By this wench Sally, our Presi-dent has had several children. . . . The African Venus is said to officiate as housekeeper at Monticello." Callender challenged the President to appear in court to challenge the truth about "the black wench and her mulatto litter."[42]

In November Callender reprinted a poem from the *Boston Gazette*:

> Of all the damsels on the green
> Of mountain or in valley,
> A lass so luscious ne'er was seen,
> As the Monticellian Sally.
> Yankey doodle, who's the noodle?
> What wife were half so handy?
> To breed a flock of slaves for stock,
> A blackamoor's the dandy.[43]

Jefferson did not let Callender continue his editorial assaults unchallenged.

*The Philosophic Cock, by political cartoonist James Akin
(1773–1846), shows President Thomas Jefferson as an admiring
rooster and his slave Sally Hemings as the hen. The text in fine
print is from Act I of Joseph Addison's drama Cato and reads,
"'Tis not a set of features or complexion or tincture of a skin that
I admire."* (AMERICAN ANTIQUARIAN SOCIETY)

"Are you not afraid, Callender, that some avenging fire will consume
your body as well as your soul?" warned Jefferson's friend, the editor of
the *Richmond Examiner*.[44]

On July 17, 1803, Callender's dead body washed ashore on the James
River.[45]

CHAPTER 11

Party Rage

As John Marshall set out for circuit court in Raleigh, North Carolina, after Christmas in 1802, he felt uncharacteristically melancholy: Thomas Jefferson had blatantly violated the Constitution—indeed, violated his oath to "preserve, protect, and defend the Constitution" by shrinking the federal judiciary and effectively emasculating the Supreme Court. He had ignored normal impeachment and trial procedures and removed federal judges from the bench because they held political views that differed from his own.

Adding to Marshall's somber mood was the news that his father, Thomas Marshall, had died in Kentucky. After John Marshall's election to Congress in 1799 he had taken the time to visit his father, knowing it might be the last time they would ever be together. They had always been close, and old age had taken its toll on Thomas Marshall.

Obsessed by his irrational loathing of the Marshalls, Thomas Jefferson imagined a dark political plot behind the Marshall son's pilgrimage to see his father. He told Virginia Senator Wilson Cary Nicholas that "the visit of the apostle Marshall to Kentucky excites anxiety" and warned of "poisons" that Marshall would introduce into Kentucky politics.[1]

"There is so much in the political world to wound honest men that I am disgusted with it." Marshall lamented to his friend Charles Cotesworth Pinckney, the retired congressman from South Carolina.

> I begin to see things and indeed human nature through a much more gloomy medium than I once thought possible. This new doctrine of the perfectibility of man . . . begins to exhibit him I think as an animal much less respectable than he has heretofore been thought.[2]

The new North Carolina capital of Raleigh lay 165 miles away from Richmond. The forty-eight-year-old Marshall covered the distance on horseback in about three days, traveling about fifty miles a day and spending two nights on the road—sometimes at a tavern, sometimes at a friend's house, sometimes simply knocking at a farmer's door.

"My dearest Polly," he wrote from Raleigh on January 2, 1803. He knew that Polly remained too fragile to ponder over his political problems.

> You will laugh at my vexation when you hear . . . I lost 15 silver dollars out of my waistcoat pocket. They had worn their way through the various mendings . . . and sought their liberty in the sands of Carolina. . . . I ordered Peter to take out my clothes that I might dress for court when to my astonishment and grief after stumbling several minutes in the portmanteau, staring at vacancy, and sweating most profusely, he turned to me with the doleful tidings that I had no pair of breeches. You may be sure this piece of intelligence was not very graciously received. However, I immediately set out to get a pair made. I thought I should be a sans culotte only one day . . . but the greatest of evils, I found, was followed by still greater! Not a tailor in town could be prevailed on to work for me. I have to pass the term without that important article of dress . . .
>
> Adieu, my dearest Polly.
> I am your ever affectionate
> J Marshall[3]

Justice Samuel Chase was even more disgusted than Marshall with Jefferson's attack on the federal courts. "I have no doubt," he appealed to Marshall, "that the circuit judges cannot . . . be deprived of their offices, or commissions, or salaries during their lives; unless only on impeachment for, and conviction of, high crimes and misdemeanors, as prescribed by the Constitution."

> As the act of Congress evidently intended to remove the circuit judges from their offices and to take away their salaries, I am of the opinion that it is void. . . . Further, all judges, by the Constitution, are required to bind themselves by oath to support the Constitution of the United States . . . and that they are bound in duty to declare acts of Congress or of any of the states contrary to the Constitution *void*. . . . Every judge of the Supreme Court . . . must, in my judgment, decline to execute the office of a circuit court judge.[4]

Although Marshall and the other justices agreed with Chase, Jefferson argued that he too had taken an oath to support the Constitution of the United States and that neither his own oath nor that of the justices permitted them to thwart the will of the people by overturning laws enacted by the people's representatives in Congress. With Jefferson's Republicans in command of Congress and the justices of the Supreme Court "in exile," the President wielded all but dictatorial powers.

Late the following spring Marshall took Polly and the children north for the summer to his boyhood home of Oak Hill, on a cool forest hillside of the Blue Ridge. In midsummer Marshall and Polly joined James and Elizabeth Monroe at Fauquier White Sulphur Springs,* a resort about forty miles from Oak Hill, where the two couples rented cottages

---

*Fauquier White Sulfur Springs was about thirty miles southwest of Washington in Fauquier County—as opposed to the more famous White Sulphur Springs resort on the eastern border of present-day West Virginia with Virginia.

next to each other. Like Polly, Elizabeth Monroe suffered chronic health problems, and the two developed a warm friendship, taking the waters together and comparing ailments and remedies, while their husbands argued politics, discussed constitutional law, or went hunting as they had when they were boys.

As summer blended into fall, storm clouds sprayed the Blue Ridge with sheets of chilly autumn rain, and the Marshalls and Monroes packed up and returned to their respective Virginia homes before resuming government service.

When Marshall returned to Washington, eleven of the judges ousted by the Judiciary Act of 1802 were petitioning Congress for reinstatement and payment of back salaries. Their dismissals, they declared, had violated their constitutional rights as federal judges to "hold their offices during good behavior and . . . receive . . . compensation." At Jefferson's direction the Republican majority in Congress rejected the petitions, declaring Congress, not the courts, sole judge of what was and was not constitutional.

"If the petitioners can bring their case before the Supreme Court," taunted Virginia's Representative John Nicholas, "let them do so. If the Supreme Court shall arrogate this power to themselves and declare our law to be unconstitutional, it will then behoove us to act. Our duty is clear."[5]

After an absence of nearly two years John Marshall reconvened an all but impotent Supreme Court. Attorney Charles Lee, the former US attorney general and brother of former Virginia Governor Henry Lee, sprang to his feet and asked the Court for a writ of *mandamus*,* or court order, to force Secretary of State James Madison to deliver William Marbury's commission as a justice of the peace. On Jefferson's instructions Madison had not appeared, and Attorney General Levi Lincoln, who represented Madison and the government's executive branch, could do nothing but sit and say nothing in the absence of his client.

---

* A judicial writ commanding (mandating) a response by a public official.

As an embarrassing silence filled the room, Marshall and the four associate justices looked to each other for a way out of the constitutional impasse. The justices realized that if they issued the writ, they had no law enforcement arm to force the secretary of state to comply. Rather than a symbol of authority, the writ would become a symbol of court impotence and prevent its emergence as a third coequal branch of the federal government. If they did not issue the writ, however, they would be complicit in undermining the foundation of the new government by allowing a President to violate Article III of the Constitution that "judges . . . shall hold their offices during good behavior."

Marshall had the good sense to adjourn and give the justices time to consider their dilemma together in the privacy of their quarters.

Two weeks later the Chief Justice pronounced the most important decision in Supreme Court history. Indeed, his decision in *Marbury v. Madison* effectively changed the Constitution and reshaped the US government by establishing the judiciary as a third, coequal branch of the federal government with the executive and legislative branches.

There were three parts to the decision, two of them restricting presidential and congressional powers and a third that expanded Supreme Court powers to put it on an even footing with the other two branches of government.

In the first part of the decision Marshall declared that the President (and his agent, the secretary of state) had violated the Constitution by withholding Marbury's commission. Marshall rejected Jefferson's argument that "delivery is one of the essentials to the validity of the deed."

"The transmission of the commission is a practice directed by convenience not by law," Marshall declared. "It cannot therefore constitute the appointment."

> It is therefore decidedly the opinion of the court that when a commission has been signed by the President, the appointment is made; and that the commission is complete when the seal of the United States has been affixed to it by the Secretary of State.

In signing Marbury's commission and affixing the Great Seal of the United States, then-President Adams and his secretary of state had "vested in the officer [Marbury] legal rights which are protected by the laws of his country. To withhold his commission . . . is an act deemed by the court not warranted by law, but a violation of a vested legal right."[6]

There it was: the Secretary of State (and, by implication, the President) had exceeded the constitutional powers of the executive branch of government. He could not remove Marbury from the bench. Marbury had a constitutional right to his commission and the right to its immediate delivery.

When, however, Marbury's lawyer asked the Court to issue the writ and *force* the secretary of state to deliver the commission, Marshall and the Court wisely backed away and responded by reminding Marbury's lawyer that the Constitution had created the Supreme Court as an appellate court. It expressly limited the Court's original jurisdiction to "cases affecting ambassadors, other public ministers and consuls, and those in which a state shall be party." Marbury, therefore, had chosen the wrong court in which to originate his case, and the Supreme Court was constitutionally proscribed from granting him a writ.

"It is the essential criterion of appellate jurisdiction," Marshall explained, "that it revises and corrects proceedings in a cause already instituted and does not create that cause." A writ of mandamus, he said, was designed to provide evidence in the discovery phase of a case. It sustains "original action . . . and therefore seems not to belong to appellate but to original jurisdiction."

Marbury's attorney protested, citing a 1789 act of Congress that, among other things, specifically gave the Supreme Court power to issue writs of mandamus. Marshall and the justices were ready with the most explosive part of their decision. As lawyers for both sides gasped in surprise, Marshall declared part of the 1789 act of Congress unconstitutional:

"The authority . . . given to the Supreme Court by the act [of Congress] . . . to issue writs of *mandamus* . . . appears not to be warranted by the Constitution. The particular phraseology of the Constitution of the United States confirms and strengthens the principle . . . that a law repugnant to the Constitution is void; and that courts as well as other departments are bound by that instrument."[7]

With those words Chief Justice John Marshall effectively amended the Constitution by assuming the power of judicial review for the Supreme Court, allowing it to void an act of Congress it deemed unconstitutional. Nowhere in the Constitution had the framers written "that a law repugnant to the Constitution is void" or given the Supreme Court power to void such a law. That the decision went unchallenged was the result of Marshall's brilliant political strategy: he and the associate justices were evidently aware they were overstepping the bounds of the Constitution, and the Chief Justice worded the decision in terms that left all parties in the case—the President, the secretary of state, Congress, William Marbury, and even the Court itself—unable to respond with either defiance *or* compliance. They could decry it, they could try to take steps around it, even try to amend the Constitution and annul it, but they could not defy it, because Marshall gave them nothing to defy.

Designed as a *fait accompli*, the decision demanded nothing of anyone and left no opportunity for anyone to respond. It set a precedent without affording any opportunity to challenge—and without depriving any of the principals of redress through constitutional action. Marbury could still ask for his writ from a lower court. Congress could rewrite the judiciary act to conform with constitutional restrictions. And the President could, if he chose, reinstate Marbury or at least stop trying to remove judges from the federal bench without due process. But no one had an avenue to challenge the decision because Marshall had left them none.

In writing the decision Marshall was simply too savvy a politician to make demands he knew the Court could not enforce. So the decision, at one and the same time, asserted that Marbury's status was not contingent on delivery of the commission and avoided ordering the President or secretary of state to deliver it or install Marbury as a justice of the peace. In voiding part of the 1789 act of Congress, the Court said it could not issue the writ of mandamus, which, in turn, left Marbury without the commission to which the Court said he was entitled. So *Marbury v. Madison* had no *immediate* impact beyond the relatively inconsequential appointment—or disappointment—of a low-level justice of the peace, essentially a sinecure.

The long-term effects of *Marbury*, however, were dramatic. It declared both the President and secretary of state guilty of violating the Constitution, and, for the first time, it voided part of an act of Congress. In effect the decision represented another in a growing list of quasi-coups d'état that each branch of government had staged since the inauguration of the first President in 1789. Each coup had altered the shape of the new American government and made the Constitution more elastic without resorting to the tedious process of amending it or the more dramatic process of using military force to renounce it.

President George Washington staged the first such coup in 1789, his first year in office, by sending Treasury Secretary Hamilton to borrow and spend funds without an appropriation or authorization from the House of Representatives as required by the Constitution. Two years later he sent troops to war with Indians in the West without a congressional declaration of war. He later issued a proclamation, then sent troops to crush a legitimate tax protest by farmers in western Pennsylvania, denying them their constitutional rights to redress of grievances. The Constitution gives the President no power to issue proclamations—in effect to legislate by executive order.

Congress staged its share of coups as well. In 1798 it scrapped the Bill of Rights with passage of the Alien and Sedition Acts to crush opposition to and criticism of the government. Later, with President Jefferson's encouragement and consent, Congress passed the Judiciary Act of 1802, removing opposition-party judges in violation of Article III, Section 1, that "judges . . . shall hold their offices during good behavior."

After a decade of unconstitutional assumptions of powers by the executive and legislative branches *Marbury v. Madison* was the first assertion of extraconstitutional powers by the judiciary. Assumption of the right of judicial review and the power to void unconstitutional laws enacted by Congress and signed by the President gave the Supreme Court equal

PÁTERSON

CUSHING

CHASE

MOORE

WASHINGTON

The associate justices of the Supreme Court who, with Chief Justice John Marshall, issued the historic Madison v. Marbury *decision. Clockwise from top left, William Paterson, William Cushing, Samuel Chase (center), Bushrod Washington (George Washington's nephew), and Alfred Moore.*
(FROM *THE LIFE OF JOHN MARSHALL*, BY ALBERT J. BEVERIDGE, VOL. III:128)

power with Congress and the President and, indeed, the power to check the actions of both the legislative and executive branches of government. Since *Marbury* the Supreme Court has voided about 200 federal laws as unconstitutional, but in doing so, it often incurred harsh criticism for overstepping constitutional boundaries into legislation.

Although *Marbury v. Madison* infuriated and frustrated President Jefferson, pressing affairs of state required his immediate attention. Spanish authorities in New Orleans had suddenly closed the port of New Orleans to American trade and provoked an economic and diplomatic crisis. Three thousand ships a year passed through New Orleans, more than half of them flying American colors. In rural areas beyond New Orleans Americans made up more than half the white population. They owned vast sugar and cotton plantations and raised huge herds of cattle on lands stretching beyond the Mississippi across the west country into Texas to the Rio Grande.

Fearful American expansion would extend into Mexico and its rich reserves of gold and silver, Spain closed the port of New Orleans and retroceded the rest of Louisiana to France, whose foreign minister Talleyrand pledged to turn the Appalachians into "an impenetrable wall of brass" with French cannons.[8]

Westerners besieged President Jefferson and Congress with demands for action against Spanish authorities, and Congress called up 50,000 militiamen to prepare an attack.

For Napoléon Bonaparte and France, reacquisition of Louisiana meant control of burgeoning commerce on the Mississippi and a huge territory to develop as a bountiful granary for France. Initially he decided to send 20,000 troops to fortify the territory, build roads, and prepare for mass colonization by French farmers and their families. They, in turn, would transform Louisiana into the motherland's primary source of grain, sugar, cattle, produce, cotton, and natural resources.

When Jefferson assumed the presidency, Napoléon Bonaparte and his advisers assumed that the new President's witless reverence for all things French would permit swift, unimpeded French occupation of Louisiana.

At first Jefferson did little to make Bonaparte question his evaluation. Indeed, more than 30 of the 150 guests he invited to his inauguration dinner in 1801 were French. When, however, Jefferson learned of Spain's retrocession of Louisiana, he suddenly abandoned his romance with Gaul.

"Every eye in the U.S.," Jefferson declared, "is now fixed on this affair of Louisiana. Perhaps nothing since the revolution has produced more uneasy sensations through the body of the nation."[9] Jefferson warned that "the produce of three-eighths of our territory must pass to market" through New Orleans and that the United States would go to war if France took possession of that city.[10]

The French ambassador sent word to Paris that "I am afraid they [the Americans] may strike at Louisiana before we can take it over."[11]

In the fall of 1802 President Jefferson ordered his secretary of war to prepare an assault on New Orleans, sending three artillery and four infantry companies to Fort Adams, near the Spanish border, about forty miles south of Natchez. Before going to war, though, Jefferson decided to demonstrate America's commitment to peace by sending his close friend and disciple James Monroe, the avowed Francophile, as special commissioner to France and Spain to try to settle the issue of Mississippi navigation amicably.[12] Ignoring the Constitution, the President asked for—and obtained—50 million livres, or $9 million, from Congress for Monroe to spend to purchase New Orleans from the French. Jefferson recognized that the purchase was "an act beyond the Constitution" and that the Constitution "made no provision for our holding foreign territory, still less for incorporating foreign territory into our Union."[13]

He nonetheless ordered congressional leaders to approve it "with as little debate as possible. The less we say about constitutional difficulties respecting Louisiana the better. . . . What is necessary for surmounting them must be done *sub-silentio* [under silence]."[14]

Even a few Federalists praised the mission, with Jefferson's longtime foe Alexander Hamilton declaring, "It belongs of right to the United States to regulate the future destiny of North America. The country is ours; ours is the right to its rivers and to all the sources of future opulence, power and happiness."[15] Senator James Ross of Pennsylvania was less patient. "Why not seize what is so essential to us as a nation? When in possession, you will negotiate with more advantage."[16]

Not everyone favored the acquisition, however. "Presently we shall be told we must have Louisiana," said Virginia's Senator S. T. Mason, "then the gold mines of Mexico . . . then Potosi—then Santo Domingo, with their sugar and coffee and all the rest. . . . But what have we to do with the territories of other people? Have we not enough of our own?"[17]

Just as opposition to acquisition of New Orleans seemed to gain momentum, news from France suddenly silenced it: James Monroe had engineered the purchase of the Louisiana territory from France, doubling the size of the nation with some 828,000 additional square miles of land for $15 million, or four cents an acre. At the time the US government was selling federal lands in the wilderness to settlers for an average price of $2 an acre.

As would-be settlers roared their approval, Federalists decried it as unconstitutional—a usurpation of power that would give southern slave states control of the federal government at the expense of commercial interests in the Northeast. Former Secretary of State Timothy Pickering of Massachusetts renewed his call for secession of New England. "The principles of our Revolution point to the remedy. . . . I do not believe in the practicability of a long-continued union."[18]

Senator Uriah Tracy of Connecticut agreed: "I am convinced that the accession of Louisiana will accelerate a division of these states," he wrote to former Secretary of War James McHenry.[19] Tracy's close friend Tapping Reeve, the renowned Connecticut lawyer who had trained Noah Webster and Aaron Burr Jr., among others, had polled area Federalists and found that "all believe we must separate and that this is the most favorable moment."[20]

Chief Justice Marshall purposely remained aloof from the debate over Louisiana to prevent any suspicion of bias ever coloring decisions on the issue that he might have to make in the Supreme Court.

The outrage in the Northeast at the Louisiana Purchase stemmed from evidence that a handful of powerful Virginia planters had already staked out large fertile tracts. With New Orleans as their outlet to world markets, they would work the land with slave labor and have a competitive advantage that would turn the entire Northeast and its small, family-run farms into an economic backwater. Vice President Burr threw his lot in with the northerners. President Jefferson had already announced he would choose a new vice presidential running mate for his second term, and Burr had countered by announcing his candidacy for governor of his home state of New York. He now pledged that if elected, he would unite New York with the New England states to form a new northern confederacy.

On October 20, 1803, Republicans silenced their opposition with a twenty-four-to-seven vote in favor of the Louisiana Purchase. Two months later, to the cheers of millions, the US government took possession of the territory, including the vital Mississippi River waterway and the gateway to world trade in the port of New Orleans.

President Jefferson then turned his attention back to the Supreme Court, vowing to throw John Marshall and other Federalists off the bench and strip the court of powers of judicial review claimed in *Marbury v. Madison.* "Nothing in the Constitution has given them the right . . . to decide what laws are constitutional and what not," Jefferson raged. Such powers "would make the judiciary a despotic branch."[21]

Jefferson's legislative puppet, Senate Majority Leader William Branch Giles of Virginia, boasted openly of his party's lust for control of the federal bench. "We want your offices for the purpose of giving them to men who will fill them better," he told freshman Senator John Quincy Adams of Massachusetts, the son of former President John Adams. Giles then warned Marshall and other justices that if they "should dare, as they had, to declare acts of Congress unconstitutional . . . it was the undoubted right of the House to impeach them and of the Senate to remove them for giving such opinions."[22]

Giles called removal by impeachment "nothing more than a declaration by Congress to this effect: 'You hold dangerous opinions, and if you are suffered to carry them into effect you will work destruction of the nation.'" An independent judiciary, he added scornfully, "is nothing more nor less than an attempt to establish an aristocratic despotism in themselves."[23]

Adams wrote warning his father that Jefferson would continue his campaign against the judiciary until the Republicans have "swept the supreme judicial bench clean at a stroke."[24]

To avoid inciting too many Federalists, however, Jefferson disguised his public remarks as "judiciary reform," aimed only at ousting "incompetent" federal judges. To rally public opinion, Jefferson selected as his first target Judge John Pickering of New Hampshire, a chronically intoxicated Federalist whose often irrational decisions provoked charges by Federalists and Republicans alike that he was insane. Asked whether insanity was an adequate cause for impeachment and removal from office, Jefferson snapped, "If the facts . . . of his intoxication . . . are proven that will be sufficient cause for removal without further inquiry."[25]

Marching in lockstep under Jefferson's orders, House Republicans impeached Pickering. Although the judge had plunged into insanity and could not appear at his Senate trial, the prosecution moved forward with its case. Massachusetts Senator John Quincy Adams protested, "The most persevering and determined opposition is made against hearing evidence to prove the man insane, only from fear that if insanity should be proved, he cannot be convicted of high crimes and misdemeanors by acts of decisive madness."[26]

The Senate's Republican majority nonetheless convicted Pickering and ordered his removal from the bench. New Jersey's Federalist Senator and former Speaker of the House Jonathan Dayton shouted in protest, denouncing the proceedings as "a mere mockery of a trial." John Quincy Adams shot to his feet to agree—only to be called out of order. Adams threatened to continue speaking "until my mouth was stopped by force."[27]

Delaware Senator Samuel White then warned, "It will not hereafter be necessary that a man should be guilty of high crimes and misdemeanors to render him liable to removal from office by impeachment, but a conviction upon any facts stated in articles exhibited against him will be sufficient."[28]

As Jefferson's program for "judicial reform" gained momentum, the President unleashed his political attack dogs on the Supreme Court. "The judges of the Supreme Court must fall," declared New Hampshire Senator William Plumer, a Jefferson ally. "They are denounced by the Executive [President] as well as the House. They must be removed; they are obnoxious unyielding men; why should they remain to awe and embarrass the administration? Men of more flexible nerves can be found to succeed them."[29]

Delaware Representative James A. Bayard, whose vote (or nonvote) had ceded victory to Jefferson in the presidential election, agreed that removal of Federalist justices from the Supreme Court "has been an object on which Mr. Jefferson has long resolved . . . since he has been in office."[30] Jefferson and his aides left no doubts that Chief Justice John Marshall was their primary target for removal because of his audacious assumption of power in *Marbury v. Madison.*

Before they could act, Associate Justice Alfred Moore resigned, giving Jefferson a chance to name a Republican to the court and influence its legal complexion without impeachment proceedings. He chose thirty-two-year-old South Carolina Judge William Johnson, a Princeton graduate who had studied law under South Carolina Federalist Charles Cotesworth Pinckney.

To Jefferson's dismay, Johnson immediately fell under the spell of Marshall's personality and brilliant legal reasoning, and the South Carolinian quickly metamorphosed from "a zealous democrat" to a champion of union, voting with Marshall in all twenty-six cases they heard that winter.

"Everyone who knew that great man [Marshall]," Federalist Oliver Wolcott laughed, "knew that he possessed to an extraordinary degree the faculty of putting his own ideas in the minds of others, unconsciously to them."[31]

Rather than risk political backlash by trying to impeach the enormously popular Chief Justice, Jefferson sent congressional Republicans after the controversial Associate Justice Samuel Chase of Maryland. A signer of the Declaration of Independence with Jefferson, Chase's acerbic personality had earned him enemies across the entire political spectrum.

As early as 1766 the *Maryland Gazette Extraordinary* called Chase—
then only twenty-five years old—"a busy, reckless incendiary . . . a foul-
mouthed and inflaming son of discord and faction, a common disturber
of the public tranquility."[32]

A member of the Continental Congress during the Revolution, Chase
had invested in a scheme to corner the market on flour, and voters turned
him out of office. A Federalist governor later appointed Chase to the
Maryland judiciary, and he served as Chief Justice of the Maryland General Court for five years until President Washington appointed him to
the US Supreme Court in 1796.

An outspoken critic of Jeffersonian Republicans, Chase had been
serving on a circuit court when he told a Baltimore grand jury that "the
bulk of mankind are governed by their passions and not by reason." He
blasted repeal of the Judiciary Act of 1801, saying it would combine with
proposals for universal (white) male suffrage in Maryland to "take away
all security for property and personal liberty" and convert America into
"a mobocracy, the worst of all popular governments."[33]

Chase went further, attacking the core principles of Jeffersonian republicanism and, indeed, the Declaration of Independence he himself
had signed. "The declarations, respecting the natural rights of man—that
men, in a state of society, are entitled to enjoy equal liberty and equal
rights—have brought this mighty mischief on us," Chase barked at the
grand jury. "I fear that it will rapidly progress until peace and order, freedom and property shall be destroyed."[34]

Jefferson believed Chase's statement warranted impeachment and
trial for "high crimes and misdemeanors" under the Constitution, but
he stepped carefully—to avoid grounds for his own impeachment. The
Constitution gave the House of Representatives sole powers to impeach,
and Jefferson chose his words and syntax cautiously in writing to Republican House Leader Joseph H. Nicholson of Maryland:

> You must have heard of the extraordinary charge of Chase to the grand
> jury at Baltimore. Ought this seditious and official attack on the princi-
> ples of our Constitution . . . go unpunished? And to whom so pointedly

A gruff, outspoken Marylander, Associate Justice Samuel Chase was the first and last Supreme Court justice to face impeachment for his political views—a target of President Thomas Jefferson's effort to dismantle the Supreme Court. (LIBRARY OF CONGRESS)

as yourself will the public look for the necessary measures? I ask these questions for your consideration. For myself, it is better that I should not interfere.[35]

On March 12, 1804, less than an hour after the US Senate had convicted Judge Pickering—and less than two months after Chief Justice John Marshall had handed down the *Marbury v. Madison* ruling—the House voted to impeach Justice Samuel Chase.

"I have just received the articles of impeachment against Judge Chase," the Chief Justice complained to his brother James Markham Marshall. "They are sufficient to alarm the friends of a pure and, of course, an independent judiciary, if among those who rule our land there are any of that description."[36]

Marshall sent word to Chase of his support, calling the House action "a very extraordinary ground for impeachment. . . . The present doctrine seems to be that a judge giving a legal opinion contrary to the opinion of the legislature is liable to impeachment." Marshall argued that rather than try to remove judges who declare laws unconstitutional, the legislature should simply rewrite the laws to make them constitutional. Marshall knew, however, that the battle Chase and the federal judiciary now faced was not with the legislature—it was with Thomas Jefferson.

"The simple truth is Mr. Jefferson has been determined from the first to have a judiciary as well as a legislature that would second the views of the executive," declared Alexander Hamilton's *New York-Evening Post* under a headline INQUISITORIAL COMMITTEE AT WASHINGTON.

> Justice is not the object. Party rage is still unsatisfied. Our courts are filled by Federalist judges. Here is the mighty crime. Here the high misdemeanor. . . . The bench in short is to be cleared of its present incumbents, no matter by what means, and filled with men subservient to the views of the powers that be . . . at the expense of all that renders a court of justice respectable.[37]

The Chase impeachment left Chief Justice John Marshall both outraged and despondent. Anticipating Jefferson's assault on the judiciary, he wrote to Charles Cotesworth Pinckney, his friend from XYZ days: "There is so much in the political world to wound honest men who have honorable feelings that I am disgusted with it and begin to see things and indeed human nature through a much more gloomy medium than I once thought possible."[38]

Marshal had good reason to be gloomy. His arch enemy Thomas Jefferson was about to emasculate the nation's Supreme Court and restore tyranny in the United States.

CHAPTER 12

❧∰❧

A Deadly Interview

"OYEZ! OYEZ! OYEZ!"* A VOICE RANG OUT IN THE US SENATE ON the morning of February 9, 1805. "All persons are commanded to keep silence on pain of imprisonment, while the grand inquest of the nation is exhibiting to the Senate of the United States, sitting as a court of impeachment against Samuel Chase, Associate Justice of the Supreme Court of the United States."[1]

Some 300 spectators had jammed the Senate chamber—Chief Justice John Marshall and 4 associate justices of the Supreme Court, all 34 senators, more than 100 members of the House, Jefferson's cabinet, the diplomatic corps, newspaper reporters, publishers, and Washington's social elite. Everyone but the President himself was there, although his brooding presence hovered over the assemblage.

When all were seated, silence suddenly enveloped the hall. All heads turned as one to stare . . . wide-eyed . . . in disbelief . . .

A short, nattily dressed man had entered and was striding down the aisle to the front bench: Aaron Burr Jr.

Still vice president of the United States and President of the Senate, Burr had come to preside over the trial of an associate justice of the US

---

* "Hear ye," from plural imperative of middle English verb *oir*, "to hear."

Supreme Court for high crimes and misdemeanors. Wanted for murder in two states, Burr had shot and killed former US Treasury secretary Alexander Hamilton in a duel less than seven months earlier in Weehauken, New Jersey, across the Hudson River from New York City.

Massachusetts Senator John Quincy Adams gasped as he watched Burr march down the aisle. "The coroner's inquest found a verdict of willful murder," Adams confided to his diary. "The grand jury . . . found a bill against him for murder. Under all these circumstances Mr. Burr appears and takes his seat as president of the Senate of the United States."[2]

Burr's appearance stunned New Hampshire Senator William Plumer. "We are indeed fallen on evil times," he lamented. "The high office of President is filled by an infidel, that of Vice President by a murderer."[3] A Federalist newspaper noted Plumer's comments, adding that courts in earlier times would "arraign the murderer before the judge, but now we arraign the judge before the murderer."[4]

Not everyone agreed. Republican Senator Robert Wright of Maryland compared Burr's duel with Hamilton to David's combat with Goliath, arguing that Federalists had condemned the duel only "because *our* David had slain their Goliath of Federalism."[5]

Twenty-eight years earlier Colonel Alexander Hamilton and Colonel Aaron Burr Jr. had been comrades in arms at Valley Forge and Monmouth, then worked as colleagues in New York's courts of law—sometimes together, sometimes against each other. Even as personal ambitions for higher office and political power pitted them against each other in opposite political parties, Federalist Hamilton and Republican Burr remained friends on a personal if not a political level.

Their relationship first began to sour after Burr unseated Hamilton's father-in-law from the US Senate in the 1791 elections and rose to the top ranks of the Republican Party. Just as Burr's political star was ascending, Hamilton's began to fall, as hints of his marital scandal forced the Treasury secretary to resign from the federal government.

The Hamilton-Burr ties frayed further when Burr showed up at Hamilton's door as a second for Virginia's former Senator James Monroe.

Hamilton had challenged Monroe to a duel for exposing Hamilton's adulterous relationship with Mrs. James Reynolds and all but destroying the Treasury Secretary's political career. All three men—Burr, Monroe, and Hamilton—had fought alongside each other in battle, however, and Burr succeeded in convincing Hamilton to withdraw his challenge.

Hamilton's suspicions festered nonetheless, and by the time Burr challenged Jefferson for the presidency, Hamilton's alienation had metamorphosed into outright paranoia. Intent on destroying Burr's political career as he imagined Burr had destroyed his, Hamilton engineered Jefferson's 1801 presidential victory in the House with a barrage of hate-filled letters to Federalist congressmen that concluded by calling Burr a man "without principles."[6]

Burr's challenge to Jefferson in the 1800 presidential election earned him Jefferson's lasting enmity as well and cost him a second term as vice president. Although his career in the federal government appeared at an end, Burr sought to retain political power at the state level when his friend New York's George Clinton vacated the New York governorship to run with Jefferson in the 1804 election.

After Burr announced for governor, however, Hamilton warned voters that Burr espoused "Jacobin principles," had no ethics "either in morals or in politics," and was "unfit to govern."[7] After Burr lost the election 30,829 to 22,139,[8] Burr allies complained, "If General Hamilton had not opposed Colonel Burr, I have very little doubt but he would have been elected governor of New York."[9]

With only ten months remaining as vice president, forty-eight-year-old Aaron Burr faced as precipitous an end to his political career as Hamilton had suffered after the Reynolds scandal. Burr, however, had done nothing to deserve his fate. He had challenged Jefferson for the presidency in a legitimate election in 1800, then campaigned for the New York governorship in another legitimate election in 1804—only to have Hamilton frustrate his ambitions in both, for no evident reason.

Burr's fury had festered as much as Hamilton's. A war of words followed, with Hamilton calling Burr "despicable" and Burr demanding an explanation. Instead of responding directly, Hamilton, who was the same age as Burr, seemed to enjoy goading his adversary:

"'Tis evident that the phrase . . . admits of infinite shades from very light to very dark." Hamilton taunted Burr, telling him to "see the matter in the same light with me. If not, I can only regret the circumstance and must abide by the consequence."[10]

Burr did not see the matter in the same light, and five days later, on June 27, the war of words turned into a war of weapons. Distraught by the undeserved attacks of both Hamilton and Jefferson, Burr refused to tolerate further assaults. He had, after all, served his country valiantly in the military arena, had continued his service to the nation in the political arena, and had received nothing but constant attacks on his character. To put a stop to them, he challenged Hamilton to a duel.

On July 11, 1804, both men crossed the Hudson River at sunrise in small boats that took them from the lower end of Manhattan Island (near present day Greenwich Village) to Weehauken, New Jersey (opposite present-day 42nd Street). After climbing a steep path up the sheer rock cliff, they reached a plateau, where, just after 7 a.m., the two heroic Men of Monmouth, once comrades in arms, stood thirty feet apart, prepared to kill each other for reasons neither man could fully explain.

Indeed, as their seconds were working out details of the duel during the previous two weeks, the two men had socialized at several dinner parties. Only a week earlier they had celebrated July Fourth together at a banquet at Fraunces Tavern, where Hamilton sang a popular drinking song solo before the Society of the Cincinnati, a fraternal organization of Revolutionary War officers.

Under accepted rules of dueling Hamilton had the option to fire first but said he bore no ill will toward Colonel Burr—"as distinct from political opposition." He therefore intended to "throw away my first fire and I have thoughts even of reserving my second fire and thus giving a double opportunity to Colonel Burr to pause and to reflect." Hamilton conceded that "I shall hazard much and can possibly gain nothing from the interview."[11]

In one of the most pointless confrontations in American history, Revolutionary War heroes Alexander Hamilton and Aaron Burr Jr. stand ready to kill each other for reasons neither man could fully explain. Once comrades in arms, the two had celebrated July 4 together at Fraunces Tavern a week earlier. (LIBRARY OF CONGRESS)

Hamilton fired, his bullet lodging in a tree limb above Burr's head. Burr then fired, intending only to wound Hamilton, he said, but the bullet penetrated Hamilton's right rib cage, tore through his liver and diaphragm, and lodged in his spine by his second lumbar vertebra.

Hamilton's seconds carried the wounded man down the cliff side to the boat, rowed him across the Hudson, and carried him to his home, where he died the following day. He left a grief-stricken widow and seven hysterical children, who had had no hint of the impending duel until Hamilton's seconds brought his nearly lifeless body home. He spent most of his last hours pleading with churchmen to give him holy communion. Absent membership in any church and given his violation of both church and civil law by participating in a duel, they refused—until he pleaded his need to die a Christian for the sake of his wife and children. A Protestant bishop relented and gave him holy communion.

In the largest such procession New York had seen since the death of George Washington, Hamilton loyalists staged a military funeral with full honors. A military detail led his coffin, followed by his horse, its boots reversed in the stirrups, stomping uneasily down Broadway to Trinity Church at the head of Wall Street, where he lies today. Ironically, Hamilton's idolaters buried him on July 14, the anniversary of the destruction of the Bastille Prison in Paris and the beginning of the French Revolution, whose excesses Hamilton despised as a mockery of the American Revolution.

As Hamilton had lain dying, Burr inquired about his fallen rival's condition and wanted to visit him but found himself more than ever the target of attacks by Hamilton supporters, who now labeled Burr an assassin. Some accused him of having hunted down his victim and shooting him without warning.

Encouraged by Jefferson, *New York Citizen* editor James Cheetham launched a furious editorial attack on the vice president. "Wrapt up in himself to appease his resentment and to gratify his ambition," Cheetham wrote, "he is capable of wading through the blood of his fellow citizens and laughing at the lamentations of widows and orphans."[12]

The fury of the attacks shocked Burr. "Thousands of absurd falsehoods are circulated with industry," he railed. "All our intemperate and unprincipled Jacobins who have been for years reviling Hamilton are the most vehement in his praise . . . and malice to me."[13]

Although they had no jurisdiction over crimes committed in New Jersey, Jefferson's Republican prosecutors in New York City called a coroner's jury and badgered it into indicting Burr for violating New York's law against dueling. Although dueling was legal in New Jersey, that state's Republican prosecutors fabricated a charge of murder, and Burr fled south to the seclusion of a friend's estate on St. Simon's Island off the Georgia coast. A few weeks later he traveled incognito to the Capitol in Washington, where he had enough supporters to prevent state authorities from trying to arrest him.

Not everyone mourned Hamilton.

"Although I have long since forgotten this arch enemy," John Adams growled, "vice, folly, and villainy are not to be forgotten because the guilty wretch repented in his dying moments."

> Nor am I obliged by any principles of morality or religion to suffer my character to lie under infamous calumnies, because the author of them, with a pistol bullet through his spinal marrow, died a penitent. . . . Born on a speck more obscure than Corsica . . . with infinitely less courage and capacity than Bonaparte, he would, in my opinion, if I had not controlled the fury of his vanity . . . he would have involved it in all the bloodshed and distractions of foreign and civil war.[14]

Jefferson was even more pleased than Adams with the outcome of the duel, which removed two of the political opponents he despised most from the political scene. With an obsequious Republican majority in Congress, the President faced no evident political opposition—except John Marshall and the Supreme Court.

A lawyer himself, Jefferson knew Marshall could—and probably would—use the *Marbury v. Madison* decision to limit the President's assertions of power over American government. Jefferson, therefore, decided to destroy Marshall and the Court. He began his assault with an attack on the Court's most vulnerable member: Samuel Chase.

As the Chase trial began, Burr seemed oblivious to the response of spectators to his presence. Although Federalists shunned him, Republicans—including President Jefferson, of all people—flocked about him, flattered him, and curried his attention. Jefferson invited the vice president to dine at the presidential mansion, then filled three important posts in Louisiana's new territorial government with Burr's stepson, brother-in-law, and closest personal friend. Although he had rejected Burr as his vice presidential running mate, Jefferson had staked much of his political future on the outcome of the Chase trial and hoped Burr would steer it in a favorable direction.

Burr, however, proved a superb presiding officer, guiding the course of witness testimony and attorney questioning with dispassion.

Before the trial began he ordered the Senate chamber "fitted up in a style beyond anything which has ever appeared in the country," according to Connecticut Senator Uriah Tracy.[15] Burr ordered a raised chair for himself placed on center stage, between two squared-off areas, surrounded by waist-high fence-like partitions—one for House managers, or prosecutors, the other for Chase and his defense attorneys.

The President's chair overlooked two rows of thirty-four desks covered in crimson cloth for the senators, while members of the House sat behind them on three tiered rows of benches covered with green cloth. Burr ordered a special area built for the President's cabinet and a temporary gallery for women. In the main spectator's gallery sat some of Washington's most important dignitaries, including Chief Justice John Marshall and the other members of the Supreme Court.

The House had served Chase with eight articles of impeachment. Four dealt with his procedures in various trials, one with his decision in the Fries trial, two with the Callender trial, and the last with his "intemperate," "inflammatory," and "indecent" charge to the Baltimore grand jury.

The trial lasted just over three weeks, from February 4 to March 1, 1805, with one day's interruption for the counting of Electoral College votes for the presidential election. To Aaron Burr fell the galling task of announcing the results and proclaiming Thomas Jefferson and George Clinton "duly elected to the respective offices of President and Vice President of the United States for four years commencing on 4th March next."[16]

As the trial of Samuel Chase continued, many senators grew uneasy.

"This prosecution," Senator John Quincy Adams of Massachusetts concluded after ten days, "is not very consistent with my ideas of impartial justice."[17] Adams complained that the articles "contained in themselves a virtual impeachment not only of Mr. Chase, but of all the judges of the Supreme Court from the first establishment of the national judiciary."[18]

Philadelphia attorney Joseph Hopkinson opened the formal Chase defense with an emotional appeal: "We appear for an ancient and infirm man, whose better days have been worn in the service of that country which now degrades him."

Hopkinson argued that none of the articles of impeachment had charged Chase with treason, bribery, or corruption, and "it is well understood and defined in law that . . . a misdemeanor or a crime . . . is an act committed or omitted in violation of a public law."[19] The Constitution, he insisted, defined high crimes and misdemeanors as indictable offenses.

A second defense counsel reinforced Hopkinson's argument. Although he admitted that Chase had used "unusual, rude and contemptuous expressions" in the Callender trial, he argued that such language represented only "a violation of the principle of politeness [rather] than the principles of law . . . the want of decorum [rather] than a high crime and misdemeanor."[20]

Chase admitted having used the word "damn," but, as his counsel said with a smile, the word had multiple meanings, "supplying frequently the place of the word 'very' . . . connected with subjects most pleasing; thus we say indiscriminately 'a very good' or 'a damned good bottle of wine,' 'a damned good dinner,' or 'a damned clever fellow.'"[21]

As for his "indecent" language to the Baltimore grand jury, Chase protested that no law existed forbidding a judge to express his opinions to a grand jury and that, absent a law, he had committed no crime, let alone a high crime or misdemeanor. He had simply exercised his right as an American citizen to express his political views. Citing instance after instance, he demonstrated the longstanding "practice in this country" of judges expressing themselves from the bench.[22]

"Is it not lawful for an aged patriot of the Revolution to warn his fellow citizens of dangers by which he supposes their liberties and happiness to be threatened?" a Chase defense attorney asked the Senate jury. "What law forbids [judges] to exercise these rights? . . . We contend that this is a criminal prosecution for offenses committed in the discharge of high official duties."[23]

Both prosecution and defense made short work of the four articles dealing with breach of procedures, with Chase admitting that he probably made procedural errors but that they had been "honest errors" with no malice intended and certainly not impeachable "high crimes and misdemeanors." Court procedures, his attorneys pointed out, varied widely from state to state, depending on whether they had been derived from common law, state laws, or British laws. The nation was still too young to have established uniform courtroom procedures.

Prosecutors charged that in fining and jailing Callender for violating the Sedition Law, Chase had violated the editor-publisher's First Amendment rights to freedom of the press. When the defense called the Chief Justice to testify, Marshall pointed out that the object of a criminal trial is to determine the guilt of the defendant, not the constitutionality of the law.

"The counsel [for Callender] persisted in arguing the constitutionality of the sedition law," Marshall testified, "in which they were constantly repressed by Judge Chase." Asked whether Judge Chase's conduct was "tyrannical, overbearing, and oppressive," as the prosecution had charged, Marshall replied, "When the counsel attempted to show the unconstitutionality of the Sedition Law, Judge Chase observed that it was a point which should not go before the jury, and he would not permit a discussion upon it."[24]

Marshall's testimony added weight to the defense attorney's argument that Chase had simply enforced the law against "one of the most dangerous libels ever published." If the courts do not protect the public against "base calumniators," defense counsel warned, the public "will become their own avengers. And to the bludgeon, the sword, or the pistol they will resort for that purpose."[25]

The prosecution turned to Chase's having sentenced Pennsylvania auctioneer John Fries to death for what President Jefferson—vice president at the time—had called legitimate tax protests. The Chase defense cited Fries's own words, however, as proof that he had led a rebellion and committed treason. In any case President Adams had pardoned Fries and his codefendants and made the case moot.

The lead prosecutor, Virginia Representative John Randolph, thought he was striking a fatal blow at the defense by arguing that many types of offenses by public officials fall outside the category of *criminal* offenses but within the sphere of *impeachable* offenses. His argument undermined his own case, however. "The wildest opinions have been advanced," he charged, "that to be impeachable, it must be indictable."

> It is possible that . . . a president of the United States may endeavor to influence Congress by holding out threats or inducements to them. . . . The hope of an office may be held out to a Senator; and I think it cannot be doubted that for this the President would be liable to impeachment, although there is no positive law forbidding it.[26]

Chase allies in the galleries and on the Senate floor hooted Randolph down, reminding everyone within earshot of Judge John Pickering's impeachment trial. After Pickering's removal from the bench, President Jefferson appointed one of the witnesses against Pickering to fill Pickering's seat, another to be clerk of the court, and a third to be district attorney in the same district.

After Burr gaveled the proceedings to order, the trial heard the last of the fifty-one witnesses, and opposing counsels summed up their arguments. John Randolph's histrionics destroyed the prosecution's chances of success with what Senator John Quincy Adams described as

> a speech of about two hours and a half without order, connection or argument, consisting altogether of the most hackneyed commonplaces of popular declamation, mingled with panegyrics and invectives . . . [and] much distortion of face and contortion of body . . . with occasional pauses for recollection and continual complaints about having lost his notes.[27]

New Hampshire Senator William Plumer agreed, calling the summation "devoid of argument, method or consistency . . . replete with invective and even vulgarity . . . a weak, feeble, and deranged harangue. After he sat down he threw his feet upon the table, distorted his features, and assumed an appearance as disgusting as his harangue."[28]

On March 1, 1805, spectators squeezed into every inch of Senate space to hear the verdict. Vice President Burr took firm command of the explosive situation, calling out firmly, "The sergeants-at-arms will face the spectators and seize and commit to prison the first person who makes the smallest noise or disturbance."

A tomb-like silence filled the hall.

"The secretary will read the first article of impeachment."

When the secretary's monotone halted, Burr's voice boomed:

"Senator Adams of Massachusetts! How say you? Is Samuel Chase the respondent guilty of high crimes and misdemeanors as charged in the article or not?"

"Not guilty!" Adams's voice rang out.

Other Federalists echoed Adams's words.

Then the Republicans had their turn—and one, two, then three Republicans shocked Jefferson by also declaring Chase not guilty.

As a body, the US Senate had rudely rejected the President's attempt to remove a justice of the Supreme Court because of his political views. Even Virginia's arch-Republican William Branch Giles, a Jefferson intimate, cried out, "Not guilty!"

"It appears that there is not a constitutional majority of votes finding Samuel Chase, Esquire, guilty of any one article," Vice President Burr announced. "It therefore becomes my duty to declare that Samuel Chase, Esquire, stands acquitted of all articles exhibited by the House of Representatives against him."[29]

New Hampshire's Republican Senator Plumer wrote to his son:

The greatest and most important trial ever held in this nation has terminated justly. The venerable judge whose head bears the frost of seventy winters is honorably acquitted. I never witnessed in any place such a display of learning as the counsel for the accused exhibited. Impeachment is a farce which will not be tried again.[30]

Despite the loathing that some Senators harbored for Burr, all agreed with Plumer that "Mr. Burr has certainly, on the whole, done himself, the Senate, and the nation honor by the dignified manner in which he has presided over this high and numerous court."[31]

Massachusetts Senator Samuel Taggart, a Federalist clergyman, agreed:

> Burr has displayed much ability, and since the first day, I have seen nothing of partiality. I could almost forgive Burr for any less crime than the blood of Hamilton for his decision, dignity, firmness, and impartiality with which he presided in this trial. He is undoubtedly one of the best presiding officers I ever witnessed.[32]

Aaron Burr Jr., had, in fact, helped the Senate crush an attempted Jefferson coup d'état. The President had been prepared to remove every justice with opposing political views and put control of the entire federal government—the executive, legislative, and judiciary branches—in the hands of a single political party, as Jacobins had done in France.

The Chase victory represented more than a personal triumph. It was a triumph for the entire Supreme Court and, indeed, for the Constitution. And it was a triumph for Chief Justice John Marshall, who left the Senate chamber after the Chase trial ready to assert himself as the most powerful jurist in the United States—defender of the Constitution and the Union against assault, from whatever the source.

Neither Jefferson's defeat nor Chase's victory were all-encompassing, however. Although the judiciary had ensured its independence from abuses of power by both legislative and executive branches, it had not achieved independence from the will of the people. Evidently chastened by his experience, Chase now recognized—with Marshall and the other justices—that although Congress could not arbitrarily remove a justice from the bench, it could impeach him and bring him before the bar of justice in the US Senate for a thorough and humiliating examination of his conduct on the bench.

Justice Chase would serve another six years until his death in 1811. He became a model of decorum, never again uttering "unusual, rude and contemptuous expressions" in court, as he had in the Callender case. Marshall convinced Chase and the other justices that public political statements seldom changed opinions and served only to provoke questions about the objectivity of judicial decisions.

Marshall pointed out that the President and members of Congress were responsible to the people who elected them and, therefore, had a responsibility to speak out on political issues. Members of the Court, however, were responsible to the Constitution—and only to the Constitution—and were duty bound to limit their public expressions to interpretations of that document.

The Chase victory chastened many Republicans as well. An unspoken truce between leaders of the three branches of government produced a prolonged, albeit uneasy calm in the capital. Even President Jefferson seemed to embrace political peace, writing to Marshall the day after the Chase acquittal to ask the Chief Justice to attend the forthcoming presidential inauguration and administer the oath of office for the President's second term. As Jefferson penned his invitation, the Republican he despised most—Aaron Burr Jr.—stood where Jefferson would take the presidential oath two days later and delivered one of the most moving addresses in US Senate history.

Speaking extemporaneously without notes for about twenty minutes, Burr apologized if, in fulfilling what he believed to be his duties as President of the Senate, he had ever wounded the feelings of any individual members. He assured his colleagues, however, that he had favored "no party, no cause, no friend [and] had always tried to be fair and impartial." He confessed his deep love for his country and its Constitution and called the Senate "a sanctuary" and "citadel of law, of order, and of liberty.

"It is here," he proclaimed, "it is here, in this exalted refuge—here, if anywhere, [that] resistance will be made to the storms of political frenzy and the silent arts of corruption."[33]

According to the *Washington Federalist*, the vice president "then adverted to those affecting sentiments which attended a fixed separation—a dissolution, perhaps forever, of those associations which he hoped had been mutually satisfactory."

> He consoled himself, however . . . that, though they separated, they would
> be engaged in the common cause of disseminating principles of freedom

and social order. He should always regard the proceedings of that body with interest and with solicitude. He should feel for their honor and the national honor so intimately connected with it, and took his leave with expressions of personal respect and with prayers and good wishes.[34]

With that, Aaron Burr Jr. resigned as vice president of the United States. New York Senator Samuel Latham Mitchell, a Jeffersonian Republican with little love for Burr, described the rest to his wife:

When Mr. Burr had concluded, he descended from the chair and in a dignified manner walked to the door. . . . On this, the firmness . . . of many of the senators gave way, and they burst into tears. There was a solemn and silent weeping for perhaps five minutes. . . . For my own part, I never experienced anything of the kind so affecting as this parting scene.[35]

The *Washington Federalist* described the "extraordinary emotions" that Burr's farewell had provoked: "The whole Senate was in tears and so unmanned that it was half an hour before they could recover themselves."[36] After Burr had left, the Senate voted unanimously for a resolution thanking Burr for "the impartiality, integrity and ability with which he had presided in the Senate."[37]

❧

WITH BURR'S FAREWELL, THE CURTAIN FELL ON THE WASHINGTON POLITICAL scene for Easter recess, its players emotionally spent. Congress and the Supreme Court adjourned, and Chief Justice John Marshall returned home to Richmond to attend his wife Polly. She was still suffering the effects of childbirth the previous January of Edward Carrington, their fourth son—actually the tenth child born to the Marshalls, but they had lost four.

As Polly's condition deteriorated, Marshall assumed all her household chores and oversaw the servants. With the indefatigable Robin Spurlock at his side, he walked to and from the market each day, buying food and other necessities. To avoid recognition, he took to wearing old, often torn work clothes. Although friendly to all and always willing to make "farm talk" about crops and weather, he sought anonymity in public, avoiding attention—and especially discussions about politics and the law.

Once, he appeared in such shabby clothes that a young dandy, new to Richmond, offered him a tip to carry a huge turkey to the gentleman's nearby home. Without a word of objection, Marshall accepted the tip and carried the bird to the young man's house as the usually voluble Robin followed behind at a distance—aghast and, for once, not knowing what to do or say.

After presiding over the circuit courts in Richmond and Raleigh in late spring, John Marshall took Polly to their summer home at Oak Hill to reunite with their oldest sons and their families. "My wife continues in wretched health," Marshall reported later. "Her nervous system is so affected that she cannot sit in a room while a person walks across the floor." When Marshall entered the house, he removed his shoes and put on slippers to avoid disturbing her. Her illness forced her withdrawal from social contact with everyone but her immediate family.

∽∾

WHEN MARSHALL RETURNED TO WASHINGTON IN 1806 FOR THE SUPREME Court's February term, the uneasy truce between the White House, Congress, and Court still held, with neither the President nor his congressional vassals willing to issue a direct challenge to judiciary independence or power. Instead, Jefferson adopted an indirect approach, with plans to install loyal Republicans on the Court as each current justice vacated his seat. He would not get his next chance until the fall, when Federalist Justice William Patterson of New Jersey died at the age of sixty-one. At the urging of Secretary of State James Madison, the President replaced Patterson with New York Supreme Court Judge Brockhorst Livingston, a staunch Republican who had been one of Madison's classmates at Princeton College.

To Jefferson's perpetual dismay, Livingston formed an instant bond with Marshall, whose warmth, constant good humor, and deep understanding and command of law won Livingston's fealty as it had that of Jefferson's previous appointee William Johnson. In the more than 400 cases they would hear together, Livingston would disagree with the Chief Justice only eight times.

Like Marshall, Livingston was "able and independent" on the bench—"luminous, decisive, earnest and impressive," according to Justice Joseph Story. Socially he and Marshall were two of a kind—both high-spirited and with "great good humor."[38] Sharing the same lodgings, the same recreation, and the same table at breakfast and dinner produced all but unshakable ties. Marshall had been raised "on Federalism and Madeira," according to Justice Story, and he soon had other justices reveling over the same diet.

In 1807 the Republican Congress gave Jefferson yet another chance to change the political complexion of the Court by filling the judicial needs of three new states—Kentucky, Tennessee, and Ohio. Jefferson responded by appointing Thomas Todd, who had been Chief Justice of the Kentucky supreme court. A fervent populist Republican, Todd had assailed the federal judiciary for favoring eastern land speculators. "A great part of the lands here are claimed by non-residents," he fumed to Kentucky Senator John Breckenridge.

> Numberless disputes will arise . . . they will bring their suits in the federal court . . . [and] appeal to the Supreme Court. The distance is so great . . . and the indigent circumstances of many of our citizens such that they will not be able to follow the appeal. They must either give up their lands or be forced into an ungenerous and unjust compromise.[39]

Marshall, however, had deep family ties to Kentucky, understood the plight of settlers there, and shared Todd's concerns for their welfare. Far from settling on the opposite pole of the legal world from Marshall—as Jefferson had hoped—Todd quickly joined other members of the court in embracing Marshall's leadership.

"Though bred in a different political school from that of the Chief Justice," Justice Story said of Todd, "he never failed to sustain those great principles of constitutional law on which the security of the Union depends. He never gave up to party what he thought belonged to the country."[40]

Infuriated by his failure to change the high court's political complexion, Jefferson would soon have another opportunity to lash out at one of his perceived enemies: the President had received a letter from General James Wilkinson, accusing former Vice President Aaron Burr of leading a conspiracy in the West to secede from the Union. Once the western territories declared independence, according to Wilkinson, Burr stood ready to lead an army of 10,000 to seize New Orleans, Mexico, and Spanish territories west of the Mississippi and declare himself emperor of a new North American nation.

Wilkinson's accusation would lead to one of the most dramatic court cases in American history, pitting a sitting President against his former vice president, and the Chief Justice of the United States sitting in judgment on both.

CHAPTER 13

The Trial

GENERAL JAMES WILKINSON HAD CLIMBED ARMY RANKS FROM CAPTAIN to brigadier general during the Revolutionary War. A sly, smooth-talking intriguer, he prowled in the shadows of ambitious officers who plotted to oust George Washington as commander-in-chief at Valley Forge. When the plot failed and its authors exposed, Wilkinson resigned and moved west to Kentucky.

During a trip to Spanish-held New Orleans Wilkinson made a secret agreement with Spanish authorities to lead Kentucky's secession and in-corporation into what was then Spain's Louisiana territory. "Wilkinson is entirely devoted to us," the Spanish minister assured his foreign minister. "He enjoys a considerable pension from the King."[1]

In 1805 Jefferson appointed Wilkinson governor of northern Louisiana—even as Wilkinson continued fomenting Kentucky secession and union with Spain. Spain gave Wilkinson title to 60,000 acres in Texas as a refuge in case the US government uncovered his plot and forced him to flee US territory. Wilkinson was convinced by then that a Spanish-American war was inevitable, and by establishing ties to both sides, he hoped to ensure his place in the winning camp at the end of the conflict.

To deflect suspicions of his involvement, Wilkinson, like Iago with Othello, whispered rumors he knew the President would eagerly

The face of evil? General James Wilkinson had plotted to overthrow George Washington as commander-in-chief during the Revolutionary war. After the war, Wilkinson secretly accepted funds from the Spanish government to organize the secession of Kentucky from the United States and convinced President Thomas Jefferson that Vice President Aaron Burr was masterminding the plot. (FROM THE LIFE OF JOHN MARSHALL, BY ALBERT J. BEVERIDGE, VOL. III: 290)

embrace—that Burr was plotting against the President, that Burr was plotting western secession. If Jefferson had any misgivings about Wilkinson's loyalties, he cast them aside and embarked on an obsessive pursuit of vengeance against Aaron Burr for Burr's defiance in the 1800 presidential election.

Causing death in a duel was a capital crime in New York, though not in New Jersey, but Jefferson pressured Republican district attorneys in both states to order Burr arrested for the murder of Alexander Hamilton. Burr, however, fled west, out of their jurisdictions after his farewell to the Senate.

"In New York I am to be disenfranchised and in New Jersey hanged," he explained to his son-in-law. "Having substantial objections to both, I shall . . . seek another country."[2]

Although he would be deeply involved in Burr's fate in the months ahead, Chief Justice John Marshall had left Washington after the Chase trial and was riding the circuit in Virginia and North Carolina, all but oblivious to and uninformed about Burr's activities.

Burr was, in fact, almost bankrupt when he left the nation's capital. Forced to abandon his lucrative New York law practice while serving as vice president in Washington, he now eyed the Louisiana Territory wilderness as a safe haven to begin life anew on vast tracts of vacant land anyone could claim for a pittance. Still a beloved—indeed, heroic—figure to many Americans, Burr had championed western interests as a US senator and found a warm welcome as he traveled west. When he reached Nashville on May 29, church bells pealed and cannons roared to welcome the former vice president and Revolutionary War hero. General Andrew Jackson staged a grand, western-style parade in Burr's honor—even urging Burr to settle in Tennessee and run for senator or President. Jackson invited him to stay at his home in Nashville, then publicly hailed Burr for defending his honor by facing death courageously against Hamilton. Far from decrying duels, Tennesseans, like most westerners and southerners, saw dueling as a basic right and obligation of all fighting men. A year later Jackson himself would kill a horse breeder in a duel that left a bullet lodged in Jackson's chest as a painful memento of the encounter the rest of his life.

On June 6 Burr reached Fort Massac, on the Ohio River, where General Wilkinson greeted the former vice president with tales of great wealth for the taking in the West. A heavy drinker, Wilkinson confided certain knowledge that Kentucky, Tennessee, Ohio, and parts of Georgia and Carolina would soon separate from the Union, form a new and independent nation, and send a combined army into Mexico to plunder Spanish gold and silver mines. Shortly after Burr left, Wilkinson wrote to President Jefferson accusing Burr of treason—of hatching the very plot

General Andrew Jackson welcomed Aaron Burr Jr. to the West, calling him a hero for his success in the duel with Hamilton and urging him to settle in Tennessee and run for the Senate. (LIBRARY OF CONGRESS)

for western secession that he himself had devised and that the Spanish government was paying him to put in motion.

New Orleans—the last stop on Burr's journey of exploration for land and opportunities—greeted him as a hero, out-cheering, out-parading, and out-feasting Nashville, with cannon fire, pealing church bells, parades, banquets, and endless greetings by and meetings with notables. By midautumn 1805 the warmth of his reception in the West convinced him that America had let his duel with Hamilton fade into history, and Burr retraced his journey to return to Washington. He stopped at Natchez to lease 40,000 acres of fertile land in northeastern Louisiana as a haven for his family and friends if he found he had to leave the East permanently.

After Jefferson received Wilkinson's letters accusing Burr of plotting secession, the President—without a single fact to support Wilkinson's charges—leaped at the chance to hang his former rival for treason. Citing unspecified information he had received, Jefferson sent Congress a message citing "an illegal combination of private individuals against the peace and safety of the Union and a military expedition planned by them against the territories of a power in amity with the United States . . . and the prime mover in these is Aaron Burr."[3]

Even former President John Adams—no friend of Burr—lashed out at Jefferson. "Politicians," he declared in a letter to his friend Benjamin Rush, have "no more regard for the truth than the devil. . . . I suspect that this Lying Spirit has been at work concerning Burr. . . . But [even] if his [Burr's] guilt is as clear as the noon-day sun, the First Magistrate [President Jefferson] ought not to have pronounced [Burr guilty] before a jury had tried him."[4]

The President's message to Congress set off a relentless wave of accusations against Burr that splashed across the pages of the nation's press. By the time Burr returned to Washington, rumors swirled in and about the capital that he was plotting every imaginable evil the human mind could conjure. President Jefferson stunned his former vice president, however, with a cordial invitation to confer for several hours at the presidential mansion—and remain for dinner. After Burr had briefed the President on ferment in the West, Jefferson invited Burr to return for another conference and dinner—and then another . . .

With each visit—and dinner—Burr and Jefferson seemed to part on good terms, with the President saying he had no objection to Burr's settling in the West and eventually returning to Washington as a representative from his new home territory. Burr left, therefore, in an ebullient mood, intending to return west to buy and settle on lands he had leased in northern Louisiana and develop a new community and constituency there.

Although rumors of Burr's activities reached the ears of Chief Justice Marshall in Richmond, he, like most Americans outside the nation's capital, paid little notice. That would soon change.

By the time Burr reached Ohio thousands of young men and women had boarded westward-bound wagons to begin new lives. Most sought—and needed—charismatic figures to lead them into the western unknown, and Aaron Burr, the son and grandson of all but saintly churchmen, stepped into that role. A few who followed him dreamed of gold and silver, but most sought only to settle and farm the rich soil he promised to sell or lease to them—in 100-acre parcels.

By the time Burr reached Nashville on his second trip west, his followers numbered about forty young men with ten hunting rifles and two shotguns on fifteen boats. More young men stood along the river's edge hoping to find boats to join his trip to the Promised Land. Andrew Jackson urged his wife's nephew to join Burr in the new settlement.

Although Burr's boys intended nothing more aggressive than tilling land in northern Louisiana, increasingly sinister rumors dogged his movements. President Jefferson urged western governors "to have him strictly watched and on his committing any overt act unequivocally to have him arrested and tried for treason, misdemeanor or whatever other offense the act may amount to."[5] The President inflated Burr's young followers into an "army" of "fugitives from justice or from their debts . . . adventurers and speculators of all descriptions."

> Burr's conspiracy . . . combined the objects of separating the western states from us, of adding Mexico to them, and of placing himself at their head. . . . He probably induced near a thousand men to engage with him. . . . The first enterprise was to have been the seizure of New Orleans.[6]

Burr expressed shock when he learned of the President's accusations. "If there exists any design to separate the West from the eastern states," he protested, "I am totally ignorant of it. I never harbored or expressed any such intention to any one, nor did any person ever intimate such design to me."[7]

In December 1806 the President set loose the bulldog Federalist District Attorney Joseph Hamilton Daveiss to hunt Burr down and bring him to bay. Burr appeared before the grand jury with his attorney, the newly appointed Kentucky Senator Henry Clay. He denied Daveiss's charges, and after Daveiss failed to produce any witnesses, the grand jury discharged Burr. A crowd waited outside the courthouse to cheer, but the cheers quickly died when the relentless Daveiss ordered Burr arrested as a traitor. Two weeks after his first court victory Burr testified before a second grand jury. Again, he was unequivocal:

> I have no design nor have I taken any measure to promote a dissolution of the Union or a separation of any one or more states. . . . I have neither published a line on this subject nor has anyone, through my agency, or with my knowledge. I have no desire to intermeddle with the government or to disturb the tranquility of the United States, or of its territories, or any part of them. My views have been fully explained to and approved by several of the principle officers of government, and, I believe, are well understood by the administration and seen by it with complacency. They are such as every man of honor and every good citizen must approve.[8]

"There have been . . . some curious stories lately," a surprised Chief Justice Marshall wrote of Burr to his brother James Markham. "Burr is . . . being denounced as a traitor."[9]

In a rare act by an attorney on either side of a proceeding, Kentucky attorney Henry Clay compared Daveiss's pursuit of Burr to the "inquisitions of Europe," then pledged his own "honor and innocence" as a state legislator on behalf of his client. Again, Daveiss failed to produce witnesses or evidence. When he called several editors to testify, they admitted they had printed rumors as if they were truths and had no evidence of any Burr conspiracy.

"When the grand jury returned the bill of indictment not true," Clay exulted, "a scene was presented in the courtroom which I had never before witnessed in Kentucky. There were shouts and applause from an audience, not one of whom . . . would have hesitated to level a rifle against Colonel Burr if he believed he aimed to dismember the Union or sought to violate its peace or overturn its Constitution."[10]

246 | JOHN MARSHALL

Fearful that Burr's back-to-back acquittals might shift the President's focus to him, Wilkinson sent Jefferson what became famous as the "cipher letter." Purportedly written in code by Burr, the cipher letter disclosed Burr's alleged plans to march southward with a force of 10,000 men to seize New Orleans and rendezvous with the British navy for a subsequent land-and-sea assault on Mexico. Wilkinson then warned the governor of New Orleans that Burr was approaching with a force that had magically shrunk to 7,000. Although he asked the governor to declare martial law, the governor refused but was powerless to prevent Wilkinson—still military commander in Louisiana—from declaring martial law himself.

Wilkinson sent troops on a campaign of terror against anyone with even the most tenuous ties to Aaron Burr. They arrested four of Burr's friends, a handful of lawyers, a dozen public officials, including a sitting judge and a former Kentucky senator, rejecting all petitions for habeas corpus and shutting down newspapers that printed even a word about the arrests.

As news of the chaos in and about New Orleans reached Washington, President Jefferson's alter-ego in the Senate, William Branch Giles of Virginia, acted to legalize Wilkinson's actions by proposing and winning passage of legislation automatically suspending habeas corpus for three months for anyone charged with "treason, misprision of treason, or other high crime or misdemeanor endangering the peace, safety, or neutrality of the United States."[11]

Chief Justice John Marshall and his Supreme Court intervened, however, issuing writs of habeas corpus for and freeing all Burr aides whom Wilkinson had arrested. There had been no evidence to support charges of treason against them, Marshall thundered. In freeing them, Marshall cited Article III, Section 3 of the Constitution:

Treason against the United States shall consist only in levying war against them or in adhering to their enemies, giving them aid and comfort. No person shall be convicted of treason unless on the testimony of two witnesses to the same overt act, or on confession in open court.[12]

Marshall barked at the President's attorneys as if he were chastising stupefied school boys: for anyone to be guilty of treason "war must actually be levied against the United States."

> However flagitious may be the crime of conspiring to subvert by force the government of our country, such conspiracy is not treason. . . . There must be an actual assembling of men for the treasonable purpose to constitute a levying of war. . . . There is not one syllable which has a necessary or a natural reference to an enterprise against any territory of the United States. . . . It is, therefore, more safe as well as more consonant to the principles of our Constitution that the crime of treason should not be extended to doubtful cases.[13]

Incensed by Marshall's decision, Senator Giles growled about impeaching the Chief Justice and introducing a constitutional amendment to strip the Supreme Court of its power of judicial review. But others called the Marshall decision "a triumph of reason and law over popular passion and injustice . . . the triumph of civil over military authority."[14]

Some members of the House responded by demanding an explanation from the President for Wilkinson's actions, and on January 22, 1807, the President disclosed what he thought were the details of the Burr conspiracy. Although he admitted that his information was based on a "mixture of rumor, conjectures, and suspicions . . . difficult to sort out from real facts," he asserted his trust in Wilkinson, who, he said, had displayed the "honor of a soldier and fidelity of a good citizen." Burr's guilt, the President emphasized without presenting evidence, was "beyond question."[15]

By then Jefferson had ordered federal marshals to hunt Burr down and arrest him. One of them reached Ohio and warned Governor Edward Tiffin of an impending attack by Burr's phantom "army"—now inflated to 20,000 men. Tiffin ordered his militia to seize Burr's boats in Marietta and install cannons on the hills in and about the city to repel any attempt by Burr to take the city. Militiamen seized and plundered the lavish Ohio River island mansion of a wealthy family that had offered Burr their hospitality on his previous trips.

As Wilkinson whipped up government authorities to repel Burr's hordes of imaginary invaders, Burr himself was in Frankfort, Kentucky, appearing before yet another grand jury, with no idea of the campaign that Jefferson, Wilkinson, and their army of aides and attorneys were mounting against him.

"Never in the history of the United States did so powerful a combination . . . unite to break down a single man as that which arrayed itself against Aaron Burr," declared historian Henry Adams. Adams's grandfather John Quincy Adams was in the Senate at the time and had led those who frustrated President Jefferson's attempt to seize control of the US Supreme Court by impeaching Justice Samuel Chase. "In the face of all this provocation," Henry Adams stated, "the vice president [Burr] behaved with studied caution and reserve."[16]

Burr did not realize the enormity of the forces arrayed against him until, exonerated of all wrongdoing and set free by a third grand jury, he set off downriver on the Ohio toward the Mississippi River and Natchez. On January 10 he learned of Wilkinson's ruthless roundup of his friends and the reward Wilkinson was offering for his capture. With a price on his head, Burr realized he faced summary execution if captured.

Ironically, Wilkinson knew the only way to avoid charges of treason himself was to silence Burr and send him to the grave bearing responsibility for Wilkinson's own plot.

Alone suddenly, at the mercy of any passing bounty hunter, Burr fled, hoping to survive long enough to surrender to civil authorities in Mississippi. Jefferson and Wilkinson cited Burr's flight as proof of guilt, and as rewards for Burr's head multiplied, he faced imminent death as he rounded every tree and turn of the river.

On March 3, 1807, a posse of civil deputies halted and searched Burr's "fleet" of nine boats and sixty would-be settlers as they sailed on the Tombigbee River in northeastern Mississippi toward Natchez. When the search revealed only a few rifles, shotguns, and supplies, the posse let them continue, and Governor Cowles Meade concluded, "His object is agriculture and his boats are the vehicles of emigration."[17]

Eager to end the manhunt, Burr went voluntarily to the US territorial district court to testify before a special grand jury—his fourth—and the jury refused to indict him.

"We are of the opinion," the jury foreman proclaimed, "that Aaron Burr has not been guilty of any crime or misdemeanor against the laws of the United States or of this territory or given any just alarm or inquietude to the good people of the territory."[18]

As a token of apology to Burr, the grand jury filed a "grievance" against Wilkinson for sending the militia after Burr and for "the destruction of personal liberty" in his round-up and imprisonment of Burr associates in New Orleans.

Jefferson's chief judge in the Mississippi Territory, Thomas Rodney, rejected the grand jury's decision and ordered Burr to remain within the court's jurisdiction. When Burr saw Wilkinson's thugs ride into the area, however, he feared for his life and fled, vanishing into the Alabama territory. After a local official recognized him two weeks later, Alabama militiamen seized him and led him under guard on the long journey to Richmond, Virginia.

On March 26 a heavy military escort led Burr into Richmond, where, after four days in jail, he appeared for arraignment before Chief Justice John Marshall, still riding circuit and sitting in Richmond Circuit Court. Almost three decades and hundreds of miles removed from the battlefield that thrust them together as comrades, two of the last surviving Men of Monmouth stood face to face, the one seeking justice, the other dispensing it.

Burr faced two charges: the first, leading a military expedition against Spain; the second, treason against the United States. Because it was an arraignment, Marshall made it clear that the prosecution did not have to prove the charges to hold Burr for trial, but it did have to show probable cause. On the charge of treason, he declared, the government had failed to present any probable cause or evidence of "an overt act" of treason.

"The assembling of forces to levy war is a visible transaction, and numbers must witness it," Marshall scolded the prosecution. "Several months have elapsed since this fact did occur, if it ever occurred. More than five weeks have elapsed since the Supreme Court declared the necessity of proving the fact, if it exists. Why is it not proved?"

As the prosecuting attorney sat in silence, Marshall answered his own question: he concluded that no evidence of treason existed and dismissed the charge. He did, however, hold Burr over for trial on the charge of leading an expedition against Spain—nothing more than a misdemeanor. He set bail at $10,000—more, perhaps, to protect Burr from retaliation by the state than the reverse.

Marshall's dismissal of the treason charge against Burr incensed Jefferson—more so because it was the second time in his presidency that both Marshall and Burr had challenged Jefferson's authority. In the belief they were in collusion, Jefferson called Marshall's decision one of many "tricks of the judges." He charged Marshall and the Federalists with "making Burr's cause their own—mortified only that he did not separate the Union or overturn the government."

Jefferson's hate seemed to know no bounds. In a sometimes irrational letter to his senatorial manservant Virginia Senator William Branch Giles, Jefferson ranted of "treason stalking through the land in open day"—only to admit in the next sentence that "our information having been chiefly by letter, we do not know of a certainty yet what will be proved." Scoffing at Marshall's insistence on "an overt act" as proof of treason, Jefferson asked Giles whether "letters and facts published in the local newspapers, Burr's flight, and the universal belief or rumor of his guilt [are not] probable ground . . . to put him on trial?"

Jefferson then raised his true political colors and displayed his disdain for civil liberties and the right to trial by jury: "The nation," he declared,

will judge both the offender and judges for themselves. . . . They will see and amend the error in our Constitution, which makes any branch independent of the nation. They will see that one of the great coordinate branches of the government, setting itself in opposition to the other two, and to the common sense of the nation, proclaims impunity to that class of offenses which endeavors to overturn the Constitution and are themselves protected in it by the Constitution itself.[19]

Jefferson urged Giles to propose a constitutional amendment to limit the terms justices could serve, to make their removal easier, and to make them directly responsible to voters.

"If their protection of Burr produces this amendment," he said of Marshall and the justices, "it will do more than his condemnation would have done."[20]

Jefferson ended his diatribe with a disingenuous remark that belied his ferocious campaign to destroy the former vice president:

"Against Burr, personally," he insisted, "I never had one hostile sentiment."[21]

As the date approached for Burr's trial for preparing an invasion of Spanish territory, Jefferson's attorney general stunned the President by withdrawing from the case. Jefferson himself took charge, turning to Virginia district attorney George Hay to lead the prosecution. The son of a cabinet maker, Hay slipped into the halls of the Virginia dynasty by marrying the daughter of Jefferson's acolyte James Monroe. With an ambitious eye focused on the attorney general's office, he complied zealously with every presidential instruction—even submitting a motion to reinstate the treason charge against Burr. In doing so, however, he inadvertently put President Thomas Jefferson on trial alongside Burr.

Although Burr acted as his own attorney, he assembled a team of skilled lawyers to help him, including the formidable Luther Martin, a renowned Maryland attorney who had walked out of the Constitutional Convention. Martin had fought ratification in his state with oratory that compared well with that of another foe of ratification, Patrick Henry of Virginia.

Noting that the Constitution required two witnesses to the same overt act as proof of treason, one of Burr's lawyers asked simply, "Is there even one solitary witness who can depose to an act of overt treason?"

There was none.

Burr then testified in his own defense, saying, "We are told by the President that the people of Ohio were alarmed.

"How were they alarmed?" he asked.

"He [the President] alarmed them," Burr answered his own question.

"How was he alarmed?" Burr asked. "By Mr. Wilkinson."

Burr said that grand juries in the West had "honorably discharged" him, with one grand jury actually censuring the government.

"There was no alarm in that part of the country!"[22]

He had gone west, he told Justice Marshall, for "purely peaceable and agricultural" purposes. "My designs were honorable and would have been useful to the United States."[23]

The grand jury, having heard testimony from forty-eight people, charged Aaron Burr—without explanation—of "not having God before his eyes . . . but being moved and seduced by the instigation of the devil . . . with a great multitude of persons . . . did falsely and traitoriously assemble . . . in a warlike and hostile manner, array and dispose themselves against the said United States." Although somewhat skeptical about the evidence presented, Marshall decided there was enough evidence to hold Burr for trial on the charge of leading an expedition against Spanish territory.[24]

"I have three rooms in the third story of the penitentiary," Burr wrote with his usual drollery to his daughter after Marshall remanded him to federal custody. "My jailor is quite a polite and civil man—altogether unlike the idea one would form of a jailer."

> My friends and acquaintances of both sexes are permitted to visit me without interruption, without inquiring their business, and without the presence of a spy. . . . If you come, I can give you a bedroom and parlor on this floor. The bedroom has three large closets. . . . Remember: no agitation, no complaints, no fears or anxieties.[25]

After three weeks in prison, however, he lost all traces of lightheartedness. "I should never invite anyone, much less those so dear to me, to witness my disgrace. I may be immured in dungeons, chained, murdered in legal form, but I cannot be humiliated or disgraced."[26]

The trial did not begin until mid-August, with the jury hearing more than a dozen prosecution witnesses. None could testify having seen "an act of levying war."

When Burr demanded to see the documents the President had said would prove Burr's guilt, the prosecution and Jefferson refused.

"The President," Martin fumed, "has undertaken to prejudge my client by declaring that 'of his guilt there can be no doubt.' He has assumed to himself the knowledge of the Supreme Being . . . to keep back the papers which are wanted for this trial, where life itself is at stake."[27]

Infuriated by Martin's attack, the President ordered prosecutors to look into indicting the lawyer as a coconspirator with Burr—"*particeps criminis* . . . [to] put down this unprincipled and impudent federal bulldog and add another proof that the most clamorous of Burr's defenders are all his accomplices."[28] The prosecutors, however, failed to find any evidence against Martin, and the case remained on track, with Burr still demanding that the President release the evidence he claimed would prove the charges against the former vice president.

On June 15, 1807, Chief Justice John Marshall issued another of his many landmark decisions. He began by addressing the issue of withholding evidence:

"The propriety of introducing any paper into a case as testimony must depend on the character of the paper, not the character of the person who holds it," Marshall declared.

> The uniform practice of this country has been to permit any individual who was charged with any crime to prepare for his defense. . . . The genius and character of our laws and usages are friendly, not to condemnation at all events, but to a fair and impartial trial. And they consequently allow to the accused the right of preparing the means to secure such a trial.[29]

Marshall cited the Sixth Amendment to the Constitution giving the accused in all criminal prosecutions "the right to a speedy and public trial and to compulsory process for obtaining witnesses in his favor."

"The right given by this article," the Chief Justice proclaimed, "must be deemed sacred by the court."[30]

Having disposed of Burr's constitutional right to obtain any and all documents relating to his case, Marshall then turned his attention to whether the subpoena to obtain such documents can be directed to the President of the United States.

"In the provisions of the Constitution . . . which give the accused a right to the compulsory process of the court," Marshall answered his own question, "there is no exception whatever . . . and it would seem that no person could claim an exemption from them."

When the prosecution retorted by citing the British constitutional principle that "the king can do no wrong," Marshall was ready:

> By the Constitution of the United States, the President . . . may be impeached and removed from office on conviction of high crimes and misdemeanors. By the constitution of Great Britain the crown is hereditary and the monarch can never become a subject. . . . The President is elected from the mass of the people, and on the expiration of the time for which he is elected, he returns to the mass of the people again.[31]

Marshall conceded that national security might dictate the President's withholding of some documents, but there was no indication that the papers Burr had requested fell into that category.

To Jefferson and every successor American President, therefore, Chief Justice Marshall proclaimed in *United States v. Burr* that the President of the United States was then and forever a citizen like every other citizen and as subject to the rule of law.

Jefferson complied and released the letters, and when General Wilkinson took the stand under oath, he admitted that he altered and forged parts of the notorious "cipher letter" to change Burr's otherwise innocent missive into a blueprint for conspiracy.

Marshal chided the prosecution, saying it had charged Burr with levying war against the United States—an overt act that must be proved by two witnesses.

"It is not proved by a single witness," Marshall declared, calling the testimony that the jury had heard inadmissible, irrelevant, and "incompetent to prove the overt act itself."[32] If Burr had, indeed, raised an army of 7,000 troops, Marshall asked, "what could veil his army from human sight? An invisible army is not an instrument of war."[33] A few minutes later the jury declared Burr "not proved guilty under this indictment by any evidence submitted to us. We therefore find him not guilty."[34]

Having called fifty witnesses, even Hay realized that all evidence pointed overwhelmingly to Burr intending only to settle and develop his lands without intent of bothering anyone in nearby Spanish territory. Hay asked Marshall to dismiss the jury *nolle prosequi*—without further charges—but Burr now shot to his feet to protest, demanding a jury verdict. Marshall agreed he could not dismiss the jury without the defendant's consent. The jury conferred and again ruled Burr *not guilty* of the original indictment.

Jefferson immediately sent the trial records to Congress, demanding that the House impeach Marshall and write a constitutional amendment that would roll back Marshall's decisions and sharply circumscribe judicial authority.

"We had supposed we possessed fixed laws to guard us equally against treason and oppression," Jefferson raged. "But it now appears we have no law but the will of the judge."[35]

Jefferson ordered aides and friendly editors to whip up public opinion against the Supreme Court.

"Let the judge be impeached," demanded the Richmond *Enquirer*, which called federal judges in general "too independent of the people" and Marshall in particular "a disgrace to the bench of justice."[36]

Jefferson's Republicans in Congress acted to dilute Marshall's powers by increasing the number of Supreme Court justices to seven to ensure a large enough Republican majority to dispatch Chief Justice John Marshall and his opinions into legal obscurity.

In Baltimore an angry mob responded to editorials condemning Marshall by hanging the Chief Justice in effigy alongside an effigy of Aaron Burr and pledging to march on the Supreme Court if Marshall ever again appeared in Washington.

CHAPTER 14

The Court Must Be Obeyed

As the press intensified its demands for Chief Justice Marshall's removal, mobs snaked through the streets of Richmond threatening to hang Aaron Burr. Terrified, not knowing where to go, he found even his oldest, most faithful friends unwilling to risk their own property or lives to help him.

Deeply in debt, fearing death at the hands of Jefferson's or Wilkinson's agents, and facing prosecution in six states by Jefferson-appointed district attorneys, Burr obtained passage on a ship bound for England in June 1808 and found both a safe haven and warm friendship at the home of the then-radical philosopher Jeremy Bentham. He busied himself with Bentham's various projects—abolition of slavery, women's suffrage, prison reform, and Latin American liberation—and engaged in endless sexual adventures.

Arrested in 1809 and ordered to leave the country for his support of Latin American liberation movements, Burr traveled about Europe, finally settling in Paris, where he pursued any and every opportunity to survive. Among other gainful activities, he translated French works into English by day and sold sexual attentions to wealthy, elderly women at night.

After Jefferson left office Burr decided it was safe to return to America, and he arrived in New York in early 1812—only to learn that his only grandson, ten-year-old Aaron Burr Alston, had just died in Charleston, South Carolina. The boy's distraught mother, Theodosia—Burr's only child—boarded a boat to rejoin her father in New York but never arrived. The ship and all its passengers and crew were lost at sea. Burr remained in New York, shunned politics, and practiced law in relative obscurity for the rest of his life.

General James Wilkinson faced court martial for his false testimony at the Burr trial but was found not guilty. He commanded an American force in the War of 1812 but was relieved of his command after two failed campaigns. He went to Mexico in 1821 to claim a Texas land grant from Spanish authorities and died there. Subsequent inquiries revealed his almost-constant ties to treasonous activities during his career as an officer in the American military.

Marshall, meanwhile, had swept his wife into their carriage after the Burr trial and ridden away to the calm and safety of their Oak Hill home in the Blue Ridge Mountains. Terrified by news of the Baltimore mob hanging her husband in effigy, Polly sank into another depression that left her clinging to her husband more than ever, pleading with him not to wander far whenever he set foot near the door.

Jefferson's efforts to impeach John Marshall and amend the Constitution to weaken the judiciary met with diminishing enthusiasm in Congress. Even Jefferson's most ardent admirers now recognized his response to the Burr trial as another in his relentless efforts to wreak vengeance on his perceived enemies and expand his personal power. That these efforts had crossed the line into paranoia became clear when he ranted about the Chief Justice having planned in advance "not only to clear Burr but to prevent the evidence from ever going before the world."[1] Even Jefferson's compliant ally Congressman William Branch Giles turned against the President, conceding that the lack of evidence had sustained "the innocence of the accused."[2]

That Jefferson's obsession with punishing political enemies was clouding his judgment in other presidential matters had become evident even before the trial began, when a barrage of citizen complaints against the President besieged Congress.

In late June 1807, more than a month before the Burr trial had started, a British frigate *Leopard* sailing in international waters near Norfolk, Virginia, ordered the American frigate *Chesapeake* to surrender four men the British captain claimed were deserters. When the *Chesapeake*'s captain refused, the British fired without warning, killing three Americans, wounding eighteen, and carrying off the four alleged deserters. When the American ship limped into port, Americans demanded that the President retaliate.

Caught by surprise by the *Chesapeake* disaster and obsessed with fears of the illusory Burr conspiracy, the President responded precipitously. In a carelessly conceived—some said irrational—move, Jefferson called on Congress to pass a broad-based embargo act that closed American ports to foreign trade—not just English or French trade, but *all* foreign trade. The President told Americans to do without imports, become self-sufficient, and rely entirely on American-made goods.

"Our commerce is so valuable to them," he asserted naively, "that they will be glad to purchase it, when the only price we ask is justice."[3]

The Embargo Act proved an instant disaster, with almost no ill effects on British foreign trade and crushing consequences for the American economy. The nation had neither the skilled workers nor the manufacturing facilities to absorb and transform the huge quantities of raw materials it produced each year into manufactured goods—and no domestic market large enough to absorb such finished goods if it could make them. Economic survival depended on exporting raw materials.

Connecticut's legislature declared the Embargo Act "unconstitutional and despotic" and ordered state officials not to enforce it.[4] Connecticut Governor Jonathan Trumbull taunted Jefferson with the President's own words from the Kentucky Resolution of a decade earlier.

"Whenever our national legislature is led to overleap the prescribed bounds of their constitutional powers," Trumbull mocked the President, "it becomes the duty [of state legislatures] to interpose their protecting shield between the right and liberty of the people and the assumed power of the federal government."[5]

Other states followed suit in mass defiance of presidential and federal authority. Across New England a huge smuggling trade emerged, driving prices up uncontrollably as merchants openly defied the American government and engaged in illicit trade with England and her colonies, paying whatever prices smugglers demanded.

In the absence of American vessels on world trade routes, British cargo ships filled the void in international commerce. Canada and South America replaced the United States as Europe's primary suppliers of lumber, grain, pelts, and other commodities. While Jefferson focused on his insane pursuit of Aaron Burr, American exports plummeted nearly 80 percent from $108 million in 1807 to $22.5 million in 1808, while imports fell nearly 60 percent, from $138 million to less than $57 million. Government revenues from duties dropped from $16 million to a few thousand dollars. The Act marooned 55,000 sailors and left 100,000 other Americans—merchants, craftsmen, laborers, and others who depended on foreign trade—without work or income. American ships trapped in foreign waters when the Embargo Act went into effect fell prey to pirates as well as the British and French navies.

Massachusetts Senator and former Secretary of State Timothy Pickering stopped just short of renewing his earlier call for secession, urging instead a convention of New England states to nullify the embargo.

"My dear sir," Chief Justice Marshall answered Pickering's invitation to the convention,

> If sound argument and correct reasoning could save our country, it would be saved. Nothing can be more completely demonstrated than the inefficacy of the embargo, yet that demonstration seems to be of no avail. I fear that the same spirit which so tenaciously maintains this measure will impel us to a war with the only power which protects any part of the civilized world from the despotism of that tyrant [Napoléon Bonaparte]. . . . But I abstain from remarks on this question.[6]

Marshall's reason for refusing Pickering's invitation became clear two months later, when he announced the court's decision voiding Pennsylvania's nullification of a federal court order as unconstitutional.

The case dated back to the Revolutionary War when Gideon Olmstead and three sailors mutinied aboard a British sloop in 1778 and sailed it toward New Jersey to sell it and its cargo. An armed Commonwealth of Pennsylvania vessel intercepted them and sailed the ship to Philadelphia, where a commonwealth court awarded Olmstead and his friends one-fourth of the proceeds from the sale of the ship and cargo and gave the rest to the state.

Olmstead sued, and in 1779 a federal Continental Prize Court awarded Olmstead all the proceeds. The Pennsylvania legislature passed a law that nullified the Continental Prize Courts award "to protect the just rights of the state . . . from any process whatever issued out of any federal court."[7]

Federal Judge Richard Peters held the funds until the Supreme Court could hear the case in 1808. A year later the High Court declared the Pennsylvania legislature's action to have been an unconstitutional assertion of state sovereignty and ordered Peters to turn the moneys over to Olmstead. In a separate case that followed soon after, a federal district court judge cited *United States v. Peters* in dismissing a state's challenge to the Embargo Act, citing the supremacy of federal over state authority.

Nor were state governments alone in challenging the Embargo Act. Merchants in every port colluded with ship owners and smugglers to undermine—indeed, make a mockery of—the Embargo Act. Jefferson reacted with angry demands that Congress pass a Force Act, requiring ship owners to load vessels in the presence of federal marshals. He told the Republican majority in Congress to ignore the Constitution and authorize customs officials to seize vessels without warrants if they suspected embargo violations. Boston officials refused to obey the Force Act, and Connecticut's governor rejected the secretary of war's request to deploy militia to force compliance in his state.

As the 1808 presidential elections approached, Republicans in New England, New York, and even Jefferson's home state of Virginia broke ranks with the President over the embargo and threatened to reject Jefferson's chosen successor for the presidency, his protégé, Secretary of State James Madison. At Madison's behest, Jefferson retreated and ended the

A Republican acolyte of Thomas Jefferson, President James Madison reversed course as the nation's chief executive and embraced Chief Justice John Marshall's Federalist philosophy. He even threatened to use troops if necessary to enforce a Supreme Court decision. (LIBRARY OF CONGRESS)

embargo. The expansion of trade that followed and the prosperity it engendered ensured an easy victory for Madison in the presidential election.

Although Jefferson, like George Washington, ceded the presidential mansion at the end of his second term, he enjoyed wielding power too much to emulate Washington by retiring quietly "under the shadow of my own Vine and Fig-tree."[8] Indeed, Madison had not finished uttering his oath of office before Jefferson attempted to impose his views on his successor.

Madison, however, did not share some of those views, and although he had served obediently as Jefferson's secretary of state, he had no intention of serving as Jefferson's President. As a symbol of his newfound independence, Madison named Chief Justice John Marshall—the man

Jefferson despised most in Washington—to administer his oath of office as fourth President of the United States.

They were an incongruous pair, Madison and Marshall. The powerful six-foot, two-inch Chief Justice—for eight years the target of Jefferson's political arrows—towered over sickly little "Jamie" Madison who stood barely five feet tall. Despite their physical differences, however, they stood as one in their support for the Constitution and for the Supreme Court and federal judiciary as an independent, coequal branch of American government.

Immediately after his inauguration Madison sent a bevy of attorneys into Marshall's court to reopen *United States v. Peters*, which Marshall thought he and his colleagues had settled. And indeed they had—*almost*. Federal Judge Richard Peters, however, had failed to obey the court's order to pay Gideon Olmstead. His failure, he said, resulted from his effort "to avoid embroiling the government of the United States and that of Pennsylvania."[9]

Marshall responded angrily, issuing another court order for Peters to pay Olmstead.

> If the legislatures of the several states may, at will, annul the judgments of the courts of the United States and destroy the rights acquired under those judgments, the Constitution itself becomes a solemn mockery, and the nation is deprived of the means of enforcing its laws by the instrumentality of its own tribunals.[10]

Judge Peters reacted quickly, ordering federal militiamen to surround the house that held the proceeds of the Olmstead mutiny and demand delivery. Pennsylvania Governor Simon Snyder, a Jeffersonian Republican and ardent proponent of states' rights, ordered Pennsylvania militiamen to stand against the federal troops, and the legislature supported him with resolutions that defied the Supreme Court and denied its jurisdiction.

Calling Pennsylvania's action "destructive of the Union," Marshall insisted that "the state of Pennsylvania can possess no constitutional right to resist the legal process which may be directed in this case."[11]

Certain of support for his resistance from fellow Republicans, Governor Snyder hoped Republican President James Madison would also support him, but to everyone's surprise and shock, diminutive "little Jamie" charged into the legal fray like Samson.

"The executive of the United States," he scolded the Pennsylvania governor, "is not only unauthorized to prevent the execution of a decree sanctioned by the Supreme Court of the United States, but is expressly enjoined by statute to carry into effect any such decree where opposition may be made to it."[12]

With that, Madison alerted federal militiamen, and, faced with the option of firing on federal troops, Snyder backed off, ordered his own troops to stand down, and temporarily ended the threat of armed conflict between a state and the federal government.

Madison's willingness to support judiciary independence with troops signaled the climax of John Marshall's eight-year struggle to defend the judiciary against submission to popular or presidential will. In effect James Madison, the man who had helped write the Constitution, now gave the judiciary the firing power to defend itself and the Constitution.

The usually inflammatory Philadelphia newspaper *Aurora* put it simply and eloquently:

> We have heard much talk about the independence of the judiciary, but here is a point at which the independence of the judiciary, in its strict and constitutional sense, exists and demands to be supported, and in which it must be supported, or there is an end to government. . . . The decree of the Court must be obeyed.[13]

In 1803 the Court had assumed power in *Marbury v. Madison* to void an act of Congress as unconstitutional. In 1809 it extended that power in *United States v. Peters* to include state laws. In response many states had issued veiled threats of secession at one time or another, but Marshall and the Court—and now President Madison—agreed that survival of the Union depended on enforcing state compliance with the federal

Constitution. The Court's next chance came in early March 1809 in *Fletcher v. Peck.*

Land speculator John Peck had sold Robert Fletcher 15,000 acres in western Georgia. The property was part of a 35 million–acre expanse of lands watered by the Yazoo River that now encompasses most of Alabama and Mississippi. Peck and a group of speculators had bribed Georgia legislators to sell them the land at a bargain price of one and one-half cents an acre. After the press exposed the scandal, voters turned the legislators out of office, and a new legislature passed a law canceling all Yazoo land sales, including the sale to Peck and, in turn, his resale to Fletcher.

Without clear title to the land he had bought, Fletcher sued to get his money back from Peck, who hired John Quincy Adams as his defense lawyer. Adams argued that cancellation of Peck's land purchases from the state and, in turn, his sale of land to Fletcher, had violated Article I of the Constitution, which prohibits states from passing "any law impairing the obligation of contracts." John Marshall and the Supreme Court stunned state lawmakers across the nation by sustaining Adams's argument and effectively shearing the powers of state legislatures over property transfers within their borders.

"All the title which the state of Georgia ever had in the premises had been legally conveyed to John Peck" in the state's original sale of Yazoo River lands, Marshall declared. He deplored evidence "that corruption should find its way into the governments of our infant republics" but insisted it was not "within the province of the judiciary to control their conduct." In any case, he went on, "this is not a bill brought by the state of Georgia. . . . The case made out in the pleadings is . . . a private contract between two individuals," and the Constitution barred the state from voiding such a contract.[14]

❧

IN 1810 THE COURT MOVED INTO NEW QUARTERS ON THE FIRST FLOOR of the Capitol in what had been the Senate chamber. Before he left office

In 1810, the Supreme Court moved into new, more spacious quarters on the first floor of the Capitol in what had been the Senate chamber. Redesigned by the great architect Benjamin Latrobe, the stately "Hall of Justice" became one of Washington's most visited sites. It served as the Supreme Court chamber until 1860. (ARCHITECT OF THE CAPITOL)

President Jefferson—putting his finger into everyone else's political pies as usual—ordered his surveyor of public buildings, the great architect Benjamin Latrobe, to redesign the Capitol interior.

Latrobe moved the Senate to a larger chamber on the second floor to accommodate expanding membership from new western states. He then moved the Supreme Court and Library of Congress from the dark, cramped quarters of the ground floor to the old Senate chamber on the first floor. Ignoring Senate refusal to appropriate funds for the Supreme Court, Latrobe redesigned part of the old Senate chamber and built a stately "Hall of Justice," furnished with gleaming mahogany amidst majestic arches. It quickly became one of the most visited sites in the capital city.

Construction of the new chambers had no sooner ended when the court lost its oldest member, seventy-eight-year-old Associate Justice William Cushing. The Massachusetts Federalist had been the first Chief Justice of Massachusetts and author of the monumental decision abolishing slavery in that state. As a symbol of his own abhorrence of slavery, President Washington made Cushing his first appointee to the US Supreme Court.

Far from mourning Cushing's death, Thomas Jefferson saw his passing as an opportunity for personal aggrandizement and a "circumstance of congratulations."

"Old Cushing is dead," he chortled to a confidante. "The event is a fortunate one, and so timed as to be a Godsend for me."[15]

To try to change the Federalist complexion of the Court, Jefferson sent President Madison his recommendations to replace Cushing, saying that "firm republicanism and known integrity will give complete confidence to the public in the long desired reformation of the judiciary."[16] But, Jefferson warned, "It will be difficult to find a character of firmness enough to preserve his independence on the same bench with Marshall."[17]

Apart from influencing national political affairs, Jefferson admitted he had a strong personal motive for influencing Madison's selection of Cushing's replacement. Former Congressman Edward Livingston had sued Jefferson in federal court for $100,000 over a land dispute—enough to leave the former President a homeless pauper if he lost. The case was on its way to circuit court and possibly the Supreme Court, and Jefferson hoped to put some allies on the bench before the case got there.

"It is little doubted," Jefferson railed bitterly, "that his [Livingston's] knowledge of Marshall's character has induced him to bring this action."

> His twistifications of the law in the case of Marbury, in that of Burr and the Yazoo [*Fletcher v. Peck*] case, show how dexterously he can reconcile law to his personal biases; and nobody seems to doubt that he is ready to decide that Livingston's right to the *Batture* [lands] is unquestionable and that I am bound to pay for it with my personal fortune.[18]

The Batture lands case began after the Louisiana Purchase, when Livingston moved from New York and established a thriving law practice in New Orleans. Once there, he invested in lands that included the Batture, a strip of islets formed by sand and other deposits by the flow of the Mississippi River, between the river's edge and nearby levees. As President, however, Jefferson had issued an executive order seizing the Batture for the federal government, including acreage for which Livingston held clear title. With the case headed for circuit court and possibly the Supreme Court, Jefferson feared "the deep-seated enmity of one judge [Marshall]."[19]

Although Jefferson insisted he would "never embarrass the President with any solicitation," he did just that, urging Madison to appoint Virginia Court of Appeals Judge John Tyler, a wealthy planter and staunch Republican to the High Court. Confident that Madison would comply, Jefferson wrote to Tyler denouncing Marshall:

"The law is nothing more than an ambiguous text to be explained by his sophistry into any meaning which may subserve his personal malice."[20]

That June seventy-year-old Samuel Chase died, leaving the Supreme Court with two vacancies, and to Jefferson's deep disappointment, President Madison, once Jefferson's loyal protégé, ignored his former patron's advice. Although Madison chose two Republicans, the President admired and respected Marshall too much not to consult the Chief Justice. Together they chose two moderates: former Maryland Chief Justice Gabriel Duvall,* fifty-nine, and thirty-two-year-old Joseph Story, the youngest member ever chosen for the Court. Already a renowned legal scholar, Story was speaker of the Massachusetts House of Representatives when Madison selected him.

Five Republicans now made up an overwhelming majority of the Court—Duvall, Story, Livingston, Todd, and Johnson. Only Marshall

---

* There are differences in the spelling of Justice Duvall's last name. My research shows it to have been derived from the French DuVal but Anglicized to Duvall by the time Justice Duvall was on the court. He preferred the Duvall spelling.

and Bushrod Washington were nominal Federalists. All seven, however, shed their allegiances to political parties and unified in a firm embrace of the Constitution and the Union—and the Supreme Court as guarantor of their sanctity. Unlike Jefferson, they all believed the Union's survival depended on a strong federal authority and stringent limits on state authority.

As Jefferson watched the High Court's Republican justices discard their political prejudices, he despaired of salvaging his fortune from Edward Livingston's lawsuit, and when the case appeared on the docket in Richmond Circuit Court before Chief Justice John Marshall, Jefferson awaited Marshall's final, fatal blow in their decades-old rivalry.

The Chief Justice's opening remarks seemed to confirm Jefferson's worst fears. Marshall called Jefferson's seizure of Livingston's Batture lands an outrageous abuse of authority by the former President. Then the Chief Justice paused. When he spoke again, he expressed his regrets that he was legally helpless to return the Batture to its proper owner.

Federal law, Marshall explained, included a strict local-action rule at the time—which meant that if Livingston wanted justice, he would have to sue Jefferson in New Orleans first and nowhere else. With that, Marshall dismissed the case, and Jefferson walked out, his fortune intact and his lust for power equally strong.

On February 3, 1812, the Supreme Court prepared to convene with a full complement of seven members for the first time. All seven would remain on the Court together for the next eleven years, drawing closer to each other than any other group of federal officials in American history. They shared their lodgings and meals in Washington during each session of the Court and rendered a body of written legal decisions called *case law*, which formed—and remains today—one of the three pillars of the American legal system with the Code of Laws of the United States of America (statutory law), and the Constitution (constitutional law).*

---

* Federal laws, or statutes, are known collectively as the Code of Laws of the United States of America.

As in England, the American system of case law combines common law, based on accepted practices, and *stare decisis*,* or precedents set in previous written judicial decisions. Thomas Jefferson detested the concept of case law, and it remains a center of controversy, with critics calling it pseudo-legislation by unelected officials who serve for life and are subject to almost no public restraints.

Members of the 1812 Marshall Court differed in age, family backgrounds, and regional origins, but all had deep ties to the American Revolution, directly or indirectly. Marshall, Washington, Todd, Duvall, and Livingston had all served in the war—Marshall as a daring officer and one of the last Men of Monmouth. Story and Johnson had been too young to serve, but they witnessed their fathers participate in revolutionary activities—Story, in Boston, and Johnson, in Charleston, South Carolina. Washington, Duvall, and, of course, Marshall, were southerners like Johnson.

All the court's members were renowned lawyers and legal scholars. Duvall and Todd had been Chief Justices of their state supreme courts, and Johnson and Story had been Speakers of their state assemblies.

When the new associate justices assembled for the first time, however, they looked about in vain for the Chief Justice. To everyone's astonishment, John Marshall failed to appear. It was some time before they learned that heavy rains had turned Virginia roads into mud, and Marshall's coach had overturned as it careened down a steep slope. When the splintered wreck came to a halt, Marshall lay in agony with a broken collarbone and assorted cuts and bruises. He did not show up at the Supreme Court for ten days.

When he returned, the Capitol—like much of the nation—was aflame with talk of war. The British navy had suddenly stepped up attacks on

---

* *Stare decisis* are Latin words meaning "to stand by decisions" and part of the Latin phrase *stare decisis et non quieta movere*—"to stand by decisions and not disturb the undisturbed." In effect it directs a court to follow precedents set by earlier courts and not till new legal ground.

STORY

JOHNSON

WASHINGTON

DUVAL

LIVINGSTON

TODD

President Jefferson's attempt to fill the Supreme Court with Republican allies failed after each of his appointees bonded with his bitter political enemy Chief Justice John Marshall. Clockwise from upper left, Joseph Story, William Johnson, Brockhorst Livingston, Thomas Todd, Gabriel Duval, and Bushrod Washington.
(FROM *THE LIFE OF JOHN MARSHALL*, BY ALBERT J. BEVERIDGE, VOL. IV:282)

American ships at sea. The economy was collapsing, and anti-British sentiment swept the nation.

"Impressments and other outrages are multiplying," President Madison worried. "The public mind is rising in a state of high sensibility."[21] With the next presidential election not far off, the administration could not afford to let British attacks on American ships go unanswered.

In the West, Indian raiders, supplied by the British, had stepped up assaults on American settlers, and, under pressure to retaliate, General William Henry Harrison, governor of the Indiana Territory, led a force of 1,000 militiamen to the Indian capital of Shawnee chief Tecumseh.

Tecumseh had organized a confederation of Indian tribes to halt American migration westward. Although Tecumseh's forces ambushed Harrison's vanguard at the confluence of the Tippecanoe and Wabash Rivers, the atrocities of the Indian warriors—scalping live captives, for one—spurred frenzied American survivors to fight with an intensity that sent the Indians fleeing for their lives. Thirsting for more blood—and Indian scalps—the Americans followed and destroyed Tecumseh's village. Across the West settlers who had envisioned peaceful coexistence with Indians now grew determined to drive the Indian from western territories, along with his British ally.

In the shifting political atmosphere of Congress, the winds of war shaped a new political bloc of western and southern "war hawks," made up mostly of younger members. Though still a minority, they nonetheless won chairmanships of the key House Foreign Affairs Committee and the Naval Committee, while their leader, Kentucky Congressman Henry Clay, won election as Speaker of the House. Declaring British impressment and seizures a challenge to national rights and honor, they called for military attacks on British Canada and Spanish Florida to ensure national security.

Older Federalists and dissident Republicans—many of them veterans of the Revolutionary War—argued for peace. Some suggested Chief Justice John Marshall as an ideal presidential candidate on a peace ticket. A brigadier general in Virginia's militia, Marshall had been an outspoken champion of Washington's neutrality policy.

The US Capitol on the morning of August 24, 1814, before the British captured Washington and burned all public buildings in retaliation for American troops having burned the public buildings in the Canadian capital of York. (now Toronto). (LIBRARY OF CONGRESS)

Responding to the outcries of war hawks, Madison went to Congress on April 1, 1812, and requested a sixty-day reinstatement of the embargo on British trade. Ten days later Congress authorized him to call up 100,000 militiamen for six months' service.

By the end of June the American embargo had combined with a French embargo on British exports to Europe to bring British industrial production and foreign trade to a near-halt. Factories and mills shut down and unemployment soared, along with the price of food. British exports dropped by one-third, and employers and workers united in demanding that Parliament restore good relations with the United States by ending impressment and other depredations against American ships. On June 23 Parliament agreed. The Americans had, at last, won their thirty-year dispute with Britain.

But victory came too late.

Four days earlier President Madison had succumbed to pressures of congressional war hawks and declared war against Great Britain. Fifty-five years before the laying of the first trans-Atlantic communications cable, it took a month or more for messages to cross the Atlantic, and Madison was unaware of Parliament's debate over peace overtures to the United States. On June 1 he sent a message to Congress citing impressment, the blockade of American ports, seizure of American ships, and incitement of Indians on American frontiers as ample reasons for war. On June 4 the House agreed, and the Senate followed suit two weeks later.

Maritime and commercial states—Massachusetts, Connecticut, New York, New Jersey, and Delaware—protested, demanding that the nation remain at peace and resume negotiations.

"There is but one way to save our country," former Secretary of the Navy Benjamin Stoddert wrote to James McHenry, who had been secretary of war and, like Stoddert, had served in both the Washington and Adams administrations. Like most Federalists, they saw national ruin as the inevitable consequence of war with Britain and agreed the nation needed new leadership under a new President.

"This can be affected by bringing forward another Virginian as the competitor of Madison," Stoddert insisted. "That man is John Marshall."[22]

CHAPTER 15

An Era of Good Feelings

CHIEF JUSTICE JOHN MARSHALL AGREED THAT NATIONAL RUIN LAY ahead if the war with Britain continued. Although he called on "all who wish peace to unite in the means which may facilitate its attainment," he nonetheless took himself out of contention for the presidency. Like his chief proponent, former Navy Secretary Stoddert, he conceded that the bitterness engendered by Jefferson's embargo and Madison's war with Britain had left the nation with its fill of Virginians.

"Virginia has already furnished more than its share of Presidents," Marshall scoffed as he pulled out of the election campaign. To remove himself and the Supreme Court from political turmoil, he snapped at an invitation from the Virginia legislature to lead a survey party into the trans-Appalachian wilderness, far from the arena of partisan politics.

At stake was a longstanding dream of George Washington to tie Virginia's navigable rivers—the Potomac or the James—with the Ohio River, with a network of canals and turnpikes. Marshall's father had explored the West with Washington when both were young surveyors looking to link the Potomac River with the Youghiogheny, Monongahela, and Ohio Rivers by just such a network. The connection would have opened an inland water route between Chesapeake Bay and the Ohio, Mississippi, and Missouri Rivers and the Great Lakes. Washington envisioned the wealth of the continent—furs, ore, timber, and grain—traveling easily, swiftly, and inexpensively to Atlantic ports for transport to England and Europe.

Washington's vision had so inspired John Marshall as he researched and wrote his massive Washington biography that he leaped at the chance to help turn the dream into reality while also distancing himself from political turmoil. He also harbored personal motives: Marshall and his many relatives and friends owned enormous tracts of land in Kentucky and stood to reap untold profits by opening commercially viable routes from western farms, forests, and mines to eastern ports.

As Marshall set off into the Kentucky wilderness, American troops surged across northern borders into Canada and met with nothing but defeat on three fronts stretching from Detroit in the West to Lake Champlain in the East, although they managed to burn the public buildings in York (now Toronto), the capital of Upper Canada (now Ontario).

By then John Marshall had returned to Richmond. His wilderness expedition had covered 250 miles over six weeks and laid out a route that would realize Washington's original dream of tying "the inland navigation of the Eastern waters with those that run to the westward."

"We shall not only draw the produce of western settlers," Washington had predicted, "but the fur and peltry trade . . . to the amazing increase of our exports, we [shall] bind those people to us—westerners and easterners—by a chain that can never be broken."[1]

Marshall's report called for improving the navigation of the James River and building a turnpike over the mountains. "Not only will that part of our own state which lies on the Kanawha and Ohio [rivers] receive their supplies and send much of their produce to market down the James River, but an immense tract of fertile country, a great part of the States of Kentucky and Ohio, will send their commerce in the same direction."[2]

Before the state legislature could act on Marshall's report, however, British ships had sailed into Chesapeake Bay and seized the town of Hampton, opposite Newport. A British squadron then sailed up the James River to within forty miles of Richmond, where memories of Benedict Arnold's burning of the city in 1781 put many citizens to flight.

Charged with effecting "defensive measures . . . for the defense of the city," Marshall—still a brigadier general—analyzed the city's resources and geography and concluded that the city lacked any "height or eminence which overlooks and commands the whole town."

> The fortification of any spot, therefore, would afford no protection to the city. . . . It is believed that no works would afford any essential advantage to the city unless the whole town . . . be enclosed and regularly fortified. Such works would require sums unattainable by us; and, if erected, would require a garrison for their defense more than sufficient to beat the enemy in the open field.[3]

Before the city could act on Marshall's report, the British withdrew and put out to sea, where America's little navy—twelve fast and highly maneuverable ships—scored significant victories over the vaunted British naval forces. The forty-four-gun frigate *Constitution* demolished Britain's thirty-eight-gun *Guerrière* off the coast of Nova Scotia, and other American ships humiliated Britain's navy off the coasts of Virginia and Brazil. On Lake Erie Captain Oliver Hazard Perry's fleet engaged the British for three hours off the Ohio coast at Put-in-Bay on September 10, 1813. Although the encounter left Perry's ship in splinters, he inflicted even more damage on the enemy and emerged from the wreckage to send his famous message: "We have met the enemy and they are ours."[4]

When news of American victories reached London, the British Prime Minister reversed course and sent President Madison's new Secretary of State James Monroe an offer to begin peace negotiations at a neutral site in Ghent, Belgium. The President appointed John Quincy Adams, the son of America's second President, to lead the negotiations.

At the time Adams was US minister to Russia at St. Petersburg, and by the time he crossed out of Russia, the Russian, Prussian, and other armies allied against Napoléon Bonaparte had captured Paris and forced the French army to surrender. Bonaparte, who had crowned himself Emperor Napoléon I by then, abdicated and accepted exile on the tiny isle of Elbe in the Mediterranean Sea off the Italian west coast. Louis XVIII, the dead king Louis XVI's younger brother, acceded to the French throne and signed a treaty of peace with his nation's European neighbors.

The end of the European war freed 14,000 British troops to sail for North America for a massive land-and-sea attack against the United States. As British and American peace negotiators prepared to meet in Europe, British ships began shelling US coastal cities, devastating the entrance to the Connecticut River, Buzzard's Bay in Massachusetts, and Alexandria, Virginia, just across the Potomac River from Washington.

In mid-August 1814 4,000 battle-hardened British troops landed along the Patuxent River near Benedict, Maryland, routed a force of Americans, and marched on the capital. As the American troops fled the oncoming British, Elias Boudinot Caldwell, the clerk of the Supreme Court and a captain in the cavalry, galloped to the Capitol to save whatever records and manuscripts he could gather in the Supreme Court chamber. The son of a Revolutionary War hero, Caldwell managed to salvage the entire Supreme Court library, which he secreted in his own home nearby before fleeing the capital with the rest of the troops minutes ahead of the oncoming British force.

Bent on avenging the burning of public buildings by American troops in York, the British began an all-night spree of destruction in Washington on August 24, setting all public buildings ablaze, including the Capitol and the President's mansion. As the Americans had done in York, the British spared most private property, although they set fire to four homes whose owners repeatedly shot at passing redcoats. They also spared the Patent Office, which contained models of inventions and records that the British commander deemed private property that might well belong to British as well as American patent holders.

A storm the following morning brought bursts of heavy winds that sent flames flying erratically in so many directions, they forced the British—for their own safety—to withdraw. By September 12 they had sailed down the Patuxent River into Chesapeake Bay, then northward toward Baltimore, landing about fourteen miles from the city, where

British troops capture Washington on August 24, 1814, and burn all public buildings, including the presidential mansion (seen here in flames). The thick white paint that restoration workers later slathered over the smoke-stained stone exterior gave the building its current name "The White House." (LIBRARY OF CONGRESS)

they laid siege to Fort McHenry. As the bombardment continued the rest of the day and into the night, attorney Francis Scott Key watched "the rockets' red glare," and "bombs bursting in air" from a nearby ship. To his amazement, "by dawn's early light . . . our flag was still there," fluttering in tatters over the fort and inspiring his poem "Defense of Fort McHenry." A newspaper published it a few days later with a new name, "The Star-Spangled Banner."

On September 14 the British abandoned their fruitless assault, withdrew their troops, and sailed out of Chesapeake Bay for the British West Indies. Their departure ended the fighting, and after a month of talks with no solutions in sight, negotiators in Ghent fixed on a way out of the impasse: they declared the war ended and relegated demands of both sides to an arbitration commission to be set up at a later date.

Agreement at Ghent. Britain's chief negotiator, Admiral Lord Gambier, holds the treaty ending the War of 1812 and shakes hands with John Quincy Adams, the chief American negotiator. Albert Gallatin stands to Adams's immediate left, while Henry Clay is seated on the right at the rear. (FROM "THE SIGNING OF THE TREATY OF GHENT, CHRISTMAS EVE, 1814," A PAINTING BY SIR AMÉDÉE FORESTIER, 1914; SMITHSONIAN AMERICAN ART MUSEUM, GIFT OF THE SULGRAVE INSTITUTION OF THE UNITED STATES AND GREAT BRITAIN)

In the end the Treaty of Ghent represented a stinging defeat for both sides. After a costly two-year war they returned to the *status quo ante bellum*, releasing all prisoners and restoring all conquered territories to prewar status, except for West Florida, which fell under American sovereignty.

On Christmas Eve of 1814, as John Quincy Adams and the other negotiators signed the Treaty of Ghent, a fleet of fifty British ships landed 7,500 battle-hardened veterans on Louisiana's southeastern coast near New Orleans. To their shock, General Andrew Jackson awaited in ambush. After a spectacular but indecisive artillery battle on January 1, the British pulled back and attacked again a week later. As redcoats advanced

The battle at New Orleans on Christmas Eve, 1814, claimed more than 2,000 lives and had no impact on the outcome of the war. American and British negotiators had signed a treaty of peace in Ghent, Belgium, ending the war two weeks before the battle. (LIBRARY OF CONGRESS)

in traditional linear style of European warfare, Jackson's Tennessee and Kentucky woodsmen—all crack marksmen—opened fire. The British troops stepped forward mechanically, toppling one by one, then by the dozens. The bodies piled higher and higher until the "horror before them was too great to be withstood: and they turned away, dropping their weapons and running to the rear."[5] After only thirty minutes the battle was over; the British commanding general and two other generals lay dead along with more than 2,000 British troops. British survivors staggered back to their ships and, on January 27, sailed away from what proved the last battle of the war and the last hostile incursion by British troops on American soil.

A few days later Secretary of State Monroe called members of Congress into the Patent Office building in Washington, the only public building the British had spared from flames. They unleashed a chorus of sustained cheers when he delivered the news of Jackson's victory. Federalists,

Republicans, hawks, and doves alike exchanged handshakes and adjourned to soak in the news with appropriate drinks.

What they did not know, however, was the utter uselessness of Jackson's victory. Two weeks earlier John Quincy Adams and his American negotiators had signed the treaty ending the war, but like the negotiations when the war began, news of the settlement did not arrive until weeks later, when a British sloop sailed into New York harbor, flying a flag of truce. The war the United States could have won without firing the first shot had ended before they fired the last.

Nonetheless Americans—almost unanimously—deluded themselves into calling the war a glorious triumph over the world's most powerful nation—a "second war of independence." The national delusion resulted from a series of coincidences: The victory at New Orleans had come just *before* they received news of peace, and in the public mind the chronology of events made the battle seem decisive in forcing the British to sue for peace and end depredations on American shipping. In fact, it was the defeat of Napoléon that allowed Britain to harbor her warships and end the need to impress seamen and seize ships with contraband.

When the Supreme Court justices returned to Washington in the winter of 1815, a maze of scaffolding and a horde of workmen filled the interior of the Capitol. Although the fire set by British invaders had left most of the interior a blackened ruin, the Supreme Court chamber beneath the Senate escaped relatively untouched. Construction work in the damaged sections of the Capitol, however, made the Court chamber inaccessible, and the justices gathered, instead, on the spacious second floor of the nearby home of Elias Caldwell, the clerk of the Supreme Court who had saved the court's records from British destruction. His home would serve as Court chambers for the next two years, 1815 and 1816.

Renowned by then for sparkling and often soaring oratory, the Supreme Court became an entertaining gathering place for Washington society in the days before card games and other pastimes filled the idle hours of wealthy American women.

"Mrs. Madison and a train of ladies entered . . . the day I was there," recalled Mrs. Samuel Harrison Smith, whose husband was editor, publisher,

*The home of Elias Boudinot Caldwell, a captain of
cavalry in the War of 1812. As his troop retreated through
Washington, Caldwell had the foresight to stop at the
Capitol and salvage the papers of the Supreme Court and
hide them in his family home. Spared during the burning
of Washington, Caldwell House hosted the Supreme Court
on its spacious second floor for two years after the war.*
(LIBRARY OF CONGRESS)

and owner of Washington's *National Intelligencer.* Mrs. Smith was convinced that one attorney "thought more of the female part of his audience than of the court."[6]

During and immediately after the War of 1812 most arguments before the High Court related to admiralty cases, captured ships, cargoes, and the rules of war more than they did to the Constitution. One case, however, proved an imposing landmark for both:

In August 1813 a Spanish merchant in London had chartered the armed English cargo ship *Nereide* to carry £10,000 worth of Spanish iron, steel, coal, tools, and dry goods to Buenos Aires. After an exchange of fire, an American privateer captured the *Nereide* and brought it to New York. The district court there awarded the ship and its cargo to their American captor as a prize of war. After the circuit court upheld the award, the Spanish merchant appealed to the Supreme Court, arguing that Spain was a neutral nation and that international law exempted neutral goods from seizure as prizes of war. The American claimant charged that the *Nereide* had been armed and belligerent—that the British flag on its mast and fearsome cannons on deck left the ship far from neutral in appearance.

Marshall and the Court disagreed, declaring neutral goods invariably exempt from seizure at sea, regardless of the character or nationality of the ship carrying the goods.

"The original law of nations," Marshall explained, stated that "the goods of an enemy in the vessel of a friend are a prize of war and the goods of a friend in the vessel of an enemy are to be restored." He said the rule evolved from the principle that war gave combatants "full right to capture the goods of an enemy, but . . . no right to capture the goods of a friend."

> The character of the property . . . depends in no degree upon the char-
> acter of the vehicle in which it is found. . . . The characters of the vessel
> and cargo remain as distinct in this as in any other case. The sentence,
> therefore of the Circuit Court must be reversed, and the property . . . be
> restored [to the Spanish merchant].[7]

Added to international law by the 1856 Declaration of Paris, Marshall's *Nereide* decision opened the seas to international free trade, permitting neutral nations to remain out of other nations' conflicts without suffering economic penalties. Marshall's decision remains a core element of international law and the laws of the sea and made possible the restoration to their owners of untold hundreds of millions of dollars' worth of art and other goods stolen by Nazi, Communist, and other twentieth-century rogue governments.

A few months after signing the Treaty of Ghent the United States and Britain signed a commercial accord that ended discriminatory duties between the two nations and catapulted the two nations' economies to record peacetime levels. Both nations subsequently acted to prevent accidental renewal of hostilities along the US-Canadian frontier by agreeing to limit naval strength on the Great Lakes to four ships each. Both nations were to limit arms aboard their ships to those needed for enforcing customs regulations but incapable of participating in naval warfare.

The war quickly became a distant memory, as Americans happily embraced the greatest peacetime prosperity they had experienced in the more than thirty-two years since victory at Yorktown. General William Henry Harrison's victories over the Indian nations of the West had opened the lands between the Appalachian Mountains and Mississippi River to American migration.

Secure from attack by British troops and Indians, tens of thousands of Americans realized Aaron Burr's dream and streamed westward to carve new farms from virgin plains, harvest furs and pelts from super-abundant wildlife, cull timber from vast forests, and chisel ores from rich mountainsides.

The land rush added six states and scores of towns to the United States, generated wealth for almost every man, woman, and child in the nation, and engendered the greatest social and economic revolution in history. Never before in the annals of man had a sovereign state transferred so much land to ordinary citizens with no claims to nobility. Regardless of their lineage, they claimed millions of acres of land that lifted them into the "propertied class"—the landed gentry—with rights to vote, serve in public office, and govern their communities, states, and nation.

With the surge of migration across the Appalachians into the Virginia wilderness, the Virginia legislature appropriated funds to implement John Marshall's recommendations in the 1812 River Commission Report to improve James River navigation and build a turnpike across the mountains.

A decade later it would charter the James River and Kanawha Company and fulfill George Washington's dream of strengthening the Union with commercial links between East and West.

Although it spawned far-reaching economic progress, the westward migration also produced thousands of disputes over land ownership—including one courtroom drama over a relatively miniscule 739 acres. The case reached the Supreme Court in 1816 and provoked a historic decision that expanded the controversy over state sovereignty and sent the nation a step closer to civil war. For once Chief Justice John Marshall had no part in the decision, having recused himself because his brother James Markham Marshall had leased the lands in the case.

In Marshall's absence it fell to Boston's Associate Justice Joseph Story to deliver the historic decision—a monumental peroration that upheld the constitutional primacy of treaties as "supreme law of the land" [Article VI]. In addition, it reiterated federal government sovereignty over foreign relations and the Supreme Court's authority to void state court decisions it deemed unconstitutional.

Martin v. Hunter's Lessee was an unsettled remnant of *Hite v. Fairfax* that John Marshall had won in 1794. During the Revolution land speculator David Hunter had purchased a 739-acre tract from the Commonwealth of Virginia which had been seizing and selling unsettled Tory lands. When the Marshalls won *Hite v. Fairfax*, Hunter claimed his property lay outside the Fairfax Manor Lands and was, therefore, unaffected by the decision that had given Fairfax title to the manor lands. Virginia's court of appeals, the state's highest court, agreed.

John Marshall's brother James Markham appealed to the US Supreme Court, which reversed the Virginia court decision and ruled against Hunter. In delivering the High Court decision, Story said the Jay Treaty had nullified Virginia's confiscation law and nullified its sale of land to Hunter. He ordered the Virginia Court of Appeals to reverse itself and restore title to the current owners of the manor lands—that is, the Marshalls.

Led by Thomas Jefferson's political parrot Judge Spencer Roane, the Virginia Court startled the nation—North and South—by rejecting the

Supreme Court order and declaring "the appellate power of the Supreme Court does not extend to this Court."

Not satisfied with defying a Supreme Court order, Roane and his court echoed the words of Jefferson's notorious Kentucky Resolution, calling the Constitution a compact between sovereign states and denying the US Supreme Court any jurisdiction in state matters.[8]

Unlike Marshall, Justice Story shied from angry confrontations and prefaced his response with a gentle apology to members of the Virginia court for the "unwelcome task" he faced. Nonetheless he and the other justices were unyielding, with a firm, collective rejection of both the Virginia and Kentucky Resolutions:

"The Constitution of the United States was established *not* by the states," Story asserted, "but, as the preamble declared, by '*the people of the United States.*'" With that, he added one more weapon to the Supreme Court's arsenal: in *Marbury v. Madison* the Court had asserted power to void federal laws it deemed unconstitutional. In *United States v. Peters* Marshall and the court asserted the supremacy of federal over state laws, denied states the right to overrule federal laws, and asserted its own power to void state laws. With *Martin v. Hunter's Lessee* Story asserted the Court's power to overturn state court decisions it adjudged in violation of the Constitution. In effect he presented the Supreme Court as the nation's final arbiter, with powers to void any and every law *and* court decision, federal or state.

DESPITE GROWING OBJECTIONS TO VIRGINIA'S OUTSIZED INFLUENCE IN the federal government, Americans elected Secretary of State James Monroe fifth President of the United States, with virtually no opposition, and his inauguration was the most joyful and elaborate since that of George Washington.

As secretary of state and secretary of war, Monroe had become the most visible, most powerful figure in the Madison administration. With some justification, Americans inflated his role in government and credited him with masterminding "victory" in the War of 1812, initiating postwar western expansion, and engineering the nation's economic recovery.

Although his hair had grayed and worry had carved furrows across his cheeks, Marshall's former comrade-in-arms remained robust, handsome, and fit, with a martial bearing that made him seem a worthy successor to George Washington.

March 4, 1817, dawned "a mild and radiant" morning, and at 11:30 a.m. Monroe and Vice President–elect Daniel D. Tompkins, the former governor of New York, stepped out of Monroe's house to the cheers of thousands. "A large cavalcade of citizens on horseback," the newspapers reported, escorted them to the temporary capitol, a building hastily constructed to house Congress while workmen repaired the fire-damaged original 100 yards away.

In the first open-air presidential inauguration in American history President Madison and the justices of the Supreme Court greeted the President-elect as the Marine Corps and several companies of artillery and riflemen fired explosive military honors into the air. The officials shuffled into the small, temporary Senate chamber for Tompkins to take the oath of office as vice president, then moved outside onto a specially built platform for the presidential ceremonies.

According to custom then, Monroe delivered his address before taking his oath, expressing his deep distress over the secessionist movement in New England and calling for "increased harmony" among Americans. "Discord does not belong to our system," he insisted. "The American people . . . constitute one great family with a common interest." Monroe pledged that "harmony among Americans . . . will be the object of my constant and zealous attentions."[9]

At Monroe's earnest request, his friend since childhood, Chief Justice John Marshall, administered the oath of office in a ceremony fraught with emotions for both. From the time they were boys in the Virginia woods Monroe and Marshall had led lives in tandem, attending the same little backwoods school, going off to the same college, enlisting and fighting heroically in the Revolutionary War, shivering through a bitter winter in the same log hut at Valley Forge, leading the charge into British lines at Monmouth. Both had studied law after the war and entered public service.

They parted ways for a while over ratification of the Constitution and Bill of Rights, but the course of their careers reunited them. Both men served their country loyally and brilliantly as congressmen, diplomats in Europe, and, eventually, as secretaries of state.

Both Marshall and Monroe had aged visibly under the burdens of heavy public and private responsibilities. They were both married with children. Monroe had two daughters, thirty-year-old Eliza, married by then, and sixteen-year-old Maria Hester. Marshall had five sons and one daughter. Marshall's oldest son, thirty-two-year-old Thomas, had graduated from Princeton College but chose to return to his roots on the family farm on the old Fairfax estate. The next oldest, twenty-eight-year-old Jacquelin, abandoned medical studies to join Thomas. Although eighteen-year-old John was still at Harvard, he would be dismissed before graduating and join his older brothers on the farm. Twenty-one-year-old Mary had married a Richmond business man and settled near the Marshall house. Only fifteen-year-old James Keith and ten-year-old Edward Carrington still lived at home.

On March 15, 1817, John Marshall administered the presidential oath to James Monroe. They were the last Revolutionary War officers to lead the nation and the last of the Virginia Dynasty that had governed the nation during all but four years since independence. Although much of the Capitol lay in ruins behind them, the Constitution they swore to uphold remained intact.

The inauguration was a personal triumph for both men, and outgoing President James Madison—a close friend of each by then—joined the estimated 8,000 spectators who roared their approval as the President uttered the last words of the presidential oath: "So help me God."

The lives of Monroe and Marshall would remain intertwined long after that first inauguration. Although Monroe's sweeping election victory relegated Marshall's Federalist Party to history's dustbin, Marshall's

With the Capitol ruins looming in the background, Chief Justice John Marshall (right, holding Bible) swears in James Monroe as the nation's fifth President. The destruction by British troops in the War of 1812 forced the inauguration outdoors for the first time. (LIBRARY OF CONGRESS)

broad Supreme Court decisions had tossed Monroe's Republican Party*
and many of its Jeffersonian concepts into the same receptacle.

As President, Thomas Jefferson had sought to give states authority over most domestic matters, but Marshall had set aside all or part of half the number of laws passed by state legislatures. "The government of the United States is supreme," Marshall asserted again and again. "Its laws, when made in the pursuance of the Constitution, form the supreme law of the land."[10]

---

* As stated earlier, Monroe's and Jefferson's Republican Party had no ties to the modern Republican Party.

Although Monroe disagreed with some Marshall decisions, he took full advantage of them as President. Like most Presidents before and after, Monroe found Marshall's brand of Federalism the only practical means for governing a nation with so diverse a population, such sharp regional differences, and so many conflicting interests. Together the two friends helped allay "the storms of party" and turn Monroe's presidency into an "Era of Good Feelings."[11] The President took advantage of the political calm to strengthen the nation's physical defenses against external foes, while the Chief Justice strengthened the nation's constitutional defenses against internal foes.

By the end of Monroe's first term political parties had disappeared, the US land mass had expanded into an empire that stretched "from sea to shining sea," and Monroe became the only President in American history other than George Washington to win reelection without opposition.

The great westward migration saw land disputes clog the Supreme Court calendar immediately after Monroe's first inauguration, but when the Court reconvened in the winter of 1819 Marshall and his associate justices began what would be the twelve most important years in Supreme Court and US government history.

CHAPTER 16

The Final Arbiter

LIKE THUNDERBOLTS FROM ON HIGH, SUPREME COURT RULINGS BEGAN crashing onto the legal landscape of the United States in early 1819, as Virginia's John Marshall, the American Law Giver, proclaimed to all Americans what thou *shalt* and *shalt* not do. Together with *Marbury v. Madison*, the decisions from 1819 to 1832 firmly established the Supreme Court of the United States as the third pillar of America's federal government and final arbiter of the nation's legal matters.

Although the Court did not and could not initiate domestic cases, Marshall's Supreme Court grew far more powerful than the appellate court described in the Constitution. To make the Constitution work—"to form a more perfect union, establish justice, insure domestic tranquility . . . and secure the blessing of liberty to ourselves and our posterity"—Marshall's Supreme Court put restraints on Presidents and governors, Congress and state assemblies, and federal and state courts.

Marshall's Court assumed so many powers so quickly, however, that southern states opposed to union and reluctant to cede state sovereignty rose in protest. First, South Carolina, then Georgia called out its state militia in 1832 to confront federal troops and prepared for civil war—thirty years ahead of history's schedule. Indeed, Marshall himself feared "that our Constitution cannot last."[1]

Thus, Marshall conceded that the Court's decisions had indeed changed the Constitution and altered the shape of the government that the Founders—from North and South—had created.

John Marshall's Supreme Court ruled America's legal landscape for thirty-five years and made him the longest-serving Chief Justice in US history. Of the court's hundreds of decisions, the following nine may have been the most far-reaching, in that they formed a new foundation for US constitutional law:

Marbury v. Madison (1803)
United States v. Peters (1809)
Fletcher v. Peck (1810)
Martin v. Hunter's Lessee (1816)
Dartmouth College v. Woodward (1819)
McCulloch v. Maryland (1819)
Cohens v. Virginia (1821)
Gibbons v. Ogden (1824)
Worcester v. Georgia (1832)

Historians and jurists may debate which were *the* most important, but each was most important in certain ways—as are so many cases the Supreme Court decided then and since. Three cases (*Marbury v. Madison*, *United States v. Peters*, and *Worcester v. Georgia*) established the Supreme Court as the nation's supreme arbiter, asserting the Court's right to review and void every law, court decision, and executive act in the land—federal, state, or local. As Chief Justice Earl Warren would put it in 1958, "The federal judiciary is supreme in the exposition of the law of the Constitution."[2]

Three other cases (*McCulloch v. Maryland*, *Martin v. Hunter's Lessee*, and *Gibbons v. Ogden*) stripped states of sovereignty beyond their borders and affirmed federal government sovereignty in national and international affairs, and extended the federal government's designated powers in the Constitution to include so-called implied powers.

And three cases (*Fletcher v. Peck, Dartmouth College v. Woodward*, and *Cohens v. Virginia*) ensured individual citizens (and private institutions) the "inalienable rights" promised by the Declaration of Independence and Bill of Rights. John Marshall and the Court defined them as life, liberty, and *property* rather than *pursuit of happiness*. The three cases re-asserted the inviolability of contracts and protected citizens and corporations against arbitrary confiscation of their property by government.

Of the nine, a full discussion of *Marbury v. Madison* (judicial review) appears on pages 195–196 and 206–210; *United States v. Peters* (federal sovereignty) on pages 261 and 263–264; *Fletcher v. Peck* (inviolability of contracts) on page 265; and *Hunter v. Martin's Lessee* (treaties as federal law and Supreme Court powers to overrule state courts) on pages 286–287.

Dartmouth College v. Woodward followed the seizure in 1816 of Dartmouth College by New Hampshire's state legislature, which took control of the private school and converted it into a public, state-run institution. After a state court upheld the takeover, Daniel Webster, the eloquent New Hampshire attorney and Dartmouth alumnus, appealed to John Marshall's Supreme Court with one of the most moving summations in Court history:

"This, Sir," Webster pleaded to the Chief Justice, "is the case not merely of that humble institution; it is the case of every college in our Land!"

> It is the case of . . . all those great charities founded by the piety of our ancestors to alleviate human misery. . . . It is, in some sense, the case of every man among us who has property of which he may be stripped. For the question is simply this: "Shall our State Legislatures be allowed to take *that which is not their own*, to turn it from its original use, and apply it to such ends and purposes as they in their discretion shall see fit!"

"Sir," the future senator all but sobbed, "you may destroy this little institution. It is weak. It is, Sir, as I have said, a small college . . . "

Webster choked on his words.

" . . . and yet, there are those who love it."[3]

Far from destroying Webster's "little institution," Marshall scolded state authorities, calling the New Hampshire law and state court ruling that turned Dartmouth into a state institution "repugnant to the Constitution of the United States."

In a decision to ensure constitutional protection of individual and institutional property rights in America, Marshall declared the original state-issued charter that created the college a *contract* protected by Section 10, Article I of the Constitution, which prohibits states from passing "any law impairing the obligation of contracts."* He declared the constitutional prohibition applicable to all contracts—including state charters that created charitable and benevolent corporations as well as private business corporations.

"The judgment of the state court," he stated, "must therefore be reversed."[4]

⤜⤛

ONLY TWO WEEKS AFTER *DARTMOUTH* THE MARSHALL COURT HANDED down another monumental decision in *McCulloch v. Maryland,* repudiating all state sovereignty over federal activities and proclaiming the federal government the ultimate sovereign in the United States. The decision would eventually provoke not only civil war, but a host of bitter confrontations between state and federal authorities in the intervening decades.

McCulloch v. Maryland began in 1818 when Maryland imposed a tax on all banks in the state, including the federally chartered Bank of the United States. James McCulloch, the manager of the Baltimore branch of the federal bank, refused to pay, arguing that the state had no right to tax the federal government. A county court disagreed and convicted him of

---

* The state seizure of Dartmouth College did not involve eminent domain or state seizure of private property for public use. At the time the state granted the charter to Dartmouth College it could have established a public institution but instead signed a contract, or charter, with the trustees of the college to establish a private college. The Supreme Court, therefore, did not rule on any question of eminent domain but on the state's breach of its contract.

"A small college . . . yet there are those who love it." When the state of New Hampshire passed a law converting Dartmouth College (seen here in 1793) from a private to a public school, John Marshall's Supreme Court voided the law, calling it "repugnant to the Constitution of the United States." (ENGRAVING BY J. DUNHAM AND S. HILL, IN MASSACHUSETTS MAGAZINE, FEBRUARY, 1793)

violating state tax law. After the state court of appeals upheld his conviction, McCulloch appealed to the US Supreme Court, where batteries of famous lawyers fired their legal arrows at each other. Among them were US Attorney General William Wirt and the demosthenic Daniel Webster, fresh off his triumph in the Dartmouth case.

Maryland lawyers reiterated Thomas Jefferson's arguments in the Kentucky Resolution. They called the Bank of the United States illegal, saying the Constitution did not give the federal government powers to charter a bank—which it did not. They argued, as Jefferson had, that the Constitution was "a compact between the states, and all the powers which are not expressly relinquished to it are reserved to the states. . . . The powers of the general government . . . are delegated by the states, who [*sic*] alone are truly sovereign."[5]

After Webster and Wirt finished their arguments for the federal government, Marshall savaged Maryland's attorneys in a unanimous decision that assailed their claims of broad state sovereignty. In perhaps the most famous—and most important—words of any Chief Justice in American history, Marshall conceded that Maryland's attorneys had been correct in only one of their assertions—that the *framers* had indeed been elected by state legislatures and not the people of the United States.

But he went on to give them a stern lesson in history, pointing out that the Constitution drafted by the framers was only a *proposal*. It did not become the law of the land until *the people* in each state elected conventions to vote it up or down.

"The government of the Union," said Marshall, "is emphatically and truly a government of the people. Its powers are granted by them and are to be exercised directly on them and for their benefit."

> Let the end be legitimate, let it be within the scope of the Constitution, and all means which are appropriate, which are plainly adapted to that end, which are not prohibited, but consist with the letter and spirit of the Constitution, are constitutional. . . . After the most deliberate consideration, it is the unanimous and decided opinion of this Court that the act to incorporate the Bank of the United States is a law made in pursuance of the Constitution and is part of the supreme law of the land.[6]

In effect Marshall reaffirmed Alexander Hamilton's contention as Treasury secretary in George Washington's first administration that the Constitution gave the federal government "implied powers" as well as specific ones. Hamilton argued that by granting Congress power "to make all laws which shall be necessary and proper for carrying into execution" its other obligations (Section 8, Article 1), the framers had extended federal authority beyond the letter of the Constitution.

Marshall agreed.

"If the measure . . . is not forbidden by any particular provision of the Constitution," Marshall declared, "it may safely be deemed to come within the compass of the national authority."[7] In effect Marshall stabilized the foundation and structure of the entire federal government, extending constitutional powers beyond the literal meanings of its words to include implied meanings.

The decision remains the center of acrimonious debate to this day, and some authors of both the Constitution and Bill of Rights (the first ten amendments to the original document) sharply disagreed with Marshall.

"The powers of the federal government are enumerated," James Madison had stated unequivocally at the Virginia ratification convention. "It has . . . defined and limited objects, beyond which it cannot extend its jurisdiction."[8] Indeed, the Tenth Amendment of the Bill of Rights, sponsored in the First Congress by Madison at the insistence of Patrick Henry, declared "powers not delegated to the United States by the Constitution . . . are reserved to the states."

The *McCulloch* decision, therefore, represented a sea change that muddied constitutional waters then and since and has often encouraged each of the three branches of the federal government to step well beyond constitutional bounds.

In 1846 President James K. Polk ordered troops into disputed territory to provoke the Mexican War—without a constitutionally required declaration of war. Abraham Lincoln—then an Illinois congressman—argued vigorously that the President had assumed powers of an absolute monarch and usurped war-making powers from Congress. A few years later as President, however, Lincoln himself mirrored Polk's constitutional violations by unilaterally expanding the military, proclaiming martial law, suspending habeas corpus, and, finally, issuing a proclamation emancipating slaves—all without congressional approval.

Nothing in the Constitution gives a President power to issue proclamations or executive orders with the force of law. Only Congress can legislate, yet presidents have issued more than 13,500 proclamations and executive orders since the founding of the Republic, while Congress has enacted only about 20,000 laws.

But the executive has not been alone in usurping powers not granted by the Constitution. Since the First Federal Congress met in 1789 the national legislature has enacted nearly 200 laws that the Supreme Court has voided as unconstitutional. Of the 20,000 laws enacted by Congress since the First Congress met in 1789, the President has vetoed more than 2,500—sometimes for political reasons, but often because he deemed them unconstitutional. And the Supreme Court itself, as Jefferson suggested, may have crossed the line between interpretation of the Constitution and amending it when it assumed the power of judicial review in *Marbury v. Madison* and gave Congress implied powers in *McCulloch v. Maryland*. Certainly the Dred Scott decision declaring African Americans noncitizens fell into that category.

President Lincoln justified his actions as necessary to preserve the *country* as opposed to the *Constitution*. Others in both the executive and legislative branches have justified their breaches of the Constitution as necessary interpretations of vague constitutional language or as essential for filling gaps overlooked or unforeseen by the framers at the time they wrote the document. And Marshall's Supreme Court justified many of its most controversial decisions as essential to the survival of the federal government.

After the Supreme Court declared the federal government's Bank of the United States constitutional, it went on to impose sharp limits on state sovereignty by denying Maryland (and every other state) the right to tax the federal government or its agencies.

"The power to tax is the power to destroy," Marshall declared, "which would defeat the operations of a supreme government. . . . If the states may tax one instrument employed by the government . . . they may tax any and every other instrument. They may tax the mail . . . the mint . . . defeat all the ends of government. This was not intended by the American people."

Marshall insisted that the Constitution did not give any government the right "to pull down what there is an acknowledged right in another government to build up." His voice then rose as he proclaimed, "We are unanimously of opinion that the law passed by the legislature of Maryland imposing a tax on the Bank of the United States is unconstitutional and void."[9]

By voiding a state law and further paring state sovereignty, *McCulloch* outraged the South. Undeterred, however, Marshall and the Court continued adding to southern outrage in case after case. As Marshall explained to social activist Thomas S. Grimke, "The assumption that our Constitution is essentially a LEAGUE [*sic*] and not A GOVERNMENT [*sic*] . . . is the true and substantial dividing line between parties in the United States. As the one opinion or the other prevails, will the Union, I firmly believe, be preserved or dissolved." He said that a league had "never been of long duration" or strong enough "to preserve a lasting peace between its members."[10]

A year after *McCulloch* the Court extended its protection to every citizen in the land by asserting its power in *Cohens v. Virginia* to overturn decisions in every court—even a local criminal court.

A Virginia court had imposed a fine of $100 on Philip and Mendes Cohen of Baltimore, Maryland, for violating Virginia's ban on sales of out-of-state lottery tickets by selling District of Columbia "National Lottery" tickets in Virginia. The Cohens appealed, arguing that the National Lottery was a federal entity like the Bank of the United States and, therefore, protected from state regulation. The state moved to dismiss, arguing that the Supreme Court had no jurisdiction in a local criminal court case.

As with so many disputes it heard, Marshall and the justices faced two distinct questions in one case: whether it had jurisdiction in a local criminal case and whether the state ban against the sale of out-of-state lottery tickets infringed on a legitimate federal activity. Marshall and the other justices found holes in all the arguments and ruled accordingly. They rejected the Cohens' argument, saying Congress had not created the National Lottery as a national institution like the Bank of the United States. The National Lottery was *national* in name only; Congress had created it as a municipal agency to raise revenues for the city of Washington. In effect it was a local gambling game with no connection to interstate commerce, and the Court had no authority to force a state to sell out-of-state lottery tickets if it chose not to.

He nonetheless issued a stern rejoinder to Virginia's lawyers, asserting the Court's jurisdiction over every court in the nation and proclaiming the rights of all Americans to the same constitutional protections in the lowest criminal courts as in the highest.

"In war we are one people," he lectured Virginia's lawyers.

> In making peace, we are one people. In all commercial regulations, we are one and the same people. . . . The constitution and laws of a state, so far as they are repugnant to the Constitution and laws of the United States, are absolutely void. These states are constituent parts of the United States. They are members of one great empire for some purposes sovereign, for others subordinate.[11]

Marshall's words outraged Thomas Jefferson, who called for a constitutional amendment converting judgeships into elective offices, thus making the Supreme Court and federal judiciary directly responsible to the public. Jefferson, however, aging as well as deeply involved in supervising construction of the University of Virginia in Charlottesville, could not leave to reenter the political fray himself. Instead, he again turned to Judge Spencer Roane to lead the attack.

Married to one of Patrick Henry's daughters, Roane invoked his father-in-law's legendary name in newspaper essays criticizing the Court's "monstrous" decisions and increasingly "despotic power. . . . Appointed in one generation, it [the Court] claims to make laws and constitutions for another."[12]

Home in Massachusetts by the time Roane's articles appeared, Associate Justice Joseph Story wrote to Marshall accusing Jefferson of attempting "to prostrate the judicial authority and annihilate all public reverence for its dignity. . . . Can he wish yet to have influence enough to destroy the government of his country?"[13]

"What you say of Mr. Jefferson," Marshall replied, "rather grieves than surprises me. It grieves me because his influence is still so great that many will adopt his opinions, however unsound they may be." Marshall warned Story that Jefferson had long plotted "to convert our government into a mere league of states. . . . The attack upon the judiciary is in fact an attack against the Union."[14]

> For Mr. Jefferson's opinion as respects this department it is not difficult to assign the cause. He is among the most ambitious and I suspect among

the most unforgiving of men. His great power is over the mass of the people and this power is chiefly acquired by professions of democracy. Every check on the wild impulse of the moment is a check on his own power and he is unfriendly to the source from which it flows. He looks, of course, with ill will at an independent judiciary.[15]

Marshall refused to acknowledge even a grain of truth to what some constitutional scholars considered legitimate criticisms of the Court and the case law it was writing. Jefferson was first to voice such criticisms, and critics continue to echo his complaint that the states—and, indeed, the American people—lack an arbiter to review and restrain the Supreme Court. Jefferson argued that Supreme Court decisions often crossed the line from constitutional interpretation to legislation—that "case law" itself represents legislation by court fiat.

"The legislative and executive branches may sometimes err," Jefferson argued time and again, "but elections . . . will bring them to rights. The judiciary branch . . . [is] like gravity, ever acting, with noiseless foot and unalarming advance, gaining ground step by step . . . engulfing insidiously the [state] governments." Jefferson complained that Supreme Court justices and the rest of the federal judiciary "consider themselves secure for life" and independent of "the will of the nation" because they do not have to face elections and are not subject to term limits.[16]

Apart from impeachment of individual justices, there were (and are) few checks on the Supreme Court's exercise of powers. The Supreme Court itself can hear—and has heard—challenges to previous court decisions, and it has, on occasion, reversed or tempered those earlier rulings. Congress can check Supreme Court powers by passing laws that negate the effects of court decisions, and it can respond to abuses of power by impeaching and removing individual justices. It can also invoke Article V of the Constitution and initiate the slow, cumbersome process of amending the Constitution to void a Supreme Court decision.

❧

THE FUROR THAT JEFFERSON PROVOKED AGAINST THE SUPREME COURT gained intensity in the South in the fall of 1823, when Associate Justice William Johnson, presiding in Charleston's circuit court, declared South Carolina's Negro Seamen Act unconstitutional. South Carolina had passed the act in response to rumors of an imminent slave rebellion in Charleston following Haiti's bloody slave uprising (see page 152). The law required imprisonment of *all* black seamen on arriving ships—free or not—for the duration of their stay and regardless of a ship's country of origin. Ship captains were held responsible for enforcing the law, and black seamen who failed to comply were to be arrested and sold into slavery.

"Our brother Johnson," Marshall wrote to Joseph Story, "has hung himself on a democratic snag in a hedge composed entirely of thorny states' rights in South Carolina."

> The subject is one of much feeling in the South. . . . The decision has been considered as another act of judicial usurpation, but the sentiment has been avowed that if this be the Constitution, it is better to break that instrument than submit to the principle.[17]

President Monroe drew some attention away from Johnson's decision by announcing plans to retire at the end of his second term. Burning with ambition to succeed him, members of his cabinet filled the press with so many attacks on each other that the newspapers and their readers all but forgot the Negro Seamen case.

Also drawing attention away from the Negro Seamen controversy was the outbreak of waterfront violence in many cities resulting from a spreading war between steamboat operators. New York State's legislators had planted the seeds of conflict sixteen years earlier in 1808, when they granted steamboat inventor Robert Fulton and his partner Robert Livingston exclusive rights to operate steamboats in New York waters. Louisiana's legislature followed suit in its waterways three years later, in 1811.

As steamboat travel and shipping increased, state after state granted monopolies to individual steamboat companies, with some states seizing vessels of unlicensed out-of-state operators. Violence erupted between

Increased steamboat traffic on the Hudson River and elsewhere set off a steamboat war, as states granted favored operators exclusive licenses and barred out-of-state firms. John Marshall's Supreme Court ruled such state monopolies unconstitutional, saying the Constitution had given Congress exclusive authority over interstate commerce. "Commerce among the states does not stop at the boundary line of each state," the Chief Justice declared in his historic decision. (Library of Congress)

seamen from competing companies for control of piers in waterfront towns in Connecticut, New York, New Jersey, and other states. Steamboat operators· and owners rushed into courtrooms, filing suits and countersuits until one legal skirmish reached John Marshall and the US Supreme Court.

The Fulton-Livingston monopoly had granted Aaron Ogden an exclusive license to operate a ferry on the Hudson River between New York City and New Jersey. Meanwhile Thomas Gibbons and the young Cornelius Vanderbilt—still years away from his legendary riches—were operating two steamboats under the Federal Coasting Act, allowing them to carry passengers and goods in coastal waters. Coastal waters, however, flowed into New York Bay and lapped both New York and New Jersey shores, putting them in competition with Ogden and infringing on his monopoly. When New York state banned Gibbons's vessels from New York waters, he sued.

Even the astute minds of John Marshall and his colleagues admitted that the steamboat wars so "perplexed the understanding as to obscure principles which were before thought quite plain." Marshall and the Court, however, restated those principles simply:

"The enlightened patriots who framed our Constitution," Marshall declared, "must be understood to have employed words in their natural sense and to have intended what they said." Citing Article I, Section 8 of the Constitution, he said the framers had given Congress power "to regulate commerce" and the word "commerce . . . describes the commercial intercourse between nations and parts of nations. . . . Commerce among the states does not stop at the boundary line of each state, but may be introduced into the interior."[18]

His conclusion was direct and blunt:

The several laws of the state of New York that prohibit vessels licensed according to the laws of the United States from navigating the waters of New York . . . are repugnant to the Constitution and void . . . and the bill [lawsuit] of the said Aaron Ogden . . . is hereby dismissed.[19]

Several historians called the 1824 *Gibbons v. Ogden* decision "the emancipation of American commerce"[20] and the legal foundation of the free enterprise system. In effect it barred states from interfering in interstate commerce by establishing state-sponsored monopolies. It also reinforced federal sovereignty over interstate affairs and commerce generally, and it gave national interests priority over state and regional interests.

❧

AS MARSHALL AWAITED ANOTHER JEFFERSON ASSAULT ON THE COURT after *Gibbons v. Ogden*, the eighty-three-year-old Sage of Monticello remained uncharacteristically silent. Jefferson was bankrupt and about to lose his beloved home and all his possessions. He organized a public lottery hoping to sell his mills and raise enough money to keep his mountain-top home at Monticello and its surrounding farms.

Jefferson had been no more profligate than other southern plantation owners of his social and political class. All lived beyond their means and accumulated enormous debts, but professional success, crop sales, and sales of excess land had always provided enough income to cover living costs and retire enough debt to keep bill collectors and sheriffs at bay. Ironically, Jefferson's own Louisiana Purchase added so much vacant land in the West to the nation's supply of unsold real estate that eastern land values plummeted and reduced proceeds from the sale of Jefferson's own unused fields.

With his retirement from the presidency, the loss of his annual $25,000-a-year salary left him drowning in debt, with unpaid interest accumulating rapidly and land sales unable to cover a fraction of what he owed. Compounding his problems, he cosigned two notes of $10,000 each for a close friend who died shortly thereafter and left Jefferson owing another $20,000 plus $1,200 a year in interest.

Whether financial ruin precipitated his final illness is unclear, but it did him no good. By midspring of 1826 he suffered from painful arthritis, swollen legs, chronic diarrhea, and a urethral obstruction. On July 2, 1826, he began drifting in and out of consciousness, and on July 4—the fiftieth anniversary of the Declaration of Independence that he had helped write—he died. Ironically, his once-despised political rival John Adams, the President under whom Jefferson had served as vice president for four years, died a few hours later on the same day.

Protagonists at their nation's birth, each had nurtured political divisions and chaos that would climax with their nation's near-destruction in Civil War, thirty-five years after their passing.

⁂

IN THE SUMMER OF 1829 VIRGINIANS ELECTED DELEGATES TO A CONVENTION to reform the state constitution—a 1776 relic that limited voting to the propertied elite with at least 100 acres. Eastern plantation owners,

therefore, could cast the votes of their slaves and easily outvote westerners on small mountain properties with only a slave or two. The growing
western population demanded universal white manhood suffrage to permit every white man—propertied or not—to vote.

Virginia's three legendary elder statesmen—seventy-one-year-old
James Monroe, seventy-four-year-old John Marshall, and seventy-eight-
year-old James Madison—easily won election to the convention. The
presence of two former Presidents and the Chief Justice gave the convention an aura of national—even international—importance, and delegates
immediately voted former President Madison president of the convention
on the basis of his seniority. Madison declined, however, pleading the discomforts and infirmities of old age. The convention elected Marshall next,
but he refused for the same reasons. Madison then nominated Monroe.

The frailest of the three statesmen, Monroe accepted the designation,
and John Marshall escorted him to the chair amidst a storm of cheers and
applause. After six weeks, however, weaknesses of advancing age combined with excruciating arthritic pains to force Monroe's resignation, and
he returned home. The convention ended in 1830 after granting added
representation in the state legislature to westerners. It was the last time
the three friends would ever meet.

Late that year Monroe's wife died and left the former President a broken man. His secretary found him sobbing hysterically at the foot of his
wife's bed "with trembling frame and streaming eye."[21]

After his daughter and son-in-law arrived and carried her coffin into the
family vault, Monroe became irrational, saying he would stay in the vault
and await his time to rejoin his wife. Deeming her father incapable of caring for himself, his daughter Eliza took the former President to New York
City to live with her and her husband. He spent most of his last months in
bed, preparing to die and writing to old friends to say good-bye.

Calling "the restoration of my health very uncertain," he wrote both
Marshall and Madison that

> I deeply regret that there is no prospect of our ever meeting again. Since
> so long have we been connected, and in the most friendly intercourse, in

public and private life, that a final separation is among the most distressing incidents which could occur.[22]

Monroe's letter left Madison distraught. "Closing the prospect of our ever meeting again afflicts me deeply," he replied. "The pain I feel. . . . I will not despair of your being able to keep up your connection with Virginia."[23]

As old as he was, Marshall retained his natural optimism, answering Monroe with hopes that "exercise and change of scene . . . had improved your health and spirits." He signed the letter "your friend . . . with the truest wish for your happiness."[24]

James Monroe died the following summer, on July 4, 1831—the third of the first five Presidents to die on the anniversary of the signing of the Declaration of Independence. Richmond's citizens named Marshall chairman of the committee on funeral arrangements. Monroe's death left John Marshall one of the last living officer-heroes of the Revolutionary War.

IN THE LATE 1820S THE DISCOVERY OF GOLD ON CHEROKEE TERRITORY in Georgia infected the souls of whites across the state with a madness that left Marshall and the Supreme Court helpless to prevent the nation's first crime against humanity.

To seize the gold fields from the Cherokees, Georgia's political leaders convinced President Jackson—once an Indian fighter himself—to ram the Indian Removal Act of 1830 through Congress. The act ended George Washington's successful, decades-old program to integrate southeastern Indians into American society. After passage of the federal Indian Removal Act, Georgia's state legislature passed its own Cherokee Acts, effectively dissolving the Cherokee nation.

The Cherokee Acts stripped Cherokees of citizenship, voided Cherokee laws, and divided the nine million acres of Cherokee properties (and the gold they contained) into state counties. No longer citizens, the Cherokees were helpless to protect their lands and homes from seizure by the state and helpless to sue for protection in state courts. Indeed, a Georgia court—in clear violation of a treaty between the Cherokees and the US government—had tried, convicted, and sentenced to death a Cherokee, George "Corn" Tassel, for killing another Cherokee.

Under the Cherokee treaty with the US government, only Cherokee courts had jurisdiction in cases of Cherokees killing each other, but when Marshall issued a writ to stay the execution, Georgia's legislature ordered the governor "and every other officer of this state . . . to disregard" it, saying it represented "interference in the administration of the criminal laws of this state . . . [and] a flagrant violation of her [state] rights." Georgia executed Tassel without granting him an appeal.

Georgia's Cherokee Acts allowed the state to confiscate thousands of Cherokee homes and properties, including many large, productive plantations they had carved out of the wilderness. In the end the state of Georgia forced 130,000 Cherokee, Chickasaw, Choctaw, Muskogee Creek, and Seminole Indians from their homes onto a terrifying "Trail of Tears" that claimed some 60,000 lives before survivors crossed the Mississippi River and found refuge in what is now Oklahoma.

In a desperate last effort to save themselves from exile, Cherokee leaders turned to the US Supreme Court and sued the state of Georgia. When *Cherokee Nation v. Georgia* came before the Court, however, Georgia's governor demonstrated his contempt for the Court and for federal authority by refusing to respond or even send a representative to appear.

"The Constitution, laws, and treaties of the United States are prostrate in the state of Georgia," former President John Quincy Adams lamented in his diary. "The Union is in the most imminent danger of dissolution."[25]

On March 18, 1831, Marshall delivered the Court's decision in *Cherokee Nation v. Georgia*, expressing deep sympathy for the plight of the Indians but regretting that the court lacked jurisdiction. The Cherokees were in a unique situation, he admitted, "unlike that of any other" people: they were no longer a foreign nation nor were they citizens of the United States. The Court could have heard the case of either a foreign nation or citizens of the United States, but their territories were now "part of the United States," and the Cherokees were "domestic dependent nations . . . in a state of pupilage" whose status the Constitution did not address. In effect there was no such legal entity as *Cherokee Nation*, making the case moot and leaving the Court with no jurisdiction.

Although the Court had determined the status—or lack of status—of the Cherokees, the case did not challenge, nor did the Court rule on, Georgia's Cherokee Acts, which had forced Indians onto their "Trail of Tears." The opportunity to do so came up in a second related suit brought by Samuel A. Worcester, a Congregationalist minister from Vermont who had worked for many years as a missionary among the Cherokees and supported himself with a job as US postmaster.

When he and several other missionaries refused to leave the state with the Cherokees, Georgia militiamen arrested them and dragged them off to prison and a sentence of hard labor. Nine missionaries agreed to leave Georgia and won their freedom, but Worcester and another missionary refused and sued the state in the US Supreme Court.

As in *Cherokee Nation v. Georgia*, the state ignored the court proceedings, but unlike that earlier case, the appellant was a white citizen of the United States and a federal official (postmaster), giving Marshall and the Court powers to rule on the Indian expulsion laws under which he was arrested.

In a decision that stunned the nation and sent it to the brink of civil war, Marshall ruled the Cherokee Acts of the Georgia legislature "repugnant to the Constitution, laws and treaties of the United States."

> The forcible seizure and abduction of [Samuel A. Worcester], who was residing in the nation with its permission and by authority of the President of the United States [as postmaster], is also a violation of the acts which authorize the chief magistrate to exercise his authority.

With that, Marshall ordered Georgia's Cherokee Acts "reversed and annulled."[26]

All but ordering rebellion against the federal government, Georgia Governor Wilson Lumpkin called Marshall's decision "usurpation" and said the state would respond with "the spirit of determined resistance."[27]

With no means of enforcing their decision, Marshall and the justices were helpless to prevent the collapse of the federal legal system they had built so carefully. Georgia state authorities had rendered two successive Supreme Court cases irrelevant and left the Court powerless to enforce its rulings.

"I yield slowly and reluctantly to the conviction that the Constitution cannot last," the dejected Chief Justice wrote to Associate Justice Joseph Story.

> I had supposed that north of the Potomac a firm and solid government competent to the security of national liberty might be preserved. Even that now seems doubtful. The case of the South seems to me to be desperate. Our opinions are incompatible with a unified government even among ourselves. The Union has been prolonged thus far by miracles, I fear they cannot continue.[28]

In Congress southerners confirmed Marshall's fears with shouts of defiance. South Carolina Senator Robert Young Hayne called Marshall's decision and other federal government measures "oppressive," and, citing Jefferson's Kentucky Resolution that the Constitution was a compact between the states, he again raised the banner of state sovereignty.

The eloquent Daniel Webster, senator from Massachusetts, fired his reply:

"It is, sir, the people's constitution, the people's government; made for the people, by the people and answerable to the people."

> The people . . . have declared that this Constitution shall be the supreme law. . . . Who is to judge between the people and the government? . . . Shall constitutional questions be left to four and twenty popular bodies,* each at liberty to decide for itself, and none bound to respect the decisions of others?

Webster said the Constitution had answered the question by declaring that "the judicial power shall extend to all cases arising under the Constitution and laws." He ended his defense of the Supreme Court and the

---

*The number of states at the time.

Constitution with the stirring words that became a rallying cry across the North:

"Liberty *and* Union, now and forever, one and inseparable."[29]

As northerners poured into the streets to protest Georgia's Cherokee Acts, southerners matched their fervor, calling for armed resistance. Facing reelection in a matter of months, President Andrew Jackson tried to steer clear of the controversy, reportedly telling journalist Horace Greeley, "John Marshall has made his decision. Now let him enforce it."[30]

❧

ADDING TO MARSHALL'S DEJECTION OVER SOUTHERN RESISTANCE TO the Court's decisions was his failing health. Approaching seventy-seven, he had been through an excruciatingly painful gall-bladder operation the previous fall. After months of increasing abdominal pain, he had consulted Philadelphia's Dr. Philip Syng Physick, then the nation's leading surgeon, who agreed to perform a lithotomy on the aging jurist. Marshall's colleagues feared he might not survive, but he said he preferred death to the agony afflicting him.

Worried that Marshall would not survive, Associate Justice Joseph Story wrote to his friend Judge Richard Peters. "He is beloved and reverenced here beyond all measure," Story said of Marshall. "Next to Washington, he stands the idol of all good men."[31]

As Marshall lay on the operating table "scarcely uttering a murmur," Physick cut into Marshall's abdomen and the neck of his gall bladder— *without anesthesia*. He inserted a pair of forceps into the open wound, and, one by one, or as many as the teeth of his instrument would hold, he extracted what he estimated were about 1,000 gall stones.*

"I have at length risen from my bed and am able to hold a pen," the exhausted Chief Justice wrote to Polly two weeks later.

---

*Considered the "father of American surgery," Dr. Philip Syng Physick (1768–1837) lived in a Federal-style house (Physick House) that can still be visited on Fourth Street in Philadelphia. His name became a synonym for the practice of medicine in America and, later, for purgatives designed to cleanse the body of illness.

The most delightful use I can make of it is to tell you that I am getting well and have well-founded hopes that I shall be entirely free from the painful disease with which I have been so long afflicted. . . . I eat heartily and sleep sound. My wounds [are] almost healed . . . God bless you my dearest Polly.[32]

Two days later he was able to walk "with a tottering and feeble step,"[33] and on November 19, five weeks after his operation, the Chief Justice boarded a steamboat at Baltimore for "a very tempestuous passage down Chesapeake Bay" and up the James River to Richmond. Polly was deathly ill when he arrived.

She died on Christmas Day.

As the Court was to reconvene in Washington a few weeks later, Justice Story found the Chief Justice in his hotel room in tears, still inconsolable over his wife's death. He confessed to Story of crying each night.

"It was the will of God," he sobbed, "to take to itself the companion who had sweetened the choicest part of my life . . . the woman I adored. From the hour of our union . . . I never ceased to thank heaven for this its best gift. . . . I have lost her!"[34]

As Marshall's wife had lain dying, President Andrew Jackson easily won reelection to a second term, and when the time came the Chief Justice, still bereft over the loss of his wife, administered the oath of office to the President for a second time. Jackson tried consoling Marshall. He too had lost his wife—shortly before his first inauguration.

In the vicious campaign that preceded Jackson's first election to the presidency, opposition newspapers alleged that Jackson's wife had entered into an adulterous relationship with Jackson before she had divorced her first husband and married the President. Shocked by what she read, she collapsed—a stroke perhaps, or a heart attack. She died several days later and was buried on Christmas Eve without seeing her husband assume the presidency.

⚮

AFTER JACKSON HAD SWORN TO "PRESERVE, PROTECT, AND DEFEND" THE Constitution a second time, South Carolina's legislature stunned the President and the nation by passing a law echoing Jefferson's belief in a state's right to nullify federal laws it deemed unconstitutional. It declared a federal tariff law on imports "null, void, and no law, nor binding" upon South Carolina.* Two states—South Carolina and Georgia—now stood in defiance of the federal government. The Union was dissolving.

"The laws of the United States must be executed," President Jackson raged, then signed a Proclamation against Nullification that remains one of the most important presidential acts in American history.

"My duty is emphatically pronounced in the Constitution," he stormed. "I have no discretionary power on the subject."

> I consider the power to annul a law of the United States assumed by one state, incompatible with the existence of the Union, contradicted expressly by the letter of the Constitution, unauthorized by its spirit, inconsistent with every principle on which it was founded, and destructive of the great object for which it was formed. . . . Those who told you that you might peaceably prevent the execution [of federal laws] have deceived you. . . . Their object is disunion. But be not deceived . . . disunion by armed force is treason. Are you really ready to incur its guilt?[35]

The President ordered Treasury Department cutters—later called the Coast Guard—into Charleston Bay to enforce the tariff law. South Carolina's legislature responded by authorizing the governor to call out the militia and, if necessary, draft able-bodied men between the ages of eighteen and forty-five. It appropriated $200,000 for military preparations for civil war.

---

*To protect cotton mills in the Northeast, Congress had imposed tariffs on foreign textiles. Southern cotton growers feared England, the biggest manufacturer and exporter of finished cotton goods—and biggest buyer of raw cotton from the American South—would retaliate by imposing tariffs on southern cotton.

The President, in turn, called on Congress for a Force Bill, authorizing him to use federal troops and ships to crush South Carolina's rebellion. After Congress enacted token tariff reductions as a sop to the South, officials from other southern states condemned South Carolina's Nullification Act, with Alabama's legislature declaring it "dangerous." Mississippi charged South Carolina with "reckless precipitancy," and Georgia's legislature surprised the nation (and the South Carolina legislature) by calling the Nullification Act "rash and revolutionary."

With that, South Carolina yielded, postponing for twenty-eight years the Civil War it would eventually thrust on the nation at Fort Sumter. After forcing South Carolina to retreat on nullification, Jackson convinced Georgia's governor to submit to the Supreme Court order for Reverend Worcester's release. The state legislature agreed to repeal the law that led to Worcester's arrest, and the governor ordered his release and that of his fellow missionary.

President Jackson's recognition of his obligation and that of all Presidents to enforce Supreme Court decisions cemented the court's foundation as the third coequal branch of the American government. Instead of resting in legal oblivion, *Worcester v. Georgia* emerged as one of the Supreme Court's most important cases, ensuring military support, if necessary, to enforce its decisions as supreme laws of the land.

"Who would have dreamed of such an occurrence," Justice Story wrote to his wife about President Jackson. "The Chief Justice and myself have become his warmest supporters."[36]

⁓

BY 1835 ASSOCIATE JUSTICE WILLIAM JOHNSON HAD DIED AND GABRIEL Duvall had grown deaf and resigned—each of them replaced with Jacksonians who might have radicalized the Court. Like the Jeffersonians before them, however, they immediately fell under Marshall's spell. The Court and its decisions remained as centrist as Marshall himself—at one and the same time liberal and conservative in the literal sense of both words. They protected and preserved individual liberties that did not infringe on the liberties of others or cross the line between liberty and license. They sustained and conserved the spirit of the Constitution "to form a more perfect union."

Late in June 1835 Marshall collapsed on his daily walk to Polly's grave, two miles outside of town. He had been suffering from liver disease for some time. His youngest son, Edward—like his brothers, a farmer on the family's Fairfax lands—took him to Philadelphia to Dr. Physick. His oldest son, fifty-one-year-old Thomas Marshall, was on his way to join them when a thunderstorm erupted, forcing him to take shelter. When a bolt of lightning hit the building, its chimney collapsed and killed him. Edward withheld the news from his father.

John Marshall died six days later, on July 6, 1835, two months short of his eightieth birthday, the last but one of the heroic Men of Monmouth.

Edward Marshall and John Marshall's other surviving children buried the Chief Justice next to their mother in Richmond's Shockhoe Hill Cemetery. Until Polly's death, Marshall had planned to retire with her at his boyhood home at Oak Hill, near the farms of his sons and grandchildren, but her death left him feeling so utterly alone that he spent his last days and hours visiting her grave.

"John Marshall died last Monday," John Quincy Adams wrote in his diary a few days later.

> He was one of the most eminent men that this country has ever produced. . . . Marshall has cemented the Union which the crafty and quixotic democracy of Jefferson had a perpetual tendency to dissolve. Jefferson hated and dreaded him. . . . Marshall, by the ascendency of his genius, by the amenity of his deportment and by the imperturbable command of his temper, has given a permanent and systematic character to the decisions of the Court, and settled many great constitutional questions favorably to the continuance of the Union.[37]

Marshall's colleague Associate Justice Joseph Story delivered a eulogy to the Chief Justice in Boston, asking, "When can we expect to be permitted to behold so much moderation united with so much firmness, so much sagacity with so much modesty, so much learning with so much experience?"

> Ambition never seduced him from his principles . . . amid the extrava-
> gances of party spirit. . . . If we were tempted to say in one word what it
> was in which he chiefly excelled other men, we should say in wisdom. . . .
> The Constitution, since its adoption, owes more to him than to any other
> single mind. . . . Whether it lives or perishes, his exposition of its princi-
> ples will be an enduring monument to his fame.[38]

Aaron Burr Jr. outlasted Marshall and the other heroic Men of Monmouth. After years of practicing law successfully but unobtrusively, Burr died in New York, on Staten Island, on September 14, 1836. He had no heirs, but the faculty, students, and alumni of Princeton College, led by a military band and a color guard, buried him with full military honors at the foot of his father's and grandfather's graves in Princeton Cemetery.

James Madison, the last living member of the Virginia Dynasty, died a few weeks before Burr, on June 28, 1836.

ON APRIL 12, 1861, SOUTH CAROLINA'S STATE MILITIA OPENED FIRE on federal defenses at Fort Sumter, in Charleston Harbor, setting off a civil war that would claim more than 600,000 American lives. New England's Nathaniel Hawthorne lamented to a friend, "We were never one people and never really had a country."[39]

Although Chief Justice John Marshall did not live to see the outbreak of civil war, he sensed its approach. "I yield slowly and reluctantly to the conviction that our Constitution cannot last," he admitted to his friend Associate Justice Joseph Story in 1832. "The case of the South seems to be desperate. Our [Supreme Court] opinions are incompatible with a united government."[40]

For once, however, Supreme Court Justice John Marshall's opinion proved wrong. The Constitution would not only last; the Marshall court decisions would prove so compatible with a united government that two centuries later—despite civil war and four presidential assassinations—both the Union and Constitution remain in place, sustaining what is now the oldest system of self-government in the history of man.

Appendix

Nine Great Cases of John Marshall's Supreme Court

JOHN MARSHALL'S SUPREME COURT HANDED DOWN 1,180 DECISIONS OVER thirty-five years, with Marshall writing 549 of them. Many formed the foundation of American constitutional law. They established the Supreme Court as supreme arbiter of the Constitution and American laws and the federal judiciary as the third coequal branch of the federal government with the executive and legislative branches.

Above all, Marshall's Court gave the American people—"We the people"—a means of redress against tyranny by federal, state, and local government. Scholars may disagree about which were *the* most important decisions and argue—correctly—that the following list omits many important ones. One renowned constitutional scholar lists more than 200 such cases.[1] This miniscule compendium, however, is arbitrary and entirely personal—the prerogative of an author. Far from all-inclusive, it includes the first decisions in three key areas: establishment of federal government sovereignty over the states, protection of individual rights against arbitrary government actions, and recognition of the US Supreme Court as "supreme in the exposition of the law of the Constitution," as Chief Justice Marshall phrased it. These are the Supreme Court decisions that transformed all other Supreme Court decisions into "the supreme law of the land."[2]

Marbury v. Madison (1803)

The case: Appointed justice of the peace by President John Adams, William Marbury asked the Supreme Court for a writ of mandamus to force Secretary of State James Madison to deliver Marbury's commission and allow him to assume his post as a justice of the peace. The Court ruled that Madison (and President Jefferson) had violated the Constitution by withholding Marbury's commission but that the federal law allowing Marbury to demand a writ of mandamus from the Supreme Court was unconstitutional and, therefore, void. It was the first time the Supreme Court declared an act of Congress unconstitutional.

What it did: Established Supreme Court power of judicial review to void federal laws as unconstitutional. The Court also denied the President authority to remove a federal judge from the bench.

United States v. Peters (1809)

The case: Pennsylvania's state legislature passed a law voiding a federal Continental Prize Court award to a privateer. The Marshall Court declared the legislature's action—and the law it passed—unconstitutional, effectively upholding the supremacy of federal courts over state courts and voiding state claims to sovereignty in areas the Constitution placed under the jurisdiction of the federal government.

What it did: Established Supreme Court powers to review and void state laws and state court decisions as unconstitutional. It asserted the supremacy of federal over state authority for the first time.

Fletcher v. Peck (1810)

The case: John Peck sold Robert Fletcher 15,000 acres of Indian lands that Peck and other speculators had bought at below-market prices by bribing Georgia legislators. When a reform legislature passed a law canceling the sales, the Court voided the law as a violation of Article I of the Constitution, which prohibits states from passing "any law impairing the obligation of contracts." The court regretted the corruption that underlay the transactions but said it did not represent a basis for violating the Constitution.

What it did: Affirmed inviolability of contracts between individuals and between governments and individuals.

Martin v. Hunter's Lessee (1816)

The case: During the Revolution land speculator David Hunter had purchased a 739-acre tract from the Commonwealth of Virginia which had seized and was selling unsettled Tory lands. Although Virginia's Court of Appeals ruled that Hunter had a right to keep the land, the Supreme Court overruled the Virginia court, saying the Jay Treaty with Britain had nullified Virginia's confiscation laws and, in turn, its sale of land to Hunter. The Virginia Court defied the Supreme Court, saying it lacked jurisdiction in state affairs, that the Constitution was a compact between sovereign states. But Supreme Court Justice Joseph Story responded that "the Constitution of the United States was established not by the states, but, as the preamble declared, by 'the people of the United States.'"

What it did: Asserted primacy of treaties as "supreme law of the land" and Supreme Court power to review and void state court decisions.

Dartmouth College v. Woodward (1819)

The case: New Hampshire's state legislature seized Dartmouth College and converted it from a private to a public institution. A state court upheld the takeover, but Marshall ruled that the state charter that created the college was a contract, protected by Article I of the Constitution, prohibiting states from passing "any law impairing the obligation of contracts." Marshall termed both the law that changed the charter and the state court ruling "repugnant to the Constitution of the United States."

What it did: Reiterated constitutional inviolability of contracts, declaring arbitrary state takeovers of private and charitable property and enterprises unconstitutional. The decision protected the property of Americans from arbitrary seizure by state or federal governments.

McCulloch v. Maryland (1819)

The case: When Maryland imposed a tax on all banks in the state, James McCulloch, the manager of the Baltimore branch of the federally chartered Bank of the United States, refused to pay, and a county court convicted him of violating state law. After the state court of appeals upheld his conviction, he appealed to the US Supreme Court, which overturned the state court decision, denying a state's right to tax a federal entity. The Court asserted a new doctrine of implied powers, saying that the Constitution gave the federal government the right to establish a bank or any other agency not specifically prohibited by the Constitution so long as it was consistent with the letter and spirit of the Constitution.

What it did: Sharply limited state sovereignty, asserting precedence of federal over state laws and declaring the Constitution "the supreme law of the land." It established principle of federal government's "implied powers."

Cohens v. Virginia (1821)

The case: When a state court fined the Cohen brothers for violating Virginia's ban on the sale of out-of-state lottery tickets in Virginia, the Cohens appealed to the Supreme Court. Virginia argued that the Eleventh Amendment* denied the US Supreme Court jurisdiction in local criminal courts, but the Court ruled that the involvement of Congress in establishing the District of Columbia lottery gave the Supreme Court jurisdiction. Moreover, it asserted power to review any and every court decision touching on constitutional issues, thus extending constitutional protection to citizens in even the lowest-level criminal court.

What it did: Extended Supreme Court protection to all citizens in every court in the land.

Gibbons v. Ogden (1824)

What it did: Declared state-sponsored monopolies that interfered with interstate commerce unconstitutional and opened American interstate commerce to free competition.

The case: When a steamboat firm with federal approval to carry goods and passengers in intracoastal waters threatened the state-granted monopoly of a steamboat company operating between New York City and New Jersey, New York state banned the intracoastal line from New York waters. Marshall ruled that the Constitution gave Congress exclusive rights "to regulate commerce," which, he said, "describes the commercial intercourse between nations and parts of nations. . . . Commerce among the states does not stop at the boundary line of each state." He called New York laws prohibiting vessels licensed by the United States from the waters of New York "repugnant to the Constitution and void."[3]

---

*Eleventh Amendment: "The Judicial power of the United States shall not . . . ex tend to any suit . . . against one of the United States by Citizens of another State."

Worcester v. Georgia (1832)

The case: After the discovery of gold on Cherokee lands in Georgia in the late 1820s, Georgia's legislature unilaterally dissolved the Indian nation, voided Cherokee laws, seized 9 million acres of Cherokee lands, and forced 130,000 Indians into exile west of the Mississippi River. Without the status of citizens, the Cherokees could not sue. When Samuel Worcester, a Congregationalist minister from Vermont who settled among them, tried to help, Georgia authorities arrested him and sentenced him to four years in prison. Worcester sued, and Marshall's Court declared Georgia's Cherokee laws unconstitutional. Marshall ordered Georgia to release the missionaries—but had no means of enforcing his order. For the first time in history a President—Andrew Jackson—backed up a Supreme Court decision with troops.

What it did: Put the power of federal troops behind enforcement of Supreme Court decisions.

Notes

Introduction

1. John Paul Frank, *Marble Palace: The Supreme Court in American Life* (New York: Alfred A. Knopf, Inc., 1958), 62.

2. Viscount James Bryce, *The American Commonwealth, American Edition*, 2 vols. (Chicago: Charles H. Sergel & Co., 1891), 1:375.

3. Preamble to the Constitution of the United States.

4. John Adams to John Marshall, August 17, 1825, *The Papers of John Marshall*, 12 vols. (Chapel Hill: University of North Carolina Press, 1984). 10:197. (Hereafter JM *Papers*)

Chapter 1: Chaos!

1. Merrill Jensen, John P. Kaminski, Gaspare Saladino, Richard Leffler, and Charles H. Schoenleber, eds., *The Documentary History of the Ratification of the Constitution*, 22 vols. to date (in progress) (Madison: State Historical Society of Wisconsin, 1976), 9:951–968. (Hereafter *DHRC*)

2. Ibid.

3. Ibid., 1115–1127.

4. Jack Lynch, "A Great Deal of Noise, Whipping and Spurring: America's First Disputed Presidential Election," *Colonial Williamsburg Journal* 34, no. 3 (Spring 2002): 30–35.

5. *DHRC*, IX:1115–1127.

6. John Marshall, *An Autobiographical Sketch*, ed. John Stokes Adams (Ann Arbor: University of Michigan Press, 1937), 12–13. (Hereafter JM *Autobiographical Sketch*)

7. JM *Autobiographical Sketch*, 3–4.

8. Ibid., 22.

9. Ibid.

10. Ibid., 4.

11. Sir William Blackstone, *Commentaries on the Laws of England*, 4 vols. (Oxford: Clarendon Press, 1765–1769).

12. JM *Autobiographical Sketch*, 4.

13. Ibid., 5.

14. William Wirt Henry, *Patrick Henry: Life, Correspondence and Speeches*, 3 vols. (New York: Charles Scribner's Sons, 1891), 1:262–268.

15. Ibid.

16. Jefferson borrowed ideas and even specific words and phrases from at least four essays of John Locke: *Two Treatises of Government* (1689), *A Letter Concerning Toleration* (1689), and *An Essay Concerning Human Understanding* (1690). Locke's Second *Treatise on Government*, for example, declares, "whenever the Legislators endeavor to take away and destroy the Property of the People, or to reduce them to Slavery . . . the People are at liberty to provide for themselves . . . as they shall find it most for their safety and good." Jefferson's words in the Declaration of Independence contend that "whenever . . . Government becomes destructive, it is the Right of the People to alter or abolish it and to institute new Government . . . as to them shall seem most like to effect their safety and happiness." In their writings both Locke and Jefferson justified overthrow of corrupt or tyrannical government by the "People." Although Locke called property an inalienable right, Jefferson preferred "pursuit of happiness."

17. JM *Autobiographical Sketch*, 5–6.

18. Nathaniel Judson to Commodore R. V. Morris, February 10, 1814, in Matthew L. Davis, *Memoirs of Aaron Burr*, 2 vols. (New York: Harper and Brothers, 1836), 1:68–69.

19. Theodore Sedgwick to Aaron Burr Jr., August 7, 1776, ibid., 1:60–61.

20. JM *Autobiographical Sketch*, 24.

21. Ibid., 6.

22. John Marshall, *The Life of George Washington*, 5 vols. (Philadelphia: C. P. Wayne, 1804–1807), 2:352.

23. Jefferson to Pendleton, July 1776, *The Works of Thomas Jefferson*, ed. Paul Leicester Ford, 12 vols. (New York: G. P. Putnam's Sons, 1904–1905), 2:219–220. (Hereafter Ford, *Works of TJ*)

24. Although Dumas Malone (*Jefferson the Virginian* [Boston: Little, Brown and Company, 1948]) refers to Unger as John Lewis de Unger, it is unlikely that his family would have adopted English spellings. Most sources refer to him as Jean Louis. The French occupation of many German-speaking areas east of the Rhine created a fad among some noble German families to give their children French Christian names.

25. George Washington to Benjamin Harrison, December 18–30, 1778, *The Papers of George Washington, Revolutionary War Series*, ed. W. W. Abbot, multiple volumes (in progress) (Charlottesville: University of Virginia Press, 1985), 18:447–452. (Hereafter *PGW-R*)

26. Jefferson to Van Staphorst and Hubbard, February 28, 1790, Ford, *Works of TJ*, 6:33.

27. George Washington to Patrick Henry, December 27, 1777, *PGW-R*, 13:17–18.

28. *DHRC*, 9:1120.

29. Marshall, *Life of George Washington*, 2:434.

30. Rev. Philip Slaughter, *A History of St. Mark's Parish, Culpeper County, Virginia* (Baltimore, MD: Innes and Co., 1877), 107–108.

31. Benson Bobrick, *Angel in the Whirlwind: The Triumph of the American Revolution* (New York: Simon and Schuster, 1997), 345.

32. George Washington Parke Custis, *Recollections and Private Memoirs of Washington* (New York: Derby and Jackson, 1860), 220.

33. Charlemagne Tower Jr., *The Marquis de Lafayette in the American Revolution*, 2 vols. (Philadelphia: J. B. Lippincott, 1895), 1:384.

34. Aaron Burr to Rhoda Edwards, September 26, 1776, Matthew L. Davis, *Memoirs of Aaron Burr*, 2 vols. (New York: Harper and Brothers, 1836), 1:70–71.

35. George Washington to John Augustine Washington, July 4, 1778, *PGW-R*, 16:25–26.

36. Anthony Wayne to _____ Delaney, July 13, 1779, in Henry B. Dawson, *Battles of the United States by Sea and Land*, 2 vols. (New York: Johnson, Fry, and Company, 1858), 1:517–523.

Chapter 2: Commotions

1. Thomas Jefferson to Brother John de Coigne, June 1781, *Writings of Thomas Jefferson*, ed. Andrew A. Lipscombe, 20 vols. (Washington, DC: The Thomas Jefferson Memorial Association, 1903–1904), 15:375.

2. Eliza Ambler Carrington to her sister Nancy, "An Old Virginia Correspondence," *Atlantic Monthly* (Cambridge, MA: Riverside Press, 1899), 134:547.

3. Ibid.

4. Ibid.

5. JM to Polly, February 23, 1824, Frances Norton Mason, *My Dearest Polly* (Richmond, VA: Garrett and Massie, 1961), 262–263.

6. Carrington, *Atlantic Monthly*.

7. Ibid.

8. Thomas Jefferson to George Washington, May 28, 1781, *The Writings of George Washington*, ed. Worthington Chauncey Ford, 14 vols. (New York: G. P. Putnam's Sons, 1891), 9:276n–278n.

9. Thomas Jefferson, *The Life and Selected Writings of Thomas Jefferson*, "The Autobiography of Thomas Jefferson," eds. Adrian Koch and William Peden (New York: Modern Library, 1993), 50–51.

10. JM to TJ, October 1, 1781, ibid., 31–32.

11. JM *Autobiographical Sketch*, 10.

12. GW to the Officers of the Army, March 15, 1783, *The Writings of George Washington*, ed. John C. Fitzpatrick, 39 vols.(Washington, DC: US Government Printing Office, 1931–1944), 26:222–227. (Hereafter Fitzpatrick, *GW Writings*)

13. JM to James Monroe, January 3, 1784, *The Papers of James Monroe*, ed. Daniel Preston, 2 vols. (Westport, CT: Greenwood Press, 2003–2006), 1:113.

14. Carrington, *Atlantic Monthly*.

15. JM to James Monroe, February 24, 1784, *Papers of James Monroe*, 1:116–117.

16. Ibid.

17. Johann David Schoeff, *Travels in the Confederation, 1783–1784*. Trans. and ed. Alfred J. Morrison (Philadelphia: W. J. Campbell, 1911), 2:64.

18. JM *Autobiographical Sketch*, 7.

19. Martha Jefferson Carr to Thomas Jefferson, February 26, 1787, *The Papers of Thomas Jefferson*, ed. Julian P. Boyd, 25 vols. (Princeton, NJ: Princeton University Press, 1950–1992), 15:634–635.

20. Carrington, *Atlantic Monthly*.

21. Lee to GW, October 1, 1786, *Papers of George Washington, Confederation Series*, ed. W. W. Abbot, 6 vols. (Charlottesville: University Press of Virginia, 1992–1997), 4:281–282. (Hereafter *PGW-C*)

22. JM to James Wilkinson, January 5, 1787, JM *Papers*, 1:199–201.

Chapter 3: "We, Sir, Idolize Democracy!"

1. JM to Levin Powell, December 9, 1783, Albert J. Beveridge, *The Life of John Marshall*, 4 vols. (Boston: Houghton Mifflin Company, 1916–1919), 1:207.

2. James Madison to Thomas Jefferson, July 3, 1784, *Writings of James Madison*, ed. Gaillard Hunt, 9 vols. (New York: G. P. Putnam's Sons, 1900), 2:62.

3. Lee to GW, October 17, 1786, *Life of John Marshall*, 4:295–296.

4. *DHRC*, 13:25.

5. William Short [citing Henry] to Thomas Jefferson, May 15, 1784, in Robert Douthat Meade, *Patrick Henry, Practical Revolutionary* (Philadelphia: J. B. Lippincott Company, 1969), 273.

6. GW to Jonathan Trumbull, Junior, January 5, 1784, Fitzpatrick, *GW Writings*, 27:293–295.

7. James Madison, *Notes of Debates in the Federal Convention of 1787 Reported by James Madison* (New York: W. W. Norton, 1987), 7.

8. John Steele Gordon, *An Empire of Wealth: The Epic History of American Economic Power* (New York: Harper Collins, 2004), 61–63.

9. Henry Knox to George Washington, January 31, 1785, *PGW-C*, 2:301–306.

10. JM to Humphrey Marshall, May 7, 1833, JM *Papers*, 12:275–276.

11. Madison, *Notes of Debates in the Federal Convention*, 7.

12. JM to Arthur Lee, JM *Papers*, 1:205–206.

13. George Washington Circular to the States, Fitzpatrick, *GW Writings*, 26:483–496.

14. George Washington to John Jay, May 18, 1786, *PGW-C*, 4:55–56.

15. Madison, *Notes of Debates in the Federal Convention*, 651.

16. *DHRC*, 9:929–931.

17. George Washington to David Humphries, October 19, 1787, *PGW-C*, 5:365–366.

18. *The Federalist No. 84*, May 28, 1788, Alexander Hamilton, John Jay, James Madison, *The Federalist* (New York: New American Library of World Literature, 1961).

19. Marshall, *Life of George Washington*, 5:105.

20. *DHRC*, IX:951–968.

21. Thomas Jefferson to W.S. Smith, February 2, 1788, in Dumas Malone, *Jefferson and the Rights of Man* (Boston: Little, Brown, 1951), 171.

22. *Papers of James Monroe*, 2:408ff.

23. Ibid.

24. W. P. Cresson, *James Monroe* (Chapel Hill: University of North Carolina Press, 1946), 101.

25. *DHRC*, 9:992.

26. Ibid., 9:951–968.

27. Ibid.

28. Ibid.

29. Ibid., 9:1150–1127.

30. Ibid.

31. Ibid.

32. Ibid., 9:1072–1080.

33. John P. Kaminski, *James Madison, Champion of Liberty and Justice* (Madison, WI: Parallel Press, 2006), 17–18.

34. *DHRC*, 9:689–698.

35. Ibid., 9:1115–1127.

36. *DHRC*, 10:1476–1477.

37. Henry, *Patrick Henry*, 3:586; George Morgan, *The True Patrick Henry* (Philadelphia: J. B. Lippincott Company, 1907), 354.

Chapter 4: Quoits Was the Game

1. From an address by Mr. Justice Joseph Story, delivered in Boston on October 15, 1835, to the Suffolk (MA) Bar (Rochester, NY: The Lawyers Co-operative Publishing Co., 1900), 16.

2. JM *Papers*, 2:461n64.

3. Henry, *Patrick Henry*, 2:376.

4. Meade, *Patrick Henry*, 420.

5. Henry, *Patrick Henry*, 2:363.

6. Ibid.

7. Ibid.

8. Samuel Mordecai, *Virginia, Especially Richmond, in Bygone Days with a Glance at the Present: Being Reminiscences and Last Words of an Old Citizen* (Richmond: C. H. Wynne, 1860), 259.

9. Beveridge, *Life of John Marshall*, 2:183.

10. Joseph Story, *Eulogy*, Boston, October 15, 1835, in John P. Kaminski, ed., *The Founder and the Founders: Word Portraits from the American Revolutionary War Era* (Charlottesville: University of Virginia Press, 2008), 403–404.

11. JM *Papers*, 2:41–42.

12. Ibid., 42–43.

13. Jean-Jacques Rousseau, *The Basic Political Writings: On the Social Contract*, trans. and ed. Donald A. Cress (Indianapolis, IN: Hackett Publishing Company, 1987), 141.

14. John P. Kaminski, ed., *The Quotable Jefferson* (Princeton, NJ: Princeton University Press, 2006), 390–391.

15. Ron Chernow, *Alexander Hamilton* (New York: Penguin Press, 2004), 216.

16. Thomas Jefferson to William Short, January 3, 1793, Thomas Jefferson, *Thomas Jefferson Writings* (New York: The Library of America, 1984), 1003–1006.

17. Dumas Malone, *Jefferson and the Rights of Man*, xvii.

18. Harlow Giles Unger, *Lafayette* (Hoboken, NJ: John Wiley and Sons, 2002), 227.

19. Chernow, *Alexander Hamilton*, 459.

20. *The Political Writings of John Adams*, ed. George A. Peek Jr. (New York: Liberal Arts Press, The American Heritage Series, 1954), 194.

Chapter 5: The Great Divide

1. JM to Patrick Henry, August 31, 1790, JM *Papers*, 2:60–61.
2. Thomas Jefferson to James Madison, September 8, 1793, Kaminski, *Quotable Jefferson*, 197.
3. Ibid., 399.
4. Chernow, *Alexander Hamilton*, 401.
5. GW to Thomas Jefferson, August 23, 1792, *Papers of George Washington, Presidential Series, September, 1788–May 1793*, ed. W. W. Abbot, multi-volumes (in progress) (Charlottesville : University Press of Virginia, 1987), 11:28–32. (Hereafter *PGW-P*)
6. Thomas Jefferson to Lafayette, April 2, 1790, *The Papers of Thomas Jefferson*, eds. Julian P. Boyd et al., multi-volumes (in progress) (Princeton, NJ: Princeton University Press, 1950), 16:293.
7. Alexander DeConde, *Entangling Alliance* (Durham, NC: Duke University Press, 1958), 181; Dumas Malone, *Jefferson and the Ordeal of Liberty* (Boston: Little, Brown and Company, 1962), 97.
8. Meade Minnigerode, *Jefferson—Friend of France* (New York: G. P. Putnam and Sons, 1928), 205.
9. GW to Thomas Jefferson, April 12, 1793, *PGW-P*, 12:448–449.
10. Douglas Southall Freeman, *George Washington*, completed by John Alexander Carroll and Mary Wells Ashworth, 7 vols. (New York: Charles Scribner's Sons, 1957), 7:36.
11. JM writing as Gracchus, in *Virginia Gazette and General Advertiser* (Richmond), October 16, 1793, JM *Papers*, 2:221–228.
12. George Wythe, *Resolutions*, August 17, 1793, JM *Papers*, 2:196–197.
13. *The Correspondence Between Citizen Genet, Minister of the French Republic to the United States of North America and the Officers of the Federal Government; to Which Are Prefixed the Instructions from the Constituted Authorities of France to the Said Minister* (Philadelphia: Benjamin Franklin Bache, 1793), 1–9.
14. Minnigerode, *Jefferson*, 221.
15. *Boston Gazette*, April 29, 1793.
16. Richard Harwell, *An Abridgment in One Volume of the Seven Volume George Washington by Douglas Southall Freeman* (New York: Charles Scribner's Sons, 1968), 622.
17. Harlow Giles Unger, *The Life and Times of Noah Webster, An American Patriot* (New York: John Wiley and Sons, 1998), 71, 183.

18. *Instructions to Citizen Genet, Minister Plenipotentiary from the French Republic to the United States, from the Executive Council*, Archives des Affaires Étrangères, Quai d'Orsay, Paris, France, vol. 38, Dossier *Correspondence Consulaire: Genet.*

19. Ibid.

20. JM *Autobiographical Sketch*, 13–14.

21. Address in Support of the Neutrality Proclamation, August 17, 1793, and printed in *Virginia Gazette and General Advertiser* (Richmond), August 21, JM *Papers*, 2:196–197.

22. James Monroe, writing as Agricola, September 4, 1793, *Virginia Gazette and General Advertiser* (Richmond).

23. John Marshall, *Aristides No. 1*, September 8, 1793, *Gazette and General Advertiser* (Richmond).

24. Ibid.

25. Ibid.

26. John Adams to Thomas Jefferson, June 30, 1813, *The Adams-Jefferson Letters: The Complete Correspondence Between Thomas Jefferson and Abigail and John Adams*, Lester J. Cappon, ed. (Chapel Hill: University of North Carolina Press, 1959), 346–347.

27. Thomas Jefferson to James Madison, May 19, 1793, *Jefferson Writings*, 1007–1009.

28. Minnigerode, *Jefferson*, 184.

29. Archives des Affaires Étrangères, Ministère des Affaires Étrangères, vol. 38, Dossier *Correspondence Consulaire: Genet.*

30. JM to Archibald Stuart, March 27, 1794, JM *Papers*, 2:260–262.

Chapter 6: The Two Happiest People on Earth

1. Minnigerode, *Jefferson*, 183.

2. John Adams to Thomas Jefferson, June 13, 1813, *Adams-Jefferson Letters*, 346.

3. The Navy remained part of the US Army until 1798, when it became a separate branch of the military.

4. *The Works of Hamilton*, ed. Henry Cabot Lodge, 2 vols. (New York: Chelsea House, 1980), 6:508.

5. Ibid.

6. Henry Ammon, *The Genet Mission* (New York: W. W. Norton, 1973), 28; Jean Tulard, Jean-François Fayard, Alfred Fierro, *Histoire et Dictionnaire de la Révolution Française, 1789–1799* (Paris: Editions Robert Laffon, S.A., 1987, 1998), 349.

7. John C. Miller, *The Federalist Era* (New York: Harper and Brothers, 1960), 161.

8. Chernow, *Alexander Hamilton*, 471.

9. George Washington to Henry Knox, March 2, 1797, ibid., 35:408–410.

10. JM to Polly, June 24, 1797, Mason, *My Dearest Polly*, 90–91

11. Patrick Henry to George Washington, October 16, 1795, Henry, *Patrick Henry*, 2:558.

12. Alexander Hamilton, *Papers of Alexander Hamilton*, eds. Harold C. Syrett and Jacob E. Cooke, 27 vols. (New York: Columbia University Press, 1961–1987), 19:254–263.

13. JM *Autobiographical Sketch*, 16.

14. Thomas Jefferson to Mann Page, August 30, 1795, Ford, *Works of TJ*, 7:24.

15. JM *Autobiographical Sketch*, 15–16.

16. Thomas Jefferson to James Madison, November 26, 1795, Ford, *Works of TJ*, 8:197–198.

17. JM to Mrs. Mary W. Marshall, February 3, 1796, JM *Papers*, 3:3–4.

18. Ibid., 3:19–20.

19. Thomas Marshall to JM, September 9, 1796, ibid., 3:44–46.

20. Malone, *Jefferson and the Ordeal of Liberty*, 267.

21. JM *Autobiographical Sketch*, 18–19.

22. GW to the House of Representatives, March 30, 1796, in Fitzpatrick, *GW Writings*, 35:2–5.

23. George Washington to Alexander Hamilton (marked "Private"), March 31, 1796, ibid., 35:6–8.

Chapter 7: X, Y, Z

1. JM to James Madison, July 5, 1796, JM *Papers*, 3:19–27.

2. Ibid., 3:52–53.

3. JM to the Secretary of State, September 10, 1796, ibid., 3:54–62.

4. Instructions from the Secretary of State to James Monroe, June 10, 1794, ibid., 2:1–9.

5. George Washington to the Secretary of State, July 8, 1796, Fitzpatrick, *GW Writings*, 35:127–128; George Washington to John Marshall, July 8, 1796, ibid., 35:182–192.

6. James Thomson Callender, *History of the United States for 1796* (Philadelphia: Snowden and McCorkle, 1797), 205.

7. Ibid.

8. Cresson, *James Monroe*, 162–164, citing Gelston's notes on the confrontation, July 11, 1797, in Gratz Collection, Historical Society of Pennsylvania.

9. Ibid., 167, citing Lodge, *Works of Hamilton*, 6:533.

10. Ibid., 164–169, citing Lodge, *Works of Hamilton*, 6:517–534.

11. GW Farewell Address, September 19, 1796, Fitzpatrick, *GW Writings,* 35:214–238, esp. 214–215.

12. Ibid., esp., 35:256–227.

13. Ibid., esp. 35:233.

14. Ibid.

15. *Philadelphia Aurora,* December 21 and 23, 1796, in Donald H. Stewart, *The Opposition Press of the Federalist Period* (Albany: State University of New York Press, 1969), 533.

16. Miller, *Federalist Era,* 196–197.

17. Ibid.

18. Freeman, *George Washington,* 7:436, citing the recollections of Philadelphia's Bishop William White in William Spohn Baker, *Washington After the Revolution, 1784–1799* (Philadelphia: J. B. Lippincott Company, 1898).

19. Ibid., 457, citing John Adams to Abigail Adams, March 5, 1797, in John Adams, *Letters of John Adams Addressed to His Wife,* ed. Charles Francis Adams, 2 vols. (Boston: 1841), 2:244.

20. Felix Maurice Hippiel Markham, *Napoleon* (New York: New American Library of World Literature, 1963), 27.

21. Michel Poniatowski, *Talleyrand aux États-Unis, 1794–1796* (Paris: Presses de la Cité, 1967), 164

22. John Adams to Elbridge Gerry, May 3, 1797, Adams Family Papers, Massachusetts Historical Society, reel 117.

23. Timothy Pickering to JM, June 6, 1797, JM *Papers,* 3:86.

24. JM to Mary W. Marshall, July 3, 1797, ibid., 3:94.

25. Joseph Létombe to Citizen Delacroix, July 7, 1797, Correspondence Politique, États-Unis, vol. 347, Ministère des Affaires Étrangères, Paris.

26. Ibid., June 24, 1797, 92.

27. Ibid., July 5, 1797, 95–95.

28. Ibid., July 10, 1797, 97–98.

29. Ibid., July 12, 1797, 100–101; July 14, 1797, 101–102.

30. "Paris Journal," October 8, 1797, JM *Papers,* 3:159–160.

31. Poniatowski, *Talleyrand,* 554–559.

32. Ibid.

33. *American State Papers. Documents, Legislative and Executive, of Congress of the United States,* selected and ed. under the Authority of Congress, 38 vols. (Washington, DC: 1832–1861), Foreign Relations, ii, 159–160.

34. "Paris Journal, October 27, 1797," JM *Papers,* 3:17–174.

35. JM to Mary W. Marshall, November 27, 1797, ibid., 3:299–301.

36. Ibid.

37. Mary Pinckney to Margaret Manigault, March 8, 1798, Manigault Family Papers, cited in JM *Papers*, 3:300n.

38. Poniatowski, *Talleyrand*, 563.

39. JM *Papers*, 3:428–459; *American State Papers*, Foreign Relations, ii, to Talleyrand, April 3, 1798.

40. Alexander DeConde, *The Quasi-War: The Politics and Diplomacy of the Undeclared War with France 1797–1801* (New York: Charles Scribner's Sons, 1966), 53.

41. Beveridge, *Life of John Marshall*, 2:327.

42. Ibid.

43. JM to Charles Cotesworth Pinckney, April 21, 1798, JM *Papers*, 3:463–464.

44. JM to Fulwar Skipwith, August 21, 1798, ibid, 3:464.

45. Thomas Jefferson to Edmund Pendleton, January 29, 1799, *Life and Selected Writings of Thomas Jefferson*, 501.

46. *Columbian Centinnel* (Boston), July 4, 1798.

Chapter 8: Our Washington Is No More

1. *Porcupine's Gazette* (Philadelphia), June 19, 1798.

2. *Claypoole's American Daily Advertiser*, June 25, 1798.

3. John Adams to Congress, June 21, 1798, John Adams, *Works of John Adams*, ed. Charles Francis Adams, 10 vols. (Boston: Little, Brown and Company, 1856), 9:158–159.

4. Abigail Adams to William Smith, July 7, 1798, quoted in DeConde, *Quasi-War*, 97.

5. "Draft of the Kentucky Resolution," *Thomas Jefferson Writings*, 449–456.

6. *The Works of Alexander Hamilton*, ed. John C. Hamilton, 7 vols. (New York: Library of Congress, 1850–1851), 5:184.

7. JM "To a Freeholder," published in the *Virginia Herald* (Fredericksburg), October 2, 1798, in JM *Papers*, 3:503–506.

8. JM to Mary W. Marshall, August 18, 1798, ibid., 3:486–487.

9. *Virginia Gazette and General Advertiser* (Richmond), August 14, 1798.

10. JM "To a Freeholder," JM *Papers*, 3:503–506.

11. Ibid.

12. Claude Gernade Bowers, *Jefferson and Hamilton: The Struggle for Democracy in America* (Boston: Houghton Mifflin, 1925), 388.

13. JM *Autobiographical Sketch*, 25–26.

14. Markham, *Napoleon*, 52

15. September 28, 1798, Talleyrand to French Ambassador to the United States Louis André Pichon, *Works of John Adams*, 8:690–691.

16. John Adams, *Correspondence of the Late President Adams, Originally Published in the* Boston Patriot *in a Series of Letters* (Boston: Everett and Munroe, 1809), 29–30.

17. JM to John Ambler, December 29, 1799, JM *Papers*, 4:49–50.

18. JM Address *To the President of the United States*, December 6, 1799, ibid., 4:39–43.

19. JM *Motion*, December 18, 1799, ibid., 4:46.

20. JM *Speech*, December 19, 1799, ibid., 4:46–48.

21. John Marshall, *The Life of George Washington, Commander in Chief of the American Forces . . . And First President of the United States, Compiled under the Inspection of the Honourable Bushrod Washington*, 2 vols. (Philadelphia: James Crissy, 1834), 2:447.

Chapter 9: Midnight Judges

1. DeConde, *Quasi-War*, 179.

2. *Annals of Congress, Debates and Proceedings, 1789–1824*, Library of Congress., 6th Congress, 1st session, 254–255.

3. Page Smith, *John Adams*, 2 vols. (Garden City, NY: Doubleday, 1962), 2:1025.

4. JM Speech to the House of Representatives, March 7, 1800, JM *Papers*, 4:82–109.

5. Ibid.

6. Ibid.

7. Alexander Wolcott to Fisher Ames, December 29, 1799, in Jean Edward Smith, *John Marshall: Definer of a Nation* (New York: Henry Holt and Company, 1996), 256.

8. Theodore Sedgwick to Rufus King, May 11, 1800, in Beveridge, *Life of John Marshall*, 2:483–484.

9. Richard N. Rosenfeld, *American Aurora: A Democrat-Republican Returns* (New York: St. Martin's, 1997), 785.

10. Alexander Hamilton to John Jay, May 7, 1800, *Papers of Alexander Hamilton*, 24:465.

11. John Adams to James McHenry, May 5, 1800, Bernard Christian Steiner, *Life and Correspondence of James McHenry* (Cleveland: Burrows Brothers, 1907), cited in Beveridge, *Life of John Marshall*, 2:485.

12. Steiner, *Life and Correspondence of McHenry*, 453

13. James McHenry to Alexander Hamilton, May 31, 1800, *Papers of Alexander Hamilton*, 24:552–65.

14. *Philadelphia Aurora,* June 16, 1798, in John Ferling, *John Adams, A Life* (New York: Henry Holt and Company), 364.

15. Rosenfeld, *American Aurora,* 804.

16. JM to John Adams, May 8, 1800, JM *Papers,* 4:148–149.

17. JM *Autobiographical Sketch,* 28–29.

18. W. P. Cresson, *James Monroe* (Chapel Hill: University of North Carolina Press, 1946), 201.

19. Ibid., 202, citing Henry Adams, *History of the United States during the Administrations of Jefferson and Madison, 1801–1817,* 8 vols. (New York: 1889–1891), 2:351.

20. Ibid., citing Helen Nicolay, *Our Capital on the Potomac* (New York: Century Co., 1924), 70.

21. JM to Mary Marshall, August 8, 1800, Mason, *My Dearest Polly,* 142.

22. JM to Rufus King, August 16, 1800, JM *Papers,* 4:225.

23. JM to Mary Marshall, August 20, 1800, Mason, *My Dearest Polly,* 143.

24. *Papers of Alexander Hamilton,* 25:173–234.

25. Abigail Adams to Mary Cranch (sister), November 10, 1800, Stewart Mitchell, ed., *New Letters of Abigail Adams, 1788–1801* (Boston: Houghton Mifflin Company, 1947).

26. John Adams to JM, July 17, 1806, JM *Papers,* 6:453–454.

27. St. George Tucker to JM, November 6, 1800, ibid., 6:4–5.

28. JM to Thomas Claxton, August 26, 1800, ibid., 4:245–246.

29. St. George Tucker to JM, November 6, 1800, ibid., 6:4–5.

30. JM to Rufus King, September 20, 1800, ibid., 4:283–297

31. John Adams to Abigail Adams, November 2, 1800, Abigail Adams, *My Dearest Friend, Letters of Abigail and John Adams,* eds. Margaret A. Hogan and C. James Taylor (Cambridge, MA: Belknap Press of Harvard University Press, 2007), 472–473.

32. Oliver Wolcott, *Memoirs of the Administration of Washington and John Adams,* ed. George Gibbs from the Papers of Oliver Wolcott, 2 vols. (New York: William van Norden, 1846), 2:349–350.

33. JM to Alexander Hamilton, January 1, 1801, Hamilton, *Works of Alexander Hamilton,* (New York: Charles S. Francis and Company, 1851), 6:501.

34. JM to Rufus King, February 26, 1801, JM *Papers,* 6:82–83

35. George Washington to John Jay, October 5, 1789, *PGW-P,* 4:137–138.

36. Thomas Jefferson to John Dickinson, December 19, 1801, *Writings of Thomas Jefferson,* 10:302.

37. JM *Autobiographical Sketch,* 30.

38. JM to John Adams, February 4, 1801, JM *Papers,* 6:73.

Chapter 10: Mr. Chief Justice

1. Frank, *Marble Palace*, 62.

2. James Bryce, *The American Commonwealth* (London: Macmillan and Company, 1891), 375.

3. Joseph Story, *Life and Letters of Joseph Story*, ed. William W. Story, 2 vols. (Boston: Little, Brown and Company, 1851), 1:217–218.

4. Aaron Burr to Sen. Samuel Smith, December 16, 1800, *Political Correspondence and Public Papers of Aaron Burr*, ed. Mary-Jo Kline (Princeton, NJ: Princeton University Press, 1984), 1:471.

5. Davis, *Memoirs of Aaron Burr*, 2:353.

6. Jefferson to William Branch Giles, April 20, 1807, *Thomas Jefferson Writings*, 1175.

7. James Monroe to Thomas Jefferson, January 18, 1801, James Monroe, *Writings of James Monroe*, ed. Stanislaus Murray Hamilton. 7 vols. (New York: 1898–1903; reprint ed.: New York: AMS Press, 1969), 3:256–257.

8. Hortensius to John Marshall, Secretary of State, in *Aurora*, February 9, 1801.

9. Thomas Jefferson to James Monroe, February 15, 1801, Ford, *Works of TJ*, 7:490.

10. Thomas Jefferson to James Madison, February 18, 1801, ibid.

11. Gallatin to James Nicholson, February 14, 1801, in Henry Adams, *Life of Albert Gallatin* (Philadelphia: J. B. Lippincott and Co., 1880), 261.

12. Hamilton, *Works of Alexander Hamilton*, X: December 16, 1800.

13. Alexander Hamilton to Oliver Wolcott Jr., December 1800, *Papers of Alexander Hamilton*, 25:286

14. JM to Alexander Hamilton, January 1, 1801, JM *Papers*, 6:46–48.

15. James Bayard to Samuel Bayard, February 22, 1801, in Miller, *Federalist Era*, 273.

16. Ibid.

17. *Niles'* [weekly] *Register*, January 4, 1823.

18. *Gazette of the United States*, February 19, 1801.

19. *National Intelligencer*, February 18, 1801.

20. Jefferson to Lafayette, March 18, 1801, *The Letters of Lafayette and Jefferson*, ed. Gilbert Chinard (Baltimore, MD: Johns Hopkins University Press, 1929), 212.

21. Jefferson to Joseph Priestly, March 21, 1801, Ford, *Works of TJ*, 8:22

22. Thomas Jefferson, *First Inaugural Address*, March 4, 1784, *Thomas Jefferson Writings*, 492–496.

23. JM to Charles Cotesworth Pinckney, March 4, 1801, JM *Papers*, 6:89–90.

24. Thomas Jefferson to Charles Hammond, August 18, 1821, Kaminski, *Quotable Jefferson*, 260–261.

25. 1 Cranch 1–46, *United States Reports* (Washington, DC: US Government Printing Office, 1801–1815), 5–13 (William Cranch, 1–9).

26. Ibid.

27. Jefferson to Associate Justice William Johnson, October 27, 1822, *Thomas Jefferson Writings*, 1459–1461.

28. Jefferson to Associate Justice William Johnson, June 12, 1823, ibid., 1469–1477.

29. Thomas Jefferson to Joel Barlow, March 14, 1801, and to Archibald Stuart, April 8, 1801, Ford, *Works of TJ*, 8:46.

30. William Branch Giles to Thomas Jefferson, June 1, 1801, Dumas Malone, *Jefferson the President, First Term*, 6 vols. (Boston: Little, Brown and Company, 1948–1977), 4:116.

31. *Annals*, 7th Congress, 1st Session, 31–32.

32. Anne C. Morris, *The Diary and Letters of Gouverneur Morris*, 2 vols. (New York: Charles Scribner's Sons, 1888), 2:147.

33. Ibid.

34. *New-York Evening Post*, March 2, 1802.

35. Alexander Hamilton to John Dickinson, March 28, 1802, Hamilton Letters, New York Historical Society.

36. Ibid.

37. James Monroe to Thomas Jefferson, April 25, 1802, *Writings of James Monroe*, 3:341–344.

38. From paragraphs omitted from Jefferson's Message to Congress, December 8, 1801, cited in Beveridge, *Life of John Marshall*, 3:605–606.

39. *Annals*, 7th Congress, 1st Session, 179–180.

40. Ibid., 181.

41. Timothy Pickering to George Cabot, January 29, 1804, Henry Cabot Lodge, *Life and Letters of George Cabot* (Boston: Little, Brown and Company, 1877), 338–340.

42. *Richmond Recorder*, September 1, 15, 22, 29, 1802.

43. Ibid., November 17, 1802.

44. Chernow, *Alexander Hamilton*, 664.

45. Callender's body was found "in the James River in three feet of water," according to Jefferson's renowned biographer, the Pulitzer Prize–winning historian Dumas Malone. Malone wrote that Callender's death was officially designated as "accidental, proceeding from intoxication, but the *Examiner* [editorial of July 27, 1803] regarded it as suicidal." Malone, *Jefferson the President*, 211–212.

Chapter 11: Party Rage

1. Thomas Jefferson to Wilson Cary Nicholas, September 5, 1799, Ford, *Works of TJ*, 9:79–81.

2. JM to Charles Cotesworth Pinckney, November 21, 1802, JM *Papers*, 6:124–126.

3. JM to Mary W. Marshall, January 2, 1803, ibid., 6:145–146.

4. Samuel Chase to JM, April 24, 1802, ibid., 6:109–116.

5. *Annals of Congress*, 11:434–436.

6. *Marbury v. Madison* Opinion, September 24, 1803, JM *Papers*, 6:160–187.

7. Ibid.

8. Alexander DeConde, *This Affair of Louisiana* (New York: Charles Scribner's Sons, 1976), 87.

9. TJ to Livingston, April 18, 1802, ibid., 114.

10. TJ to Pierre Samuel du Pont de Nemours, Harlow Giles Unger, *The French War Against America* (Hoboken, NJ: John Wiley and Sons, 2005), 228.

11. Louis André Pichon to Talleyrand, October 15, 1801, Archives du Ministère des Affaires Étrangères, Correspondence Politique, États Unis.

12. DeConde, *This Affair of Louisiana*, 136.

13. TJ to John Breckenridge, August 12, 1803, Ford, *Works of TJ*, 10:7.

14. TJ to Robert Carter Nicholas, September 7, 1803, ibid., 10:10.

15. *New York Evening Post*, January 28, 1803.

16. *Annals*, February 16, 1803.

17. S. T. Mason, quoted in William Duane, *Mississippi Question: Report of a Debate in the Senate of the United States, on the 23d, 24th, & 25th February, 1803, on Certain Resolutions concerning the Violation of the Right of Deposit in the Island of New Orleans* (Philadelphia: W. Duane, 1803), 152.

18. Timothy Pickering to George Cabot, January 28, 1804, Lodge, *Life and Letters of George Cabot*, 338.

19. Uriah Tracy to James McHenry, October 19, 1803, Steiner, *Life and Correspondence of James McHenry*, 522.

20. Tapping Reeve to Uriah Tracy, February 7, 1804, Henry Adams, ed., *Documents Relating to New-England Federalism* (Boston: Little, Brown and Company, 1877), 242.

21. Thomas Jefferson to Abigail Adams, September 11, 1804, ibid., 12:162.

22. December 21, 1804, John Quincy Adams, *Memoirs of John Quincy Adams*, ed. Charles Francis Adams, 12 vols. (Philadelphia: J. B. Lippincott and Company, 1874–1877), 1:322–323.

23. Ibid.

24. John Quincy Adams to John Adams, March 8, 1805, *Writings of John Quincy Adams*, ed. Worthington C. Ford, 7 vols. (New York: Macmillan, 1917), 3:108.

25. Thomas Jefferson to William Plumer, January 5, 1804, The Plumer Papers, Library of Congress, cited in Beveridge, *Life of John Marshall*, 3:165.

26. *Memoirs of John Quincy Adams*, 1:299.

27. Ibid., 302.

28. *Annals*, 8th Congress, 1st Session, 365.

29. William Plumer to (New Hampshire attorney) Jeremiah Mason, January 14, 1803, Plumer Papers, Library of Congress.

30. James A. Bayard to (Delaware Senator) Richard Bassatt, February 12, 1802, James Asheton Bayard Papers, 1796–1815, ed. Elizabeth Donnan, in Annual Report of the American Historical Association for the year 1913, vol. II (Washington, DC: 1913), as cited by Beveridge, *Life of John Marshall*, 3:160.

31. Wolcott, *Memoirs of the Administration*, 349–350.

32. *Maryland Gazette Extraordinary*, June 19, 1766.

33. *Report of the Trial of the Hon. Samuel Chase . . .*, Taken in shorthand by *Charles Evans* (Baltimore, MD: Samuel Butler and Charles Keating, 1805), 61.

34. Ibid.

35. Thomas Jefferson to Joseph H. Nicholson, May 13, 1803, Library of Congress Jefferson Papers, 22701, cited by Malone, *Jefferson the President*, 467.

36. JM to James Markham Marshall, April 1, 1804, JM *Papers*, 6:277–278.

37. *New York Evening Post*, January 20, 1804.

38. JM to James M. Marshall, April 1, 1804, JM *Papers*, 6:277–279; JM to Charles Cotesworth Pinckney, November 21, 1802, ibid., 6:124–126.

Chapter 12: A Deadly Interview

1. Sergeant-at-Arms of the National Senate, *Annals*, 8th Congress, 1st session, 319.

2. John Quincy Adams, *Diary of John Quincy Adams*, November 5, 1804, Adams Family Papers, Massachusetts Historical Society, an Electronic Archive, www.masshist.org.

3. Plumer to Norris, November 7, 1804, cited in Beveridge, *Life of John Marshall*, 3:180.

4. *New York Evening Post*, February 6, 1805.

5. *Memoirs of John Quincy Adams*, 1:360.

6. Alexander Hamilton to Oliver Wolcott Jr., December 1800, *Papers of Alexander Hamilton*, 25:286.

7. *American Citizen*, March 1, 1804.

8. Chernow, *Alexander Hamilton*, 677.

9. Ibid.

10. Alexander Hamilton to Aaron Burr Jr., June 20, 1804, ibid., 248.

11. "Statement on Impending Duel with Aaron Burr," June 28–July 10, 1804, ibid., 279–280.

12. *American Citizen*, July 21, 23, 1804.

13. Aaron Burr Jr., to Charles Biddle, July 18, 1804, Aaron Burr Jr., *Political Correspondence . . . Aaron Burr*, 2:885–887.

14. John Adams, *Diary and Autobiography*, ed. L. H. Butterfield, 4 vols. (New York: Atheneum, 1964), 3:434.

15. Uriah Tracy to James Gould, February 4, 1805, cited in Nancy Isenberg, *Fallen Founder: The Life of Aaron Burr* (New York: Penguin Group, 2002), 276.

16. *Memoirs of John Quincy Adams*, 1:351. Passage of the Twelfth Amendment allowed each member of the college to cast but a single vote each for a presidential and vice presidential candidate. Under the previous system each elector cast both votes for a presidential candidate, with the winner of the most votes becoming president and the second-most votes vice president. The old system had produced an equal number of votes for Burr and Jefferson in the 1800 elections and led to the acrimonious voting in the House of Representatives to determine the President.

17. Ibid., 353.

18. John Quincy Adams to John Adams, March 14, 1805, *Writings of John Quincy Adams*, 3:116.

19. *Memoirs of John Quincy Adams*, 1:354–394; "Chase Trial," *Writings of John Quincy Adams*, 3:116–149.

20. *Memoirs of John Quincy Adams*, 1:429–482; *Writings of John Quincy Adams*, 3:173ff.

21. *Memoirs of John Quincy Adams*, 1:488–489; *Writings of John Quincy Adams*, 3:224.

22. *Annals*, 8th Congress, 2nd session, 105–151.

23. *Memoirs of John Quincy Adams*, 1:556; *Writings of John Quincy Adams*, "Chase Trial," 3:205–244.

24. JM *Papers*, 6:350–357.

25. Ibid., 6:488.

26. Ibid., 6:562ff.

27. Ibid., 6:359.

28. Plumer, February 27, 1805, Plumer, "Diary," Library of Congress, cited in Beveridge, *Life of John Marshall*, 3:217n.

29. *Annals*, 8th Congress, 2nd session, 669.

30. Plumer to his son, March 3, 1805, Beveridge, *Life of John Marshall*, 3:222.

31. Plumer, March 1, 1805, Beveridge, *Life of John Marshall*, 3:219n.

32. Samuel Taggart to John Taylor, February 17, 25, 1805, Samuel Taggart Papers, American Antiquarian Society, Worcester, MA, cited in Isenberg, *Fallen Founder*, 277.

33. From the *Washington Federalist*, March 13, 1805, Davis, *Memoirs of Aaron Burr*, 2:236–238.

34. Ibid.

35. Burr, *Political Correspondence*, 2:910–911.

36. *Washington Federalist*, March 13, 1805, Davis, *Memoirs of Aaron Burr*, 2:236–238.

37. *Memoirs of John Quincy Adams*, 1:367.

38. Story, *Life and Letters*, 167. See also Smith, *John Marshal*, 350–351.

39. Thomas Todd to John Breckenridge, February 17, 1802, cited in Smith, *John Marshal*, 303.

40. Charles Warren, *The Supreme Court in United States History*, 3 vols. (Boston: Little, Brown and Co., 1922), 1:301.

Chapter 13: The Trial

1. The Marqués de Casa Yrujo to Don Pedro Antonio de Cevallos, January 28, 1807, Adams, *History of the United States*, 3:342–343.

2. Aaron Burr to Joseph Alston, March 22, 1805, Davis, *Memoirs of Aaron Burr*, 589–590.

3. Special Message to Congress on the Burr Conspiracy, January 22, 1807, *Thomas Jefferson Writings*, 532–538.

4. John Adams to Benjamin Rush, February 2, 1807, in Beveridge, *Life of John Marshall*, 3:338n.

5. Thomas Jefferson, October 22, 1806, *Anas*, in Ford, *Writings of TJ*, 1:318–319.

6. Thomas Jefferson to Monsieur DuPont de Nemours, July 14, 1807, Koch and Peden, *Life and Selected Writings of Thomas Jefferson*, 536.

7. Aaron Burr to Peter Taylor, October 26, 1806, in Adams, *History of the United* States, 3:276.

8. Aaron Burr to Henry Clay, December 1, 1806, Henry Clay, *The Private Correspondence of Henry Clay*, ed. Calvin Colton (New York: A. S. Barnes and Co., 1855), 13–14.

9. JM to James M. Marshall, February 2, 1804, JM *Papers*, 6:255–256.

10. Henry Clay to James Pindell, October 15, 1828, Clay, *Private Correspondence*, 207.

11. *Annals of Congress*, 10th Cong. 1st session, 44.

12. US Supreme Court, 4 Cranch 75ff.

13. Ibid.

14. Judge William Cranch, cited in Smith, *John Marshall*, 637n60.

15. Thomas Jefferson's "Special Message to Congress," January 22, 1807, Ford, *Works of TJ*, 9:14–20.

16. Adams, *History of the United States of America*, 2:185.

17. Smith, *John Marshall*, 358.

18. *Orleans Gazette*, February 20, 1807.

19. Thomas Jefferson to William Branch Giles, April 20, 1807, *Thomas Jefferson Writings*, 1173.

20. Ibid.

21. Ibid.

22. Aaron Burr, *The Examination of Col. Aaron Burr Before the Chief Justice of the United States, upon the Charges of a High Misdemeanor and of Treason Against the United States* (Richmond: S. Grantland, 1807), 6–8.

23. Ibid., 23.

24. Aaron Burr Jr., *Reports of the Trials of Colonel Aaron Burr for Treason and for a Misdemeanor, Taken in Shorthand by David Robertson, Counselor at Law*, 2 vols. (Philadelphia: Hopkins and Earle, 1808), 1:430–432.

25. Aaron Burr to Theodosia Burr Alston, July 3 and July 6, 1807, Davis, *Memoirs of Aaron Burr*, 620–621.

26. Ibid., July 24, 1807, 621.

27. Burr, *Reports of the Trials*, 1:127–128.

28. Thomas Jefferson to George Hay, June 19, 1807, Ford, *Works of TJ*, 10:403–404.

29. *United States v. Burr*, Opinion, US Circuit Court, Virginia, June 13, 1807, JM *Papers*, 7:37–50.

30. Ibid.

31. Ibid.

32. Burr, *Reports of the Trials*, 2:446.

33. Burr, *The Examination of Col. Aaron Burr*, 34–35.

34. Ibid.

35. Thomas Jefferson to William Thompson, September 26, 1807, Ford, *Works of TJ*, 10:501–502.

36. *Enquirer* (Richmond), December 1, 4, 8, and 12, 1808.

Chapter 14: The Court Must Be Obeyed

1. Thomas Jefferson to George Hay, September 4, 1807, *Writings of Thomas Jefferson*, 11:360.

2. *Annals*, 10th Cong. 1st session, 321–324.

3. Harold Underwood Faulkner and Tyler Kepner, *America, The History and People* (New York: Harper and Brothers, 1942), 180.

4. Kaminski, *James Madison*, 100.

5. Governor Jonathan Trumbull at the opening of the Special Session of the Connecticut State Legislature, February 23, 1809, *State Documents on Federal Relations: The States and the United States*, ed. Herman V. Ames (Philadelphia: University of Pennsylvania, 1906), 40–41.

6. JM to Timothy Pickering, December 19, 1808, JM *Papers*, 7:188.

7. US Supreme Court, 5 Cranch 133, 1803.

8. George Washington to Lafayette, February 1, 1784, *PGW-C*, 1:87–90.

9. US Supreme Court, 5 Cranch 133, 1803.

10. JM *Papers*, 7:190–196.

11. *United States v. Peters*, 5 Cranch 115.

12. JM *Papers*, 7:196n15.

13. Philadelphia *Aurora*, Virginia *General Advertiser*, March 28, April 6, 13, 17, 20, 1809.

14. Ibid., 230–241.

15. Thomas Jefferson to Albert Gallatin, September 27, 1810, Ford, *Works of TJ*, 11:152–155.

16. Thomas Jefferson to James Madison, October 15, 1810, ibid., 11:150–154.

17. Thomas Jefferson to James Madison, October 25, 1810, ibid., 11:140.

18. Thomas Jefferson to James Madison, May 25, 1810, ibid., 11:139–141.

19. Thomas Jefferson to William Branch Giles, November 17, 1810, cited in Jean Edward Smith, *John Marshall*, 398.

20. Thomas Jefferson to John Tyler, May 26, 1810, ibid., 141–149n.

21. Madison to JM, December 26, 1803, Ammon, *The Genet Mission*, 227.

22. Stoddert to McHenry, July 15, 1812, Steiner, *Life and Correspondence of James McHenry*, 581–583.

Chapter 15: An Era of Good Feelings

1. George Washington to Jacob Read, November 3, 1784, Fitzpatrick, *GW Writings*, 27:489.

2. River Commission Report, December 26, 1812, JM *Papers*, 7:361–379.

3. Report on Fortifications, June 28, 1813, JM *Papers*, 7:412–414.

4. Dispatch from Oliver Hazard Perry aboard U.S. Brig *Niagara* to General William Henry Harrison, September 10, 1813, in Benson J. Lossing, *The Pictorial Field-Book of the War of 1812* (New York: Harper and Brothers, 1868), 530.

5. *Memoirs of John Quincy Adams*, 3:2.

6. Mrs. Samuel Harrison Smith to Mrs. Kirkpatrick, March 13, 1814, Mrs. Samuel Harrison Smith, *Forty Years of Washington Society*, ed. Gaillard Hunt (London: T. Fisher Unwin, 1906), 96.

7. The *Nereide*, Opinion, US Supreme Court, March 11, 1815, JM *Papers*, 8:67–81.

8. William Munford, *Virginia Reports*, 6 vols. (1, 2, 3, 5, and 6 by other publishers) (Philadelphia: James Webster, 1817), 4:25–54.

9. JM Inaugural Address, March 4, 1817, JM *Writings*, 6:6–14.

10. B. R. Curtis, ed., *Reports of Decisions in the Supreme Court of the United States*, 6th ed., 22 vols. (Boston: Little, Brown and Company, 1881), 4:415–439; Noble E. Cunningham Jr., *The Presidency of James Monroe* (Lawrence: University Press of Kansas, 1996), 82.

11. Cunningham, *Presidency of James Monroe*, 228, citing Massachusetts *Centinnel*, July 19, 1817.

Chapter 16: The Final Arbiter

1. JM to Joseph Story, September 22, 1832, JM *Papers*, 12:237–238.

2. US Supreme Court, *Cooper v. Aaron*, 358 U.S. 1 (1958), 18.

3. Daniel Webster Peroration, *Dartmouth College v. Woodward*, March 10, 1818.

4. *Dartmouth College v. Woodward*, Opinion, US Supreme Court, February 2, 1819, JM *Papers*, 8:217–239.

5. Thomas Jefferson, the Kentucky Resolution of 1798, *Thomas Jefferson Writings*, 449–456.

6. *McCulloch v. Maryland* Opinion, US Supreme Court, March 6, 1819, JM *Papers*, 8:259–279.

7. Ibid.

8. *DHRC*, 9:689–998.

9. Ibid.

10. JM to Thomas S. Grimke, October 6, 1834, JM *Papers*, 12:419–420.

11. JM *Papers*, 9:143–147.

12. Richmond *Enquirer*, May 25, 29, June 1, 1821.

13. Joseph Story to JM, June 27, 1821, JM *Papers*, 9:174–178.

14. JM to Joseph Story, September 18, 1821, ibid., 9:183–185.

15. JM to Joseph Story, July 13, 1821, ibid., 9:178–182.

16. Thomas Jefferson to Spencer Roane, March 9, 1821, and Thomas Jefferson to Thomas Ritchie, December 25, 1820, Ford, *Works of TJ*, 201–202 and 175–178.

17. Ibid., September 26, 1823, 338–339.

18. *Gibbons v. Ogden*, Opinion and decree, US Supreme Court, March 2, 1824, JM *Papers*, 10:7–34.

19. *Gibbons v. Ogden*, Opinion and decree, US Supreme Court, March 2, 1824, JM *Papers*, 10:7–34.

20. Jean Edward Smith, *John Marshall*, 473, citing Charles Warren, *History of the American Bar* (Boston: Little, Brown and Co., 1911), 396.

21. Daniel Coit Gilman, *James Monroe* (Boston: Houghton Mifflin Company, 1898), 225.

22. JM to Madison, April 11, 1831, JM *Papers*, 7:231–234.

23. Madison to JM, April 21, 1831, ibid., 7:231n, 232n, 233n.

24. JM to James Monroe, December 16, 1830, JM *Papers*, 11:394–395.

25. John Quincy Adams, *Memoirs*, 8:262–263.

26. Richard Peters Jr., *United States Reports* (*Reports of Cases . . . in the Supreme Court of the United States, 1828–1843*), 17 vols. (Philadelphia), 6:534–563.

27. Lumpkin's "Annual Message to the Legislature," November 6, 1832, Letter Books of the Governors, 1832, Georgia Department of Archives and History.

28. JM to Joseph Story, September 22, 1832, JM *Papers*, 12:237–238.

29. *Debates*, 21st Congress, 1st session, 78–80.

30. Horace Greeley, *The American Conflict*, 2 vols. (Hartford, CT: O. D. Case and Company, 1864, 1867), 1:106.

31. Justice Joseph Story to Judge Richard Peters, October 29, 1831, Story, *Life and Letters*, 2:70.

32. JM to Mary W. Marshall, November 8, 1831, ibid., 2:121–122.

33. JM to Joseph Story, November 10, 1831, ibid., 2:124.

34. JM to Polly, December 25, 1832 (a year after Polly's death), Mason, *My Dearest Polly*, 343–345.

35. President Jackson's Proclamation Regarding Nullification, December 10, 1832, Library of Congress.

36. Joseph Story to Sarah W. Story, January 27, 1832, Story, *Life and Letters*, 2:119.

37. *Diary of John Quincy Adams*, July 10, 1835.

38. Joseph Story, Eulogy, Boston, October 15, 1835, John P. Kaminski, ed., *The Founders on the Founders*, 403–404.

39. Nathaniel Hawthorne to Commodore Horatio Bridge, May 26, 1861, in Horatio Bridge, *Personal Recollections of Nathaniel Hawthorne* (New York: Harper and Brothers, 1893), 169–170.

40. JM to Joseph Story, September 22, 1832, JM *Papers*, 12:237–238.

Appendix: Nine Great Cases of John Marshall's Supreme Court

1. Herbert A. Johnson, *The Chief Justiceship of John Marshall, 1801–1835* (Columbia: University of South Carolina Press, 1997).

2. US Supreme Court, *Cooper v. Aaron, United States Reports* 1 (1958), 358.

3. *Gibbons v. Ogden*, Opinion and decree, US Supreme Court, March 2, 1824, JM *Papers*, 10:7–34.

Bibliography

Adams, Abigail. *New Letters of Abigail Adams, 1788–1801.* Edited by Stewart Mitchell. Boston: Houghton Mifflin Company, 1947.

Adams, Abigail and John. *My Dearest Friend, Letters of Abigail and John Adams.* Edited by Margaret A. Hogan and C. James Taylor. Cambridge, MA: The Belknap Press of Harvard University Press, 2007.

Adams, Charles Francis, ed. *Letters of John Adams Addressed to His Wife.* 2 vols. Boston: C. C. Little and J. Brown, 1841.

Adams, Henry. *History of the United States During the Administrations of Jefferson and Madison, 1801–1817.* 8 vols. New York: Charles Scribner's Sons, 1889–1891.

———. *Life of Albert Gallatin.* Philadelphia: J. B. Lippincott and Co., 1880.

Adams, Henry, ed. *Documents Relating to New-England Federalism.* Boston: Little, Brown and Company, 1877.

Adams, John. *The Adams-Jefferson Letters: The Complete Correspondence Between Thomas Jefferson and Abigail and John Adams.* Edited by Lester J. Cappon. Chapel Hill: University of North Carolina Press, 1959.

———. *Correspondence of the Late President Adams, Originally Published in the* Boston Patriot *in a Series of Letters.* Boston: Everett and Munroe, 1809.

———. *Diary and Autobiography.* Edited by L. H. Butterfield. 4 vols. New York: Atheneum, 1964.

———. *Letters of John Adams Addressed to His Wife.* Edited by Charles Francis Adams. 2 vols. Boston: Charles C. Little and James Brown, 1841.

———. *The Political Writings of John Adams.* Edited by George A. Peek Jr. New York: Liberal Arts Press, The American Heritage Series, 1954.

———. *Works of John Adams*. Edited by Charles Francis Adams. 10 vols. Boston: Little, Brown and Company, 1856.

Adams, John Quincy. *Diary of John Quincy Adams*. Adams Family Papers, Massachusetts Historical Society. An Electronic Archive, www.masshist.org.

———. *Memoirs of John Quincy Adams*. Edited by Charles Francis Adams. 12 vols. Philadelphia: J. B. Lippincott and Company, 1874–1877.

———. *Writings of John Quincy Adams*. Edited by Worthington C. Ford. 7 vols. New York: Macmillan, 1917.

Ames, Fisher. *Works of Fisher Ames*. Edited by Seth Ames. 2 vols. Boston: T. B. Wait, 1854.

Ammon, Henry. *The Genet Mission*. New York. W. W. Norton, 1973.

Baker, William Spohn. *Washington After the Revolution, 1784–1799*. Philadelphia: J. B. Lippincott Company, 1898.

Beveridge, Albert J. *The Life of John Marshall*. 4 vols. Boston: Houghton Mifflin Company, 1916–1919.

Blackstone, Sir William. *Commentaries on the Laws of England*. 4 vols. Oxford: Clarendon Press, 1765–1769.

Bobrick, Benson. *Angel in the Whirlwind: The Triumph of the American Revolution*. New York: Simon and Schuster, 1997.

Bowers, Claude Gernade. *Jefferson and Hamilton: The Struggle for Democracy in America*. Boston: Houghton Mifflin, 1925.

Bridge, Horatio. *Personal Recollections of Nathaniel Hawthorne*. New York: Harper and Brothers Publishers, 1893.

Bryce, Viscount James. *The American Commonwealth, American Edition*. 2 vols. Chicago: Charles H. Sergel and Co., 1891.

Burr, Aaron. *Political Correspondence and Public Papers of Aaron Burr*. Edited by Mary-Jo Kline. Princeton, NJ: Princeton University Press, 1984.

———. *The Examination of Col. Aaron Burr before the Chief Justice of the United States, upon the charges of a High Misdemeanor and of Treason Against the United States*. Richmond, VA: S. Grantland, 1807.

———. *Memoirs of Aaron Burr*. Compiled and edited by Matthew L. Davis. 2 vols. New York: Harper and Brothers, 1836.

———. *Reports of the Trials of Colonel Aaron Burr for Treason and for a Misdemeanor, Taken in Shorthand by David Robertson, Counselor at Law*. 2 vols. Philadelphia: Hopkins and Earle, 1808.

Callender, James Thomson. *History of the United States for 1796*. Philadelphia: Snowden and McCorkle, 1797.

[Chase, Samuel.] *Report of the Trial of the Hon. Samuel Chase . . . , Taken in Shorthand by Charles Evans*. Baltimore, MD: Samuel Butler and Charles Keating, 1805.

Chernow, Ron. *Alexander Hamilton*. New York: Penguin Press, 2004.

Chinard, Gilbert, ed. *The Letters of Lafayette and Jefferson*. Baltimore, MD: Johns Hopkins University Press, 1929.

Clay, Henry. *The Private Correspondence of Henry Clay*. Edited by Calvin Colton. New York: A. S. Barnes and Co., 1855.

Clinton, Robert Lowry. *Marbury v. Madison and Judicial Review*. Lawrence: University Press of Kansas, 1989.

Corwin, Edward S. *John Marshall and the Constitution: A Chronicle of the Supreme Court*. New Haven, CT: Yale University Press, 1919.

Cresson, W. P. *James Monroe*. Chapel Hill: University of North Carolina Press, 1946.

Cullop, Floyd G. *The Constitution of the United States: An Introduction*. New York: New American Library, 1984.

Cunningham, Noble E. Jr. *The Presidency of James Monroe*. Lawrence: University Press of Kansas, 1996.

Curtis, B. R., ed. *Reports of Decisions in the Supreme Court of the United States*, 6th ed. 22 vols. Boston: Little, Brown and Company, 1881.

Custis, George Washington Parke. *Recollections and Private Memoirs of Washington*. New York: Derby and Jackson, 1860.

Davis, Matthew L. *Memoirs of Aaron Burr*. 2 vols. New York: Harper and Brothers, 1836.

Dawson, B. *Battles of the United States by Sea and Land*. 2 vols. New York: Johnson, Fry, and Company, 1858.

DeConde, Alexander. *This Affair of Louisiana*. New York: Charles Scribner's Sons, 1976.

———. *Entangling Alliance*. Durham, NC: Duke University Press, 1958.

———. *The Quasi-War*. New York: Charles Scribner's Sons, 1966.

de Lafayette, Gilbert Motier. *The Letters of Lafayette and Jefferson*. Edited by Gilbert Chinard. Baltimore, MD: Johns Hopkins University Press, 1929.

Duane, William. *Mississippi Question: Report of a Debate in the Senate of the United States, on the 23d, 24th, & 25th February, 1803, on Certain Resolutions Concerning the Violation of the Right of Deposit in the Island of New Orleans*. Philadelphia: W. Duane, 1803.

Dunn, Susan. *Jefferson's Second Revolution: The Election Crisis of 1800 and the Triumph of Republicanism*. Boston: Houghton Mifflin Company, 2004.

Farrand, Max. *The Fathers of the Constitution: A Chronicle of the Establishment of the Union*. New Haven, CT: Yale University Press, 1921.

Farrand, Max, ed. *The Records of the Federal Convention of 1787*. 4 vols. New Haven, CT: Yale University Press, 1911.

Faulkner, Harold Underwood, and Tyler Kepner. *America: The History and People*. New York: Harper and Brothers, 1942.

Ferling, John. *Adams vs. Jefferson: The Tumultuous Election of 1800*. New York: Oxford University Press, 2004.

———. *John Adams: A Life*. New York: Henry Holt and Company, 1992.

Frank, John Paul. *Marble Palace: The Supreme Court in American Life*. New York: Alfred A. Knopf, 1958.

Franklin, Benjamin. *Papers of Benjamin Franklin*. Edited by Leonard W. Labaree et al. 38 vols. to date [in progress]. New Haven, CT: Yale University Press, 1959.

Freeman, Douglas Southall. *George Washington*. Completed by John Alexander Carroll and Mary Wells Ashworth. 7 vols. New York: Charles Scribner's Sons, 1957.

[Genet, Citizen.] *The Correspondence Between Citizen Genet, Minister of the French Republic to the United States of North America and the Officers of the Federal Government; to Which Are Prefixed the Instructions from the Constituted Authorities of France to the Said Minister*. Philadelphia: Benjamin Franklin Bache, 1793.

Gilman, Daniel Coit. *James Monroe*. Boston: Houghton Mifflin Company, 1898.

Gordon, John Steele. *An Empire of Wealth: The Epic History of American Economic Power*. New York: Harper Collins, 2004.

Greeley, Horace. *The American Conflict: A History of the Great Rebellion, 1862–1865*. 2 vols. Hartford, CT: O. D. Case and Company, 1864, 1867.

Hamilton, Alexander. *Papers of Alexander Hamilton*. Edited by Harold C. Syrett and Jacob E. Cooke. 27 vols. New York: Columbia University Press, 1961–1987.

———. *The Works of Alexander Hamilton*. Edited by John C. Hamilton. 7 vols. New York: Library of Congress, 1850–1851.

———. *The Works of Hamilton*. Edited by Henry Cabot Lodge. 12 vols. New York: G. P. Putnam's Sons, 1904.

Hamilton, Alexander, John Jay, and James Madison. *The Federalist*. New York: The New American Library of World Literature, 1961.

Harwell, Richard. *Washington: An Abridgment in One Volume of the Seven Volume George Washington by Douglas Southall Freeman*. New York: Charles Scribner's Sons, 1968.

Henry, William Wirt. *Patrick Henry: Life, Correspondence, Speeches*. 3 vols. New York: Charles Scribner's Sons, 1891.

Hobson, Charles F. *The Great Chief Justice: John Marshall and the Rule of Law*. Lawrence: University Press of Kansas, 1996.

Howe, Henry. *Historical Collections of Virginia*. Charleston, SC: Wm. R. Babcock, 1852.

Isenberg, Nancy. *Fallen Founder: The Life of Aaron Burr*. New York: Penguin Group, 2002.

Jefferson, Thomas. *The Complete Anas of Thomas Jefferson*. Edited by Franklin B. Sawvel. New York: Da Capo Press, 1970.

———. *The Letters of Lafayette and Jefferson*. Edited by Gilbert Chinard. Baltimore, MD: Johns Hopkins University Press, 1929.

———. *The Life and Selected Writings of Thomas Jefferson*. Edited by Adrienne Koch and William Peden. New York: The Modern Library, 1993.

———. *The Papers of Thomas Jefferson*. Edited by Julian P. Boyd. Multi-volumes (in progress). Princeton, NJ: Princeton University Press, 1950.

———. *The Works of Thomas Jefferson*. Edited by Paul Leicester Ford. 12 vols. New York: G. P. Putnam's Sons, 1904–1905.

———. *Thomas Jefferson Writings*. New York: The Library of America, 1984.

———. *The Writings of Thomas Jefferson*. Edited by Andrew A. Lipscombe. 20 vols. Washington, DC: The Thomas Jefferson Memorial Association, 1903–1904.

Jensen, Merrill, John P. Kaminski, Gaspare Saladino, Richard Leffler, and Charles H. Schoenleber, eds. *The Documentary History of the Ratification of the Constitution*. 22 vols. to date (in progress). Madison: State Historical Society of Wisconsin, 1976.

Johnson, Herbert A. *The Chief Justiceship of John Marshall, 1801–1835*. Columbia, SC: University of South Carolina Press, 1997.

Kaminski, John P. *James Madison, Champion of Liberty and Justice*. Madison, WI: Parallel Press, 2006.

———, ed. *The Founders on the Founders: Word Portraits from the American Revolutionary Era*. Charlottesville: University of Virginia Press, 2008.

———, ed. *The Quotable Jefferson*. Princeton, NJ: Princeton University Press, 2006.

King, Rufus. *The Life and Correspondence of Rufus King*. Edited by Charles R. King. New York: G. P. Putnam's Sons, 1896.

Koch, Adrienne. *Jefferson and Madison: The Great Collaboration*. New York: Alfred A. Knopf, 2007.

Koch, Adrienne, and William Peden, eds. *The Life and Selected Writings of Thomas Jefferson*. New York: The Modern Library, 1944.

Konefsky, Samuel J. *John Marshall and Alexander Hamilton: Architects of the American Constitution*. New York: The Macmillan Company, 1964.

Labunski, Richard. *James Madison and the Struggle for the Bill of Rights*. New York: Oxford University Press, 2006.

Larson, Edward J. *A Magnificent Catastrophe: The Tumultuous Election of 1800, America's First Presidential Campaign*. New York: Free Press, 2007.

Linklater, Andro. *An Artist in Treason: The Extraordinary Life of General James Wilkinson*. New York: Walker and Company, 2009.

Lipsky, Seth. *The Citizen's Constitution: An Annotated Guide*. New York: Basic Books, 2009.

Lodge, Henry Cabot. *Life and Letters of George Cabot*. Boston: Little, Brown and Company, 1877.

Lomask, Milton. *Aaron Burr: The Years from Princeton to Vice President, 1756–1805*. New York: Farrar, Strauss, Giroux, 1979.

———. *Aaron Burr: The Conspiracy and Years of Exile, 1805–1836*. New York: Farrar, Strauss, Giroux, 1982.

Lossing, Benson J. *The Pictorial Field-Book of the War of 1812*. New York: Harper and Brothers, 1868.

Madison, James. *Writings of James Madison*. Edited by Gaillard Hunt. 9 vols. New York: G. P. Putnam's Sons, 1900.

———. *Notes of Debates in the Federal Convention of 1787, Reported by James Madison*. New York: W. W. Norton, 1987.

Malone, Dumas. *Jefferson and His Time*. 6 vols. Boston: Little, Brown and Company, 1948–1977. Individual titles:
    Vol. 1. *Jefferson the Virginian*. 1948.
    Vol. 2. *Jefferson and the Rights of Man*. 1951.
    Vol. 3. *Jefferson and the Ordeal of Liberty*. 1962.
    Vol. 4. *Jefferson the President: First Terms, 1901–1805*. 1970.
    Vol. 5. *Jefferson the President: Second Term, 1805–1809*. 1974.
    Vol. 6. *Jefferson, the Sage of Monticello*. 1977.

Markham, Felix Maurice Hippiel. *Napoleon*. New York: The New American Library of World Literature, 1963.

Marshall, John. *An Autobiographical Sketch*. Edited by John Stokes Adams. Ann Arbor: University of Michigan Press, 1937.

———. *The Constitutional Decisions of John Marshall*. New York: G. P. Putnam's Sons, 1905.

———. *The Life of George Washington*. 5 vols. Philadelphia: C. P. Wayne, 1804–1807.

———. *The Papers of John Marshall*. 12 vols. Chapel Hill: University of North Carolina Press, 1984.

Mason, Frances Norton. *My Dearest Polly*. Richmond, VA: Garrett and Massie, 1961.

Meade, Robert Douthat. *Patrick Henry, Practical Revolutionary*. Philadelphia: J. B. Lippincott Company, 1969.

Miller, John C. *The Federalist Era*. New York: Harper and Brothers, 1960.

Minnigerode, Meade. *Jefferson—Friend of France*. New York: G. P. Putnam and Sons, 1928.

Monroe, James. *The Papers of James Monroe*. Edited by Daniel Preston. 2 vols. Westport, CT: Greenwood Press, 2003–2006.

————. *The Writings of James Monroe.* Edited by Stanislaus Murray Hamilton. 7 vols. New York: 1898–1903; reprint ed.: New York: AMS Press, 1969.

Mordecai, Samuel. *Virginia, Especially Richmond, in Bygone Days with a Glance at the Present: Being Reminiscences and Last Words of an Old Citizen.* Richmond, VA: C. H. Wynne, 1860.

Morgan, George. *The True Patrick Henry.* Philadelphia: J. B. Lippincott Company, 1907.

Morris, Anne C. *The Diary and Letters of Gouverneur Morris.* 2 vols. New York: Charles Scribner's Sons, 1888.

Morris, Richard B. *Witnesses at the Creation: Hamilton, Madison, Jay, and the Constitution.* New York: Holt, Rinehart and Winston, 1985.

Munford, William. *Virginia Reports.* 6 vols. (vols. 1, 2, 3, 5, and 6 by other publishers). Philadelphia: James Webster, 1817.

Newmeyer, R. Kent. *John Marshall and the Heroic Age of the Supreme Court.* Baton Rouge: Louisiana State University Press, 2001.

Nicolay, Helen. *Our Capital on the Potomac.* New York: The Century Company, 1924.

Oster, John Edward, ed. *The Political and Economic Doctrines of John Marshall.* New York: Neale Publishing Company, 1914.

Parton, James. *The Life and Times of Aaron Burr.* New York: Mason Brothers, 1858.

Poniatowski, Michel. *Talleyrand et le Directoire, 1796–1800.* Paris: Librairie Académique Perrin, 1982.

Remini, Robert V. *The Life of Andrew Jackson.* New York: Penguin Books, 1988.

Rogow, Arnold A. *A Fatal Friendship: Alexander Hamilton and Aaron Burr.* New York: Hill and Wang, 1998.

Rosenfeld, Richard N. *American Aurora: A Democrat-Republican Returns.* New York: St. Martin's Press, 1997.

Rousseau, Jean-Jacques. *The Basic Political Writings: On the Social Contract.* Translated and edited by Donald A. Cress. Indianapolis, IN: Hackett Publishing Company, 1987.

Schminke, Frederick A. *Genet: The Origins of His Mission to America.* Toulouse: Imprimerie Toulousaine Lion et Fils, 1939.

Schoeff, Johann David. *Travels in the Confederation, 1783–1784.* Translated and edited by Alfred J. Morrison. Philadelphia: W. J. Campbell, 1911.

Simon, James F. *What Kind of Nation: Thomas Jefferson, John Marshall, and the Epic Struggle to Create a United States.* New York: Simon and Schuster Paperbacks, 2002.

Slaughter, Rev. Philip. *A History of St. Mark's Parish, Culpepper County, Virginia.* Baltimore, MD: Innes & Co., 1877.

Smith, James Morton, ed. *The Republic of Letters: The Correspondence Between Thomas Jefferson and James Madison, 1776–1826*. 3 vols. New York: W. W. Norton, 1995.

Smith, Jean Edward. *John Marshall: Definer of a Nation*. New York: Henry Holt and Company, 1996.

Smith, Page. *John Adams*. 2 vols. Garden City, NY: Doubleday and Company, 1962.

Smith, Mrs. Samuel Harrison. *Forty Years of Washington Society*. Edited by Gaillard Hunt. London: T. Fisher Unwin, 1906.

Steiner, Bernard Christian. *The Life and Correspondence of James McHenry*. Cleveland, OH: Burrows Brothers Company, 1907.

Stewart, Donald H. *The Opposition Press of the Federalist Period*. Albany: State University of New York Press, 1969.

Story, Joseph. *A Discourse upon the Life, Character and Services of the Honorable John Marshall, Chief Justice of the United States and America, Pronounced on the fifteenth day of October at the Request of the Suffolk Bar*. Cambridge, MA: Nabu Public Domain Reprints, 1835.

———. *Life and Letters of Joseph Story*. Edited by William Wetmore Story. 2 vols. Boston: Charles C. Little and James Brown, 1853.

Tagg, James. *Benjamin Franklin Bache and the Philadelphia Aurora*. Philadelphia: University of Pennsylvania Press, 1991.

Tower, Charlemagne Jr. *The Marquis de Lafayette in the American Revolution*. 2 vols. Philadelphia: J. B. Lippincott, 1895.

Tulard, Jean, Jean-François Fayard, and Alfred Fierro, *Histoire et Dictionnaire dela Révolution Française, 1789–1799*. Paris: Editions Robert Laffons, S. A., 1987, 1998.

Unger, Harlow Giles. *The French War Against America*. Hoboken, NJ: John Wiley and Sons, 2005.

———. *John Quincy Adams*. Boston: Da Capo Press, 2012.

———. *Lafayette*. Hoboken, NJ: John Wiley and Sons, 2002.

———. *The Last Founding Father: James Monroe and a Nation's Call to Greatness*. Cambridge, MA: Da Capo Press, 2009.

———. *The Life and Times of Noah Webster, An American Patriot*. New York: John Wiley and Sons, 1998.

Van Doren, Carl. *The Great Rehearsal: The Story of the Making and Ratifying of the Constitution of the United States*. New York: Viking Press, 1948.

Warren, Charles. *History of the American Bar*. Boston: Little, Brown and Co., 1911.

———. *The Supreme Court in United States History*. 3 vols. Boston: Little, Brown and Co., 1922.

Washington, George. *The Papers of George Washington, Confederation Series, January 1784–September 1788*. Edited by W. W. Abbot. 6 vols. Charlottesville: University Press of Virginia, 1992–1997.

———. *The Papers of George Washington, Presidential Series*. Edited by W. W. Abbot. Multi-volumes (in progress). Charlottesville: University of Virginia Press, 1985.

———. *The Papers of George Washington, Revolutionary War Series*. Edited by W. W. Abbott. Multi-volumes (in progress). Charlottesville: University of Virginia Press, 1985.

———. *The Writings of George Washington*. Edited by Worthington Chauncey Ford. 14 vols. New York: G. P. Putnam's Sons, 1891.

———. *The Writings of George Washington*. Edited by John C. Fitzpatrick. 39 vols. Washington, DC: US Government Printing Office, 1931–1944.

Wharton, Anne Hollingsworth. *Social Life in the Early Republic*. Williamstown, MA: Corner House Publishers, 1970.

Wolcott, Oliver. *Memoirs of the Administration of Washington and John Adams*. Edited by George Gibbs from the Papers of Oliver Wolcott. 2 vols. New York: William van Norden, 1846.

Manuscripts and Manuscript Collections

American State Papers. Documents, Legislative and Executive, of Congress of the United States. Selected and edited under the authority of Congress. 38 vols. Washington, DC: 1832–1861.

Annals of Congress, Debates and Proceedings, 1789–1824. 38 vols. Washington, DC: Library of Congress, 1831–1861.

Archives des Affaires Étrangères. Dossier *Correspondence Consulaire*, Ministère des Affaires Étrangères. Quai d'Orsay, Paris, France.

State Documents on Federal Relations: The States and the United States. Edited by Herman V. Ames. Philadelphia: University of Pennsylvania, 1906.

United States Reports (Reports of Cases . . . in the Supreme Court of the United States). Washington, DC: US Government Printing Office, 1801–1835.

Note: The US Government Printing Office did not begin publishing Supreme Court Cases until 1874. Prior to that, the Court's Reporter of Decisions published the cases privately for his own profit, and these early case reports carry the name of the Court Reporter in bibliographic references—for example, "Cranch," for William Cranch, 1801–1815, "Wheaton," or "Wheat," for Henry Wheaton, 1815–1827, and "Peters" for Richard Peters, 1827–1842.

Periodicals

American Citizen
Atlantic Monthly
Boston Gazette
Claypoole's American Daily Advertiser
Colonial Williamsburg Journal
Columbian Centinel
Gazette of the United States
Maryland Gazette Extraordinary
National Gazette
National Intelligencer
New-York Evening Post
Niles's *Weekly Register* (Baltimore)
Orleans Gazette
Philadelphia Aurora
Porcupine's Gazette (Philadelphia)
(Richmond, VA) *Recorder*
(Richmond, VA) *Enquirer*
Virginia Gazette and General Advertiser
Virginia Herald
Washington Federalist

General References

Bartlett, John, and Justin Kaplan, eds. *Familiar Quotations*, 16th ed. Boston: Little, Brown and Company, 1992.
Dictionary of American Biography. Edited by Dumas Malone. 10 vols. New York: Charles Scribner's Sons, 1946.
Morris, Richard B., ed. *Encyclopedia of American History*. New York: Harper and Brothers, 1953.
The New Encyclopedia Britannica, 15th ed. Chicago: Encyclopedia Britannica, 1985.
Webster's American Biographies. Edited by Charles Van Doren. Springfield, MA: Merriam-Webster, 1984.

Index